LANDSCAPES

OF THE HEART

Vignettes of Family
and North Africa

Peggy Call

With my very best wishes
Peggy Call

Torchflame Books
An imprint of Light Messages

CONTENTS

ACKNOWLEDGMENTS

I need to thank many people for the encouragement they have been to me. First of all, Cristina, she's a real pusher. When I asked her to tell me why she thought that I should record my stories, she actually wrote out a list of supporting reasons.

Then there is a group of young people who came to see us from time to time and they would ask me to read a story or two after dinner. They didn't give me much specific feedback but they helped me push ahead because the next time they came they made the same request. From this group I would like to thank especially Michelle and Caitlin.

And then there are those who served as editors. They corrected and made suggestions. Thank you so much Jessica, Jeannie and Mary Fran and Bill. Just little remarks like, "This section is too long," "Change the order of these stories," "I was not bored," or, "I enjoyed reading them," gave me a boost.

I could not have done the technology involved to make these stories a reality by myself. Thanks for those hours of help, Billy and Jess and Steve.

And finally, I thank my friends at the Saturday afternoon Memoir Writing Group. We are about fourteen ladies plus Bill. Thanks for your inspiration and laughs as we reminisce together. Several stories were inspired from subjects suggested in this group.

PREFACE

Some years ago I started telling stories of Bill's and my past experiences to anyone who would listen and even to those whom I mistakenly thought were listening. I was unaware that I was telling stories so often. I was shocked once by the immediate reaction of some ladies to whom I had recounted one of these experiences. They thought that I was making a point and decided to apply my story to their own situation. This was in no way my intention. The discussion had simply clicked in my mind reminding me of a similar event from our past.

Occasionally after I finished a story, someone would say, "Have you written that down?" I think that you should write a collection of stories." Sometimes just a statement or comment would remind me of something my mother used to say, or of an automobile accident, or a run-in with a sorcerer, or the time we were lost just a few miles outside the capital city in the Sahara because a sand storm blocked our vision and we couldn't find our car, or just an insignificant event, and I would launch out enjoying telling, and then perplexed and flattered that my hearers thought that they should be recorded. Someone might listen to them, but who would read them?

Stories. Everyone has them. What or where would we be without them? They are like a cup filled to the brim of our lives just bursting to overflow. For me writing of our past and of God's faithfulness is simply fun. I guess I like to turn a small insignificant event into entertainment. And I'm happy and encouraged each time they are enjoyed. I am also encouraged by the admonition, "We shouldn't be ashamed of our experiences. They are the only ones we have."

When telling a story with your audience before you, you automatically change the account drastically if your hearer is a child, or an adult who knows you well, or someone from a different culture, or a person who doesn't know you at all or even someone who doesn't agree with you. Not only do the details change, but the moral, the point, the vocabulary, the style changes from audience to audience. You see your hearers before you and adapt subconsciously. That freedom disappears in writing. You don't know who your audience will be. That is my dilemma. I don't have an idea of who you might be.

These written words are glued to the paper. Maybe a few will please you. Others you are free to leave stuck there.

Jackie Kennedy said that she wanted to live her life, not record it. I have chosen to do both.

INTRODUCTION

I have a fear. I fear I may be guilty of choosing stories that are sanitized, or accentuate the positive, or are self-flattering. I do hope that those included here represent honest memories - as honest as I can write them. But still I think we are all guilty of looking at the world and events around us, not as they really are, but as we are. How can we help it?

God created me an optimist and then He changed that optimism into faith and hope. On occasion He filled both Bill and me with faith that expected the impossible. We were not alone. We had friends who felt as we did, who were as passionate about a nascent national church plant as we were. So we learned to pray the impossible into reality. Once Jesus' disciples said to Jesus, "If salvation is so difficult, who then can be saved?" Jesus answered, "With man this is impossible, but not with God. With God, all things are possible." Even though many stories do not mention the Lord's role in a particular event, overlying and underlying these stories is gratitude to God who called us to North Africa and promised never to leave us no matter where He led. He was faithful in every way. We would not hesitate to return if age permitted.

God also created all of us with a natural tendency to forget the painful. Bill and I have consciously tried to laugh through our tears. When he felt overly discouraged Bill would get on his knees and tell the Lord of his pain. These times were often followed by exciting events. They needed to be prayed into reality.

These stories are miscellaneous events from our past that I have placed basically in chronological order. For details and dates I have sometimes been able to refer to letters, newspaper clippings and sketchy diaries.

I regret that a few of the most significant, rewarding and happiest events must remain untold. They are too personal or might have repercussions on our friends. I will just quote the statement from an old radio broadcast that assured us that "names have been changed to protect the innocent."

What is impossible with man is possible with GOD.
Luke 18:27

This is what the kingdom of God is like:
A man scatters seed on the ground.
Night and day, whether he sleeps or not,
The seed spouts and grows
Although he does not know how.
Mark 4:26

NORTH AFRICA

CHAPTER ONE - FAMILY

Troubled Times

Peggy at five years

Ionce read that the greatest gift parents can give their children is a happy childhood. I was a happy little girl. A happy girl born in troubled times. I had two brothers back then and one sister. My mother said that when I was born on July 5, 1932, she thought she had the perfect family - two boys and two girls. Then in 1936 at age 40 she gave birth to another boy. So we were David Hugh, Malcolm Douglas, Edith Ellen, Margaret Drusilla, and Bruce Ritchie, all with the exciting last name of Brown.

6

My sister claims I was spoiled. I was not aware of that of course. But I was aware that I wasn't a sharp thinker like the others. I didn't teach myself to read when I was four like Bruce. I didn't skip a grade like Edith. And I didn't become a champion chess player at the age of 15 like Malcolm, or build my own radio at the age of 12 like David. I also remember hearing, "She's four years old and she doesn't even know how to tie her shoes yet!"

Along with all of the other lack of accomplishments, I did not succeed at eating hot oatmeal. That was the preferred breakfast in our family and we were supposed to face our day with hot oatmeal in our stomachs and grow strong and healthy. I sat at the breakfast table till mid-morning trying to swallow that thick cold, lumpy, gummy stuff. It was the lumps that made me gag. Try as I would, it only came out and not down.

Finally, Mother decided that Peggy would eat Shredded Wheat. That went down so easily, but not so well with my sister and brothers. This only reinforced Edith's feelings that I was spoiled. It may also have reinforced Malcolm's conviction that I was different, expressed years later in his answer to his son Doug's question, "Why is Peggy so different from the rest of you?" Malcolm replied, "Well, she is not as bright as the rest of us, but we always knew that she would be the happiest." He had also told me when I was in high school that I had a "butterfly brain."

During those years of our youth, while David and Malcolm were solving problems of one kind or another, sometimes playing chess in bed in the dark of night where the only board was in their brains, or Edith, aspiring to become a doctor, was out picking up worms and rabbit skeletons, I would sit on the floor with a coloring book or at a small stand-up blackboard drawing pictures, usually of horses with a piece of chalk.

In high school I had lots of friends, played on sports teams, and was class treasurer. I became president of the choral society as the result of a joke. I was out of the room when the singers voted. When I came back they were laughing at having elected me when I didn't even know I was a candidate.

And despite my saying that I hated high school physics, I did graduate valedictorian and walked away with the Math Award, and was also president of our little high school chapter of the National Honor Society. This butterfly brain had won out over the huge graduating class of 17 members, the Class of 1950 from Buckingham High School in Bucks County, Pennsylvania.

The troubled times started in 1929 with the stock market crash and lasted into the decade following. There were few people who did not suffer from the shame of unemployment. Many had invested all they owned in the stock market. Some had even borrowed to invest.

Malcolm, Peggy, Bruce, Edith and David

Daddy had attended Rutgers University and then graduated from New York Law School. He was working as a lawyer for a construction company in New York City. His company was in the process of building multiple houses, each one in different stages of completion. When the financial world crashed, his boss, deeply in debt, closed himself in the kitchen of the only completed house and turned on the gas stove. His company folded.

Daddy struggled to find work to be able to feed the family. He painted a house here and took odd jobs there. I remember that our next-door neighbor, Mr. Briar, gave Daddy odd jobs as he could. Mother cooked in the coal furnace and melted all of her cookware because the gas and electricity had been turned off from lack of payment. She sold her stock in Bell Telephone and hocked her engagement ring. We ate raisin sandwiches for lunch in school.

My mother went to work for my father's oldest brother and his wife. I didn't like Aunt Emma and Uncle Rob very much. It was not because they were both employed and consequently had two salaries when so many people were hungry. I didn't like the way my mother had to serve them and because their son hurt me.

They had two children who were older. Robby used to catch hold of us in their back stairwell. He thought it was fun to pick us up by our cheeks or ears. That hurt. When I was three or four I used to walk down to their house with my mother when she went to work, only to stand in the doorway between the kitchen and dining room watching my mother cook and serve Aunt Emma and Uncle Rob. She was literally their maid. They sat at either end of their long dining room table like royalty. Aunt Emma had a tic in her cheek and her eye used to jump at a regular pace. That was fun to watch. Then mother would return home to cook for all of us.

During that time Mother and Daddy could not pay the mortgage on the cute little house they had bought at 5 Wilson Park, Hastings-on-Hudson, New York. Evidently the renters in Daddy's other two houses which he had inherited, couldn't pay their rent either, so all three houses went into foreclosure. Many men reacted to the stock market crash by committing suicide when they realized that they would have to face the shame of not being able to repay the money they had borrowed.

Illness Strikes

Sometime during the early 1930's Daddy got pneumonia; my sister Edith also became very sick as a tiny baby. And then in 1936 I too fell sick. I was four years old. I still have memories of the pain in my ears. Edith and I usually shared a bed, but I remember waking up in the middle of the night lying between Mother and Daddy. One day the doctor came and shot a liquid into my ears and then I held my head over the edge of the bed to let the liquid run out into a basin, hopefully with some of the infection.

Peggy and Bruce

9

My condition continued to deteriorate with the infection spreading throughout my body. So much thick puss accumulated in my left hip that the ball of the hip popped out of the socket. I was taken to the hospital in Yonkers where I stayed for six weeks. Daddy came to visit me. Once he brought a pull-toy that I could only look at. I was bedridden all of that time. I had long red pigtails parted in the back but when the rubbing against my pillow wore the hair off the back of my head, it was decided that I would be better off with short hair. I still have those pigtails. The ingenious doctors built a high construction at the foot of my bed. They attached my legs to cables with sixteen pound weights hanging down the other side, with the hope that my legs would be the same length once the infection was cured.

My doctor looked like a giant to me. He had a big black bushy mustache. I was very afraid of him. Once when he tried to humor me by pulling my pull-toy around the room, I yelled at him to leave that alone. There was one nurse who came most mornings to take blood samples. She became the love of my life. When I was able to go home she gave me a flowerpot with a Sweet William flower in it. Her name was Miss Williams.

I was fortunate to have been treated in Yonkers near New York City. Sulfa Drugs were still in the experimental stage. I was one of the numerous guinea pigs. They saved the life of hundreds of people including Franklin Delano Roosevelt and perhaps even Winston Churchill, and they saved my life. When I left the hospital I was fitted with a leg brace with two metal bars that were attached to the outsides of my left shoe. These shiny bars climbed up both sides of my calf and were attached to my leg with a leather pad. I wore that brace for the whole year I was in kindergarten. I wasn't able to bend that leg but I ran as fast as I could with the other children on the playground. When we played "horsey" at home I too bent over and ran around on all fours with my rear end sticking high in the air. I remember that position all too clearly because one day my mother told me that I was to return to the Yonkers hospital to see the doctors.

Oh, the humiliation of that visit. I was led into a room that turned out to be a lecture hall. The seats climbed up nearly to the ceiling on my right and were full of white coated doctors-in-training. The man up front talked about my illness and how well I was healing. To prove it he asked me to get down on all fours and walk across the room! Who had told him that I could do that? I did it in front of all of those interns and the room erupted in laughter. It made no difference to this four year old that they were learning to save children's lives and my doing as I was told was intended to prove a teaching point. Of course, I was wearing a skirt.

The Farm - Getting There

We kids were packed into the back seat of the car leaving Hastings-on-Hudson, New York, approaching the tunnels to New Jersey. We would have to choose between the Holland or the Lincoln Tunnel to cross under the Hudson River on our way to Bucks County, Pennsylvania. I loved those tunnels. How could any man-made construction hold back that mighty river above? The headlights reflected on the shiny white tiles on the walls as they flew by. Often there would be a maintenance man walking on the raised walkway that ran along the side above the level of the road. Why was he there and how long would he have to stay down there? What would he do if the tunnel sprang a leak? What would we all do? And then all of the sudden we could see the light of the New Jersey sky in the opening in front of us. The New Jersey air on the Pulaski Skyway was polluted, gray and stinky. We pinched closed our noses with one hand and wound up the windows with the other.

We impatiently anticipated these trips each summer as soon as school was out because we were headed to my Aunt Edith and Uncle Robert's Cherry Lane Farm, which we called simply "The Farm." By the time we crossed the little bridge over the Delaware River into the artist's colony of New Hope, we knew we were close. The scenery changed immediately. The gaudy road signs of New Jersey, advertising everything you could imagine, disappeared. Here the countryside was green and lush with corn, alfalfa and wheat bending in the breeze. Cows grazed here and there. The old farm houses were built of beautiful stone, some a yellowish red and some a deep red creek-bed stone. Many of these beautiful houses were pre-Revolutionary War. George Washington had slept at an inn made of the same stone up in Buckingham, just a few miles away. At least that's the way the story goes.

But in our eyes, the house on Cherry Lane surpassed them all. This farm was the best place for children and Aunt Edith and Uncle Robert didn't have any. That may be the main reason that we went there every summer. They needed help and we were kept busy. Aunt Edith was 16 years older than my mother. She replaced the grandmothers that I had hardly known.

As we turned the corner at the Buggy Wheel, a small quaint diner, we only had minutes more to wait. We could see the barn first with its bull pen, enclosed barnyard, milk house, the shed which protected the 1936 Dodge and the farm machinery. Then the corn crib came into view; all of these buildings were to the left of the long red hued lane, and there, set straight ahead farther up the lane was the beautiful red stone, two story house with it's four chimneys, three front doors, white shutters, and flagstone porch. The walls were 12 inches thick. There were two huge maples and two larger sycamore trees with their white speckled trunks and hanging pompoms spread in a line across the front lawn. The tired old walnut tree sat in the side yard, the lilac bush and another maple tree just at the back corner.

Aunt Edith came out to the porch to hug us all. She must have pulled off her apron and flung it over a chair when she heard us drive in. We entered the screened door from the flagstone porch, into the flagstone paved kitchen. These stones in the kitchen had been washed for two hundred years and were black and shiny. Our favorite slide was just to the right - the slanted door to the cellar. The tree trunk beams overhead held their secrets. Above them was the original smoke house. We didn't pay much attention to the chute open at both ends built into the stonewall of the kitchen just above the dry sink. It was made of matching flat stones that pierced through the twelve-inch thick wall and protruded about ten inches outside from the side of the house. In the absence of plumbing it was used by the early owners to get rid of dirty dishwater without having to go outside. We learned years later when the house was declared a historic site that this chute is unique. The present owners have been told by the Historical Society that there is not another like it in the United States.

All of the rooms were laid out in a line. You could walk in one of the front doors, cross the room and go out into the backyard. Each room, upstairs and down, had its own fireplace. A child could easily stand up straight in the two that included bake ovens. There were two enclosed staircases. Perhaps the early owners had built one two-story section at a time, adding the next as the farm prospered.

The Farm - The House and Its Mysteries

I was afraid to go down into the cellar alone, as it was a dark, shadowy, damp place even in the summer. The floor was unpaved and the ground slippery. But the temperature made it ideal for the jars of the food stored there. By the end of summer there were row upon row of canned peaches, pears, applesauce, tomatoes, elderberries, blackberries and endless rows of vegetables that Aunt Edith and Mother had canned. And of course we kids played our part in their preparation. We picked the strawberries and peeled the peaches. We climbed the trees and picked the cherries. This was, after all, Cherry Lane Farm. Aunt Edith had a hand-turned pitter.

Cherry Lane Farm House

Aunt Edith and Mother also canned the chickens that Uncle Robert slaughtered in the side yard. The professionally slaughtered pigs provided hams and bacon and our version of Philadelphia Scrapple. Aunt Edith served us a slice of fried scrapple for breakfast or even supper. Morning coffee was served fresh ground. The hand turned grinder, already an antique, was attached to the door of the kitchen pantry. I can still hear the sound of that grinder.

If I was afraid of the dark cellar, I loved the attic. There were two small windows at each end. The sloping slate roof meant that we could stand up in the center, but only there. The attic was divided by the chimneys. There was one very small room in the back corner, but otherwise it was one big room with the openings of the two staircases rising from the second floor. There were no railings around them to protect someone from taking a wrong step. In one section the hams and bacon hung. Aunt Edith would climb the two flights, choose the one she wanted, go back down to the kitchen, slice off just enough and hike the remainder back up to the attic. I can't remember that she ever asked us to save her a few steps.

Hidden in the old trunks were dresses from the 1800's complete with bustles and huge hats with feathers from tropical birds. My mother's hair trunk with her initials, HLB in brass, was full of family photos. There was another trunk nearly full of letters from family living in Cuba, among those from other relatives. To my knowledge I never opened one to read it. My deepest regret today is that those letters were disposed of when the house was sold. Imagine the surprises and history they contained. The dresses and hats were sent to the Mercer Museum in Doylestown, the county seat.

One day my sister and I crawled under the bed in my aunt and uncle's bedroom. We found a cloth-padded box. We sneaked a peek. In it were lots of old coins. Some of them were pure gold, and as I remember were dated in the 1850's. Finding and opening that box we kept a secret.

The Farm - Work and Play

Some of my most vivid memories were outside: running back and forth from the barn to the house in the pouring rain with burlap bag capes on our heads, the arrival for the summer of the Stackhouse family with their children, David and Catharine, and sometimes their cousins, Hide and Seek in the dark with the kids from Wycombe village who came the 3/4ths of a mile after supper to play with us, catching lightning bugs in jars and letting them go before they died, sleeping on the front lawn and then being awakened way too early when Uncle Robert let Toby out of the barn. He made a beeline to the front lawn to lick every cheek in sight.

Peggy, David S., Bruce, pigeons, Toby and Fluffy

Back from the field

We played house or hospital by the hour in a parked hackney. It was black with four huge wheels and a black canvas roof and sides with steps to make it easy for the ladies to climb up. Uncle Robert used it to deliver milk until he got his 1936 Dodge. A neighbor sitting up high and straight in his hackney still drove his beautiful trotting horse in front of the farm on his way into Wycombe. My imagination made him into a country squire that I had read about in books like "Black Beauty."

Sometimes in the evenings we would just run in the dark, across the roads, up the hills or down along the creek. One night I was lagging behind the larger group and didn't see them all duck as they ran under the electrified barbed wire fence. It caught me on my right shoulder. I carried the scar for years.

When the hay was high in the barn we could reach the rafters to capture the squabs (baby pigeons) whose nests were on the crossbeams. There was always a pair. We put them in chicken cages; fed them with our little fingers trying to dupe them into thinking they were their mother's beak. We watched their hairy bodies change to feathers and then we tried to teach them to fly. Their mother knew how that should be done but we were ignorant of her techniques. We put them on the clothesline and let them go, hoping that as they fell they would stretch their wings out. They must have learned because they followed us around sometimes riding on our shoulders. Uncle Robert helped us name them: Kate and Duplicate, Pete and Repeat, Nip and Tuck, Jack and Jill.

From time to time in the evening some neighbor would stop by and report that our heifers were out of their pasture. Uncle Robert sent us out to round them up. One night someone took a picture as we kids trudged across the hill. We were kind of lined up according to size with Toby, a cat and David Stackhouse's pet pig trailing behind. A neighbor had given David the runt of his litter that, without very special care, would have died. David cared for him like a baby and he became a hanger-on in a lot of our activities.

But another reason we were there was to help with the farm work. No one kept a diary so there is no way to know how many days we spent in the fields or in the barn. Suffice it to say that some summers Uncle Robert did not employ a hired hand. The fields had already been fertilized, plowed, harrowed and planted by the time school was out and we arrived. But very shortly haying would start. Maintaining 80 acres, with about 15 to 20 cows to be milked by hand twice a day, the pigs and chickens to be fed and watered and the hay and alfalfa to be cut and stored and the corn to be ground and the feed to be mixed, there was plenty to do to say nothing of the back breaking work of cleaning up after the animals. At least in the summer they spent their days in the pastures.

We didn't go out to the barn at 4:30 in the morning to do the milking, but we had our tasks around the afternoon milking. I was in charge of feeding and watering the chickens. That included gathering the eggs. One old hen refused to give hers up. The others flew down to eat the delicious grains I had lured them with, but she sat in total defiance glued into her nest. I was afraid to put my hand under her and steal her egg because she would peck at me with all her might. So I stood there, talked to her - and prayed. Nothing worked. She battered my arm every day.

I also was the driver of the horses, in the hay field as well as the single horse that pulled the hayfork loading the hay from the wagon into the haymow and to the mill in town. On the return trip I would just drop the reins and let them take us home. Edith, who was two years older than I, had tasks which were much more strenuous. She stacked the hay on the wagon and in the mow as Uncle Robert guided the huge fork that heaved it up. She ran the mower and probably other heavy machines. One day my brother Bruce came to the barn to watch all of the activity. He was four years younger than I so was very young. He was standing to the side but unfortunately had one leg straddling the rope as Malcolm started driving the horse down the incline. The rope jerked up and caught him just behind the knee tearing a good section of flesh from behind the joint.

I was in love with the horses. These were tired, worn out discarded workhorses with stocky legs that had delivered milk along the cobblestone streets of Philadelphia. Uncle Robert was able to buy them for a song. They gradually regained their strength in the country air and gave years of service. I would stand under their soft velvety noses petting them and talking to them, but only when I was alone.

Uncle Robert's cows except for the one Guernsey were all registered Holsteins. He asked me to reproduce the black and white colorings on their registration papers. In order to be sure my design was correct I would climb up into the haymow to look at their backs from above. They looked so different from up there with their fat bellies shooting out on both sides.

Aunt Edith spent a lot of time weeding her vast vegetable garden. I didn't mind joining her. It was there that I learned to love the feel of dirt and the satisfaction of seeing a clean row of tomato plants or beans. I can still spend many hours weeding in anticipation of that satisfaction. I painted the shutters on the house probably twice over the years. I guess she thought that I did a good enough job because she had me continue painting furniture and floors.

The Farm - Faith Reinforced

Uncle Robert was a devout Christian. He believed wholeheartedly that man should imitate the pattern of working six days a week and resting on Sunday. Even if rain was coming on a Monday he would not take the horses out haying on Sunday. They needed to rest as much as he did. But that didn't mean that the milking could be laid aside or that all of the animals didn't need to be fed.

We had a Bible reading all together in the kitchen each night. My seat was on the flagstone steps. He read consecutive chapters, and there was no skipping around. It seemed to me that we were often there when so-and-so begat so-and-so, who begat...., those Old Testament genealogies. We giggled when he came to funny sounding names, especially what we heard as 'Pegleg,' my nickname. He would then intone a prayer that sounded the same each night, finishing, "Give us rest, we pray thee, in sleep and fit us for what thou hast for us on the morrow."

The Farm - Tragedy Strikes

There was one July I will never forget. The sky looked very strange late one afternoon as though there was a crazy storm headed our way. I was standing in the kitchen doorway when I saw a dark cone shaped pillar in the sky. My first and last intimate experience with a tornado passed us by, but it hit the farm just next to us. Mrs. Naylor was in her milk house. She lifted her head in reaction to the sudden intense noise, just as the roof lifted and she found herself looking up into the sky. Those stonewalls had held firm and she was not hurt.

Some time later we were out in the front yard after supper when a small plane flew overhead. There were flames shooting out of the wing. This was no movie. The pilot jumped, his parachute exploded above him and he landed in the pasture across the road directly in front of our house. The plane crashed in Mr. Naylor's cornfield. The villagers came out to see the wreckage and to tear off pieces of the yellow canvas. The pilot hurt his knees. He said that was the first time he had agreed to wear a chute.

The third incident that same month was a fire. It was Saturday night and Mr. and Mrs. Love were heating bath water in a huge tub under the staircase. They lived only one mile away from Cherry Lane Farm, across from the Buggy Wheel. The six children were finished and already upstairs in bed when the stairway caught fire. Mr. Love was only able to save one son as access to the upstairs was completely cut off. Uncle Robert and Aunt Edith took in Mr. and Mrs. Love and their boy and settled them in the little cottage at the end of our farmhouse. I still cry when I think of this tragedy. I didn't know how to express to the family the sadness I felt. They had lost five children in the course of a few minutes.

I was born while we were at the Farm. I spent every summer of my childhood on the farm except 1938 when we went to up-state NY to my grandmother's house. In 1947 as I entered 10th grade we moved there so that Mother could be with and eventually care for Aunt Edith and Uncle Robert full time. The barn was already emptied of animals and machinery. When Bill and I went overseas to Tunisia in 1961 we packed and loaded our trailer with our luggage under those maple trees. Within two years my aunt and uncle died and the farm was sold.

Today when we drive through Wycombe and turn down Park Avenue to Cherry Lane, my heart longs to be able to walk up that lane, across the flagstone porch through the screen door to the flagstone kitchen where so many of my childhood memories took place and hug Aunt Edith and laugh as she shakes her shoulders because she doesn't like it when I touch those little curls on the back of her neck, and sit on Uncle Robert's knee while he sings "The Bear Went Over the Mountain," dropping us through his knees.

But the cherry trees have been cut down; the creek pasture is almost a forest. The bullpen is gone, as are the milk house, the sheds, and the corncrib. The cow stanchions have been removed and the haymow where we stole the squabs and where we climbed the ladder and jumped into the hay yelling, "I am the queen of the world!" as we hurtled through space to the bed of hay below, is now a fancy apartment. Many of the original 80 acres have been sold and newer looking houses have been built in at least two of the pastures and in the field behind the orchard.

The house now has red shutters and the maple trees are gone. But the view from the road to the house is still about the same. The lawns are manicured and the flowers are beautiful. The present owners don't rely on the calves to mow their lawn. They have opened the fireplaces and placed antiques everywhere. They and their two sons love it as much as we did.

Change has come, landmarks are missing, but those overwhelmingly happy memories refuse to fade.

My Home Town

My most memorable hometown is a small country village 30 miles north of Philadelphia in Bucks County by the name of Wycombe, named after High Wycombe in Great Britain. As happened to many other geographical namesakes in the U.S., either the pronunciation or the spelling diverged from the original. Instead of saying 'Wickom' as they do in England, we called it 'Wy-comb.' My university friends from New England liked to call it, "Why come to Pennsylvania?"

That is where my Aunt Edith and Uncle Robert lived. Every summer except 1938 until my adulthood, my sister Edith, brother Bruce and I helped with the haying, loading the hay wagon, packing it into the mow, caring for the animals, those with injuries became our pets, and playing with squabs, going berry and cherry picking, playing hide and seek with the town kids after dark, sleeping on the front lawn with friends until Toby was released from the barn and came tearing up the lane to lick our faces.

That is until school started and we had to return back to our real home leaving this fairyland of work, play, friends and fresh air. On reflecting back it seems to me that my best memories, fantasies, my nighttime dreams, of fun and adventure were in some way related to those 80 acres. My life was knit into the fabric of that land vibrating with life, good food, and the warmth of summer air. And that land was knit into me.

The town of Wycombe, about ¾ of a mile away, played a lesser role in those memories. Uncle Robert sometimes took us to see Mr. Overpeck. He was the tinsmith. His dark dingy house, right next to the lovely Baptist Church, was what we thought of as a dump of unused or partly cut piles of metal, tools and junk that laid helter-skelter on the floor, table and shelves. Where in there he and his wife lived, we could only speculate. But if he made his living repairing and tool making in a small town like Wycombe, he must have been a very clever man. No doubt it was the surrounding farmers who were his best customers.

We didn't see the Funeral Director, Mr. Varcoe very much, but he lived in a pretty nice house with a large front porch. It was in other buildings around back where he plied his trade!

I drove the horses to the mill during the summer to get the corn and wheat and maybe the soybeans ground. Handsome Mr. Carver was the manager. There were big holes in the floor, with no guardrails, where we could stand on the edge and watch the big grinding machinery do their work. Imagine if my mother had gone with us and had seen her two little girls standing there leaning over!

There was an adorable two-room train station by the tracks. The three-car train took a steady stream of passengers to Hatboro and then on to Philadelphia or in the other direction to New Hope, the county artists' colony on the Delaware River. Wycombe had been a vacation destination at the turn of the century for tourists from Philadelphia with this easy access by train. That was when the Wycombe Inn was in its heyday. Across the gravel parking space from the station stood the General Store/U.S. Post Office. Mr. and Mrs. Landes ran the store. Their son Stover Landes eventually became the Post Master.

Dr. Roberts lived in a large Victorian house on the corner across the street. But we didn't have to come to his office because he made house calls. The Victorian Inn was around the corner.

The main street was lined with trees and houses with large front porches. It crossed the single train track, over the stone hump-shaped bridge that spanned the 25-foot wide stream. Wycombe was more than a crossroads. There were, in addition to Main St, Washington Avenue, Smith Rd, Furlong Road, Park Ave and Cherry Lane. The town was Victorian, but the beautiful red stone farmhouses surrounding it were pre-Revolutionary.

Daddy and Our Family

In some ways Daddy's family is a bit of a mystery. We lived in Hastings, NY where Daddy had been raised and where many of his family still lived, but we did not seem to have the same emotional ties to his relatives that we had to Mother's family who lived so much farther away. I don't know the reason. Was there an 'event' that had happened in the past? Or was the family just divided naturally from the busyness of life? Was it because his mother Hughanna Ritchie (known as Annie) had died when he was born? Daddy had been given an adaptation of her name, Hugh Ritchie. His father remarried and it was the new wife Elizabeth, who raised the younger children.

When I was in elementary school, Daddy was often far away job hunting because work was so hard to find. He had a family of seven to support. As the depression years faded away he found a job in Upper New York State painting ships to help the war effort. Before I entered sixth grade, Daddy transferred to eastern Pennsylvania. We left Hastings and moved to Prospect Park, west of Philadelphia, so that we could all be together. Mother and Daddy did not share their problems with us so we were protected from their worries. When we were young my mother's brother, Uncle Edgar had remarked, "You would think that Helen's children were princes and princesses with no cares to carry on their shoulders."

My oldest brother David was already away at university and then in the Air Force and only came home when he was on leave. Malcolm was a senior in high school.

One day Daddy came home from work with a puppy, a little black and white fox terrier. We had had a cat named Penny because she came from Pennsylvania so we named the puppy, Nickel. We thought that that was clever.

It was during this time that I remember that we laughed a lot at home. Daddy joined in our Sunday dinner games of Bible Characters but with less enthusiasm. He certainly didn't share mother's vast knowledge of the Bible, but he had his idea of what Christians should do and not do. The not-does were playing cards, drinking alcohol or smoking, dancing and going to the movies. In some ways I think that these restrictions were the opposite of his personality.

I was so glad when I realized that Christianity was not what you didn't do, but more internal - what you believe, what you are, what your motivations are and how much you care for other people. I longed to get over my inhibitions about dancing while in high school, but especially overseas where weddings were just that, dancing parties, women with women and men with men. We were living in the culture where belly dancing originated and I longed to be able to just let go. But that doesn't mean I didn't dance at all!

Eventually Daddy started working for Land Title Bank and Trust Company in Philadelphia. As I started tenth grade we moved to The Farm and he changed again working at Fischer and Porter Company in Warminster, PA, with much more convenient access from the farm. This meant only taking one train instead of two. Fischer and Porter was a young thriving company with innovative ideas and a concern for the welfare of its employees. Daddy thrived there. He came home with a turkey at Thanksgiving and beautiful Christmas presents from his employer. He was so proud when he survived the annual medical check-up with flying colors year after year, all paid for by Mr. Fischer.

During my high school years Bruce and I had Mother and Daddy to ourselves. Aunt Edith and Uncle Robert lived downstairs and I often spent time sitting in Aunt Edith's kitchen when I came home from school. Mother was working in a factory helping keep both Malcolm and Edith in college. Uncle Robert had sold off the farm animals and machinery; the farm was no longer functioning. I loved my new high school and new friends. Daddy worked in his flower garden after work. He had champion irises, which he nursed as his babies. The days of Aunt Edith's huge vegetable garden were over, but every spring the Burpee Catalogue arrived so Mother and Daddy could plan and choose the seeds in preparation for the last frost. When Mother retired she added hooking rugs and quilting to her knitting, crocheting, and dressmaking.

David married Coral Jander. They had small children when they came to visit. We loved their visits. We recounted the cute things the children said over and over. David told us on one of these trips they had seen a large bridge. One of the little boys asked how anyone could construct a bridge over water like that with such big arches. When I asked how he had answered, he said, "I told them!"

Helen Bullock Brown   Hugh Ritchie Brown

I waited till Malcolm graduated from college before I went off to the University of Vermont in the fall of 1951. Malcolm married Florence Stewart, and Edith married Finlay McCormick. Several years later Bruce married Shirley Storie. Malcolm studied at Hope College and Westminster Seminary, University of Pennsylvania and Oxford University in England. Bruce studied at Temple University and at Westminster Seminary in Philadelphia, continued at Gordon Conwell Seminary in Boston. Florence and Edith taught school in the Philadelphia area.

For several years the family and our friends came and went. Edith brought her college friends home and I brought three of mine down from New England. Mother exhausted herself keeping the table filled with food but both she and Daddy reveled in the laughter and craziness in those cramped quarters. Even today I can't imagine where everyone slept. Malcolm and Bruce could hardly say anything without citing a private family joke. Malcolm told me that if either of them was in the pulpit and the other was in the congregation, they would have to avoid each other's eyes in order to keep from bursting into laughter.

After my graduation in 1955, Edith and I spent a summer with David and Coral for summer school session at Penn State in State College. I was already receiving mysterious letters. Coral asked me who they were from. She seemed satisfied when I replied that they were, "Oh just from my roommate's brother." I taught for one year at Central Bucks High School in Doylestown, PA, in 1955/56 and then at Philadelphia Montgomery Christian Academy for three years.

My Mother

She was short, not particularly beautiful in appearance except for her soft smooth skin. Perhaps her chin protruded too much or her nose was a bit stubby. She used to say that she had the Bullock chin. But it didn't take long to discover the depth of character and beauty that made up who she really was. I don't remember her beautiful head of auburn hair but her pictures during her courting years give ample evidence to what Daddy spoke of and loved so much.

My more vivid memories of her appearance are when she was tired from the cares that the Depression forced on her, of her concerns over feeding five children when Daddy was away looking for a job, then later in life when she was responsible for the drawn out care of her older sister and husband, my Aunt Edith and Uncle Robert. That care would have overwhelmed most anyone, especially someone in her sixties. That changed when she was free from caring for others and had her white hair cut and curled around her face. She used to tell me that no one cut her hair as well as I did. And of course that encouraged me to do the best I knew how.

That's the way she was, encouraging. She was gentle and wise, concerned for others, humble and deeply spiritual and had a brilliant mind. Despite her tremendous potential, her life is a story of sacrificing herself and her gifts for the benefit of others. What does one say of a person who always took the smallest portion or none at all when money was tight? Everyone loved her, and I think I loved her more than anyone. She was the anchor of my life, always there when I needed advice or simply help with my homework. And I was sure of hers and Daddy's love for me.

My remembrances render her too perfect. I realize that this may not result in a picture of a real person, but these are my real memories and she seems so real in my memory.

She was born Helen Louise Bullock on July 30, 1895 in Penn Yan, NY. Her parents had established a basket making business in Crosby, ten miles away on Lake Keuka. In 1908 when she was 13, they decided on a new venture and moved to the Isle of Pines, just south of mainland Cuba, taking some of their children with them. An older brother, Edgar, an engineer, later joined the family setting up a fruit packing business.

Leaving her parents behind she came back from Cuba to the U.S. to complete her schooling, graduating from Hastings-on-Hudson High School in 1914. It was there that she met my father, Hugh Ritchie Brown. Daddy said that the first day he saw her with her beautiful swept back head of auburn hair and blue eyes, he fell in love with her. She was a shy gentle girl with all of the traits he admired, but she didn't visibly respond to him. His persistence won the day and the pictures we have of their courting days are very sweet.

Her report card grades from high school make boring reading as the New York State Regents exam grades were included: 98, 99, 100, 99, 100. . . . We used to joke that she had studied her own six years of Latin and then added ten more years as she helped us kids through our two years each. You certainly didn't want to challenge her to a game of Scrabble.

It was unusual to hear her criticize anyone, much less complain, so when she began reminiscing about how unhappy she had been during her high school years, I felt very sad for her. Upon her return from Cuba she had moved in with her brother William who was superintendent of the schools in Hastings-on-Hudson, New York. He and his wife, Alta, had no children. They were very stiff and straight laced and seemed to have little idea what her needs were or how to be considerate of her. He and his older brother, my Uncle Joe were graduates of Colgate University. They did not keep their promise to care for their youngest brother, Homer, or pay my mother's expenses as a student at Adelphi University, so she had to leave after a short time.

The first time I realized how seldom she complained was when I was in the third or fourth grade. I came home at noon for lunch to change my dress because I was invited to a birthday party after school. She was shaking all over and having difficulty holding a needle. I had never seen her so upset. She explained that she had decided to make me a party dress that morning but it wasn't finished yet.

She was in obvious agony over something else. Bruce, who wasn't old enough to go to school, had run down the stairs, out onto the front porch slamming the door. Our downstairs neighbor came out of her apartment and scolded him with a harsh tone. Mother went down immediately and told Mrs. Walsh that if she was unhappy with any of the children's behavior, she was to speak only to their mother!

She finally sewed me into the dress, as she had no time to sew on snaps or buttons. All of her life she delighted in making clothes for her two daughters. She made my winter coat when I went off to the University of Vermont. She sewed Edith's wedding gown and my bridesmaid's dress, as well as my dusty rose silk going-away suit. I wore that suit when we sailed from New York City, destination Tunis, Tunisia in 1961.

She taught us mutual respect. Perhaps we younger children benefitted from her experiences with the older ones. But in some instances, we had to learn the hard way. One evening when I was in the seventh grade she was washing the dishes and I was drying. Some of the dishes were coming into the dish rack with spots of food on them. I must have criticized her. I never forgot her reaction.

Her hot soapy hand shot out of the dishwater across my face as she said, "You will never speak to me like that again!" I had four finger imprints on my left cheek. And then, she apologized, but I knew I deserved more than just one slap. I wanted to please her. I wanted her to be proud of me.

I respected her deep spiritual life, her understanding of the Bible. Once Bruce was directing Daily Vacation Bible School. We planned a slogan for the two weeks. Each day the children were to select a Bible verse to memorize beginning with the letters in the slogan. We had a hoot reading their choices because they just opened their Bibles and chose the first verse they found beginning with the day's letter. We were laughing as Bruce read, "Moab is my wash pot and...." Mother interrupted and finished the OT verse, "and over Edom have I cast out my shoe." Our hilarity paused astounded. Then she explained its context and meaning! We still chose another child's verse!

Sometimes after baby-sitting I would arrive home very late, usually early morning. I woke her up to tell her that I was home, but I didn't stop there. I then stood by the bed to tell her every cute thing the children had said. She never told me she needed to sleep but listened and responded from her pillow.

Shortly before I graduated from high school she told me I would have to delay college. Edith and Malcolm were both in school. Financing a third simultaneously was out of the question. She was already working in a factory and sending every cent she could to pay tuition. So I joined her for a year in what I dubbed "Pineville Finishing School." Surely we both would be finished off sitting in front of soldering irons assembling electrical plugs and fittings under that corrugated roof in the dead of summer and through the cold of winter. My mother continued there for years, again sacrificing for the benefit of her children.

Grandma Drusilla Fenton Bullock with Malcolm, David, Peggy and Edith

When we first went overseas she wrote us a wonderful letter every week She was the best letter writer. When Aunt Edith and Uncle Robert died a few months from each other, the big farmhouse was to be sold and needed to be emptied. A daunting task, and yet she still wrote us letters. They moved to New York to be near Bruce and Shirley and their children. There she was happy with a large group of ladies her age.

Mother and Daddy had a bit of inheritance from the farm sale, so they planned a trip to visit Edith in North Dakota and then later to us in Algeria. After caring for so many: Daddy's parents, Aunt Edith and Uncle Robert, her own family, she arrived in Algeria for that once-in-a-lifetime trip in 1965. But once again she slipped into that role of caregiver. Shortly after their arrival I came down with hepatitis. When I did not improve, it was decided that I should come home to the U.S. Mother aborted the remainder of her dream trip to accompany me back to the U.S. where I spent six weeks in the hospital. Daddy continued on to Paris, London, Ireland and Scotland.

As my condition worsened, we became aware that Mother herself was suffering from increasingly severe headaches. We arrived back in the U.S. mid June 1965. She died of a brain tumor on February 9, 1968. She was only 72 years old.

Fond and Not so Fond Memories - Grandmas

Daddy was the youngest of seven children. Mother was also the youngest of six and I was the fourth of five. This accounts for a good many years difference in age between my grandparents and me. Consequently I have almost no memory of them except through photos - with one or two exceptions.

My grandmother, Hughanna Ritchie Brown (Annie) died after my father's birth. His father remarried a lady named Elizabeth. I was three years old when they came to live in our house at the end of their lives. As I stood in the hallway looking at these two elderly people lying in my brothers' twin beds, I felt no emotional tie. I don't remember even going in to talk with them. Perhaps my step grandmother's reticence during these difficult years to help Mother or in just enjoying the company of us children was caused by the realization she was not really our grandmother.

Memories of Mother's mother Drusilla are soft and sweet and loving, of her diminutive frame sitting in a rocker mending socks, her white hair pulled up in a bun. It is possible of course that these memories come more from pictures and from a few letters. We visited her on Lake Keuka, one of New York's Finger Lakes, when I was six. I remember the lake and the dock but not much else. This dock reappears from time to time in my dreams.

It was my mother's sister, Aunt Edith, 16 years older than my mother, who played more the roll of the traditional grandma in my life. We spent our summers with her on the farm. She wore her long hair pulled stylishly up in a large bun on the top of her head. I remember once watching in awe as she took out the pins and it cascaded down to her thighs. I had no idea that it was so long. She combed it out and then deftly swirled it back into that chic style. If any hair stayed in the comb she carefully gathered it up, wound it around her finger and hid it in a porcelain hair dish on her dresser.

Family Legend -
The Campbells Are Coming!

Some say that legends are good in and of themselves, whether based on truth or not. I guess they bolster our ego or sense of pride and self worth. But I don't like the idea of being caught up in believing as true something that never actually happened, even if it is labeled "a legend."

My family had its legends. Daddy said his ancestry went back to Robert the Bruce, the famous king of Scotland. That was why he wanted to name my youngest brother Bruce. But if the images on the Internet are accurate, Robert the Bruce's appearance was not too much to be proud of! Daddy had a sense of Scottish and British history and its pivotal historic events. He often linked the Sepoy Rebellion in India to his ancestry through his mother's father. Unfortunately some of my memories are vague as to just what he told us about the role his ancestors actually played in that event and the final victory during the siege of Lucknow, India, in 1857. But one thing is clear. It was a heritage that was very important to him.

Evidently his mother's father, named Ritchie, was fighting alongside General Henry Havelock. The Army reached the besieged city of Lucknow, but the Sepoys resurged and Havelock's army was trapped inside. They were eventually relieved once and for all by an arriving relief force under the leadership of General Colin Campbell. The first sign that help was on its way was the sound of bagpipes playing "The Campbells are Coming." He reminisced that one of our ancestors trapped in that city was the first to hear that music over the chaos of gunfire. Daddy loved to sing, "The Campbells are coming, Hurrah, Hurrah." When we were in London with him he wanted his picture taken beside General Havelock's memorial in Trafalgar Square. I remember how many pigeons wanted theirs taken too.

The DOBBS FERRY REGISTER of 1918, Dobbs Ferry, NY recounts: "Hugh Ritchie [Brown] gets his middle name, Ritchie from his grandfather on his mother's side, who was one of that heroic band of Britishers who, after the British had made a desperate defense in Lucknow, India, during the Sepoy mutiny in 1857, brought relief to the beleaguered garrison under General Havelock. After Havelock had fought his way into the town and relieved the garrison, the siege was continued until succor was finally brought by the troops under General Colin Campbell. "Dinna ye hear the bagpipes, the Campbells are coming, hurrah, hurrah," is a reminder of the heroic days when Ritchie, the grandfather of Hugh Brown, fought behind the wall of Lucknow to hold off the bloody Sepoys while watchers in the tower strained their eyes for the coming of the Campbells and relief."

Family Legend - Saints or Strangers

I had a feeling of pride in my mother's family, the Bullocks. She told us the family lore, recounted as fact, that our distant ancestor had braved the Atlantic on the Mayflower. We were descendants of history making heroes!

In the 1990's my cousin, Paul Bullock decided to research the Bullock legend and its Mayflower connection. Word reached us overseas that he had done the best he could but there was still one generation missing. I assumed this meant he had lost the trail of our ancestry, or the line switched to a woman whose name had been dropped from the genealogy listings and that would explain that lost generation. But I was wrong.

It was clear and simple. There was no Bullock on the Mayflower. There was another name on that Mayflower passenger list to which our family is connected. John Billington was the scoundrel among scoundrels on that ship. The passengers were divided into Saints, those seeking religious freedom, and Strangers, those coming for monetary gain or for escape from punishment for a crime committed, or for adventure. John was one of the Strangers. He was traveling with his wife Elinor and two sons, John, Jr. and Francis. John, Jr. made a name for himself when he almost blew up the Mayflower, as she lay moored close to land, by shooting off a gun in the ammunition room. His father was often in trouble as well. His rough language and coarse behavior did not suit the saintly saints and he was duly punished.

One day during the years that followed, he lay in wait out in the woods for another hunter with whom he had had an argument. That fateful day he gained further renown as the first murderer in the Massachusetts Bay Colony.

His son, Francis, married Christian Penn Eaton and had nine children whom he could not feed, so he farmed them out to other families as workers or servants. Other ships arrived. On board in 1643 was our ancestor Richard Bullock. When his first wife Elizabeth Ingraham died leaving him the care of six children, he married one of Francis Billington's daughters, Elizabeth. She bore him more children all with the name of Bullock.

Our line of ancestry, however, comes not from the second Elisabeth's children, the granddaughter of John Billington, but from one of Richard's children, Samuel, born in 1648, by his first wife. So we cannot claim a blood line to the Mayflower, only a stepmother line. If we insist on the original family legend we must also claim to be descendants of renown of a different order - from the first murderer in the colonies. I wonder how my mother would have felt had she known that her family legend had been dashed to pieces. And replaced with such an uncomfortable truth!

World War II through the Eyes of a Child

I was nine years old when Japan bombed Pearl Harbor. Even I realized that that day foretold a scary future. Germany had already invaded Poland and was on its way to taking over Europe. But Germany was far away and I had never heard of Poland or those other countries in the news. But mother explained that Pearl Harbor was part of us. Even though it too was far away, we soon knew where it was and how many Americans had been killed. The country switched into total mobilization, labeled the WAR EFFORT.

I still looked at issues in black and white, right and wrong, good and bad. This war had clear guidelines and a clear purpose. Even the adults saw this war in black and white. We were on the side of RIGHT. We didn't initiate the war; our friends and we had been attacked. Everyone was expected to participate in this effort to combat wrong and everyone we knew did, with willing hearts. Our friends in Great Britain and France were dying and now our soldiers too were dying. Who our enemy was, was clear. The ALLIES were our friends. The AXIS powers were the enemy. The guilty must be punished.

So we used food stamps, which allotted us limited amounts of food for a month for a family of six. We bought margarine in a plastic bag of white grease with a little bubble of yellow dye, which had to be broken and pinched through till the whole mass imitated butter. When the sirens sounded the alarm, we were told to walk to the basement of our school and to sit lined along the wall with our knees up so that we could hide our heads between them in the case of an air attack. Thankfully these turned out to be only trial exercises. We kept our shades drawn at night. We didn't want the enemy to find its target. We turned off all lights when the sirens blew.

And then my oldest brother left college to join the Air Force. That brought the war even closer. He looked wonderful in his uniform with its brass buttons and emblems on his sleeve. Mother went to Connecticut to pin on his "Wings."

We scanned the newspapers whenever we could, and listened constantly to the radio. Rumor had it that a German U-Boat had come up the Hudson River and set a fire, which finally sunk the Normandie right in NY harbor. My parents took us to see the damage. What audacity! All the way across the Atlantic Ocean! This was all the more real to us as we lived only a few miles north in Hastings-on-Hudson. The truth, heard much later, was that an American welder had accidentally set that fire as the luxurious ocean liner was being transformed into a troop ship.

I remember where I was standing in the kitchen when the radio announcer said that Pearl Harbor had been bombed. This enemy, Japan, struck greater fear into our hearts. These strange Asians were cruel and heartless and worshipped Hirohito as their God. Germany was in cahoots with Japan who had the same goal: to rule the world! Now we had double justification to support the war effort because our country was fighting on two fronts. We saved our pennies and bought war bonds.

Our German neighbors disappeared. We wondered why, and where they had been taken. Was this right? And then we thought well, they were Germans after all. It helped that we didn't know them very well.

We kids had to find an outlet, so we planned our own vengeance on both Germany and Japan. My sister and I drew caricatures of Hitler and Hirohito. That was easy. Hirohito had a round face and slanted eyes and Hitler had plastered black hair down the side of his forehead along with his stubby, black, ugly, mustache. We fastened our pictures to the old Sycamore tree near the front porch. Our darts landed pretty accurately and we cheered each other on as our violence gradually shredded their faces. We knew we would win that war!

The Philadelphia Inquirer's front-page headline screamed, "D-DAY!" The Allied Forces had stormed the Normandy beaches. That must be really important, but where in the world was Normandy? The loss of life was terrible but we had duped the Germans. General Eisenhower was our hero and we found Churchill to be a remarkable man. We children didn't know what to think of President Roosevelt because Daddy was a staunch Republican, but it was sad that he died before the final victory. The European campaign finished and the Battles of the Pacific ruled the day.

Edith, Bruce and Peggy

Peggy

After the war, mother made Edith and me "Eisenhower Jackets" with their bands just at our waists. I was so proud. And through it all we held our right hand high imitating Churchill, with the forefinger and middle finger spread apart: 'V' IS FOR VICTORY! Soldiers brought home foreign wives. I met a Latvian woman who had had a harrowing escape from the Russians hiding out for weeks in the woods only to be captured and put in a concentration camp by the Germans.

She and her fellow prisoners were liberated by our G.I.'s. She said that the ladies there were so glad to finally be liberated. They told the G.I.'s that they had been horridly mistreated, but they had heard that the Americans were good and wouldn't touch them, and they didn't. She had married one of them. Another, a close neighbor, married to a vet, was British. I was fascinated by her accent and used to lie out on the lawn after one of her visits trying to imitate her. She once told us she wasn't feeling well and thought she needed "a complete overhaul."

Influencers

My fourth grade teacher, Mrs. Woodcock, taught me to love history through her enthralling teaching about Macedonia, Egypt, Greece, Carthage, and Rome. I was awed when she said that some vestiges from the past still existed. She set up a long table filled with sand on the side of our classroom. We carved pyramids and obelisks, and sphinxes out of big bars of Ivory Soap to place in the sand. I learned about the Parthenon and the Coliseum and the Appian Way and even about Hannibal and his elephants.

Many years later my memory returned to that classroom as I walked onto the stage of a Greek theater in Sicily and then Roman theaters in North Africa. The acoustics were fantastic. We dressed up as Romans and I belted out lines from Anthony's speech at Caesar's funeral. It was really Shakespeare's speech, which I had memorized under the tutelage of my high school English teacher. I was shocked that the scattered tourists, sitting and walking around, paying absolutely no attention to my speech, were not as moved as I was. When I actually saw the pyramids across the Cairo skyline, and the Parthenon in Athens, the Pantheon in Rome and visited ancient Carthage, I experienced an indescribable emotion as a direct result of Mrs. Woodcock's teaching.

And then there was Miss Berger, my high school English teacher who instilled in me a love of literature. I still remember some of the novels we read, some of the poems we memorized, and the plays we acted out in class. I wonder how many high school classes today have the privilege of reading three Shakespearean plays. The meter of his lines stayed in my brain so that one time after reading aloud to my sister at home, she said, "Peggy, you're talking like Shakespeare!"

The friends we choose when we are young have an important influence on the foundation building of our personalities, opinions, and values. I had a special friend, Marjorie Maier in elementary school, and Mary Bryant in junior high, and Ann Carver through senior high school. Ann and I both lived in Wycombe, and rode the bus to school together. She played the piano in our little church so I always sat down front to keep her company. We used to attend special youth meetings together. While I was in university her family moved away. I had little idea where she was for the next 61 years, but was able to track her down a few years ago. In 2011 we spent some hours together in Colorado and then a few hours again in 2012 in Durham trying to fill in the events of those 61 years.

There were others who made a difference in my spiritual development. The student pastor of our little Baptist Church when I was in elementary school preached the Bible with conviction and touched all of our lives. His preaching initiated a life-changing event in my life when I realized what Jesus had done for me. Daddy, Edith and I were baptized one summer in that little church.

I am grateful to Kat Eckel who helped me overcome my reticence to draw and paint. She was the best encourager in helping me and the other women in her classes develop latent talents by guiding us through the learning process.

But then I suspect that the person who had the most influence on my life was my mother. She was an example of frugality, integrity, honesty, and self-sacrifice. She was proud of her children, (I hope) and happy in her role of motherhood. She didn't vacillate changing the rules according to her fancy or the stresses of the moment, as I'd seen other parents do. She didn't speak to us in anger. She did not scold over accidentally spilled milk. She and my father established a stable, safe home for us. I suppose that the greatest gratitude in my heart springs from the fact that she was always there for us, ready to listen or ready to settle a problem, whether it was to mend a hole in a sock, or to find a lost ball, or to give counsel or comfort.

I am grateful for each one, for the foundation they laid for me in my most formative stage.

Yoo Hoo

"YOO HOO!" Only one person announced her arrival like that. It had to be Mrs. Loux. "YOO HOO!" the voice called out again from the bottom of the lane. We ran around the house and yard yelling, "Mrs. Loux is coming." "Mrs. Loux is here," as though we kids were the only ones who had heard her. There was no way to know ahead of time when she would arrive. Aunt Edith came out of the kitchen to the flagstone porch to greet her, and they walked into the kitchen together.

Mrs. Loux lived in a lovely house up on "The Hill." She loved to come down to Cherry Lane Farm as much as we liked to see her come. She had spent most of her married life alone. I suppose that when she married that ship's captain she must have known that he would be leading an exciting life on foreign shores crossing seas while she waited at home. To compound her loneliness, as far as we knew, she had no children. Maybe her love for us was one of the drawing cards for her visits.

Sometimes she invited my sister and me to go back home with her. Her three-story house was made of red brick with white trim. We passed through the high hedges that bordered the road, to the front door and into the living room. It was dark, mostly because there were tapestries and a dark woven tablecloth that hung to the floor on the table in the middle of the room. The room looked old fashioned, maybe Victorian. One time her husband sat almost hidden in a large chair, talking to his pet parrot! He had a wrinkled, leathery tanned face. I wish we had stopped and sat with him to hear his adventure stories, but we were a bit wary of such a man. We could have brightened his day and in turn learned so much. He invited us to talk to his parrot. We'd never seen anything like it. It actually answered us!

But the attic was our destination. Mrs. Loux always let us play in the attic. The painted room was bright and cheery with light coming in the dormer windows. Fantastic children's toys were spread around the room: dolls in pink dresses, pull toys, puzzles, games, and above all a little child's record player which we wound up over and over again. "This is the way we wash our clothes, wash our clothes....This the way we wash our clothes so early on Monday morning. This is the way we bake our bread, bake our bread.... so early on Tuesday morning." After a few times Edith and I would sing the week through, turning the handle to revive the sagging dying voice.

There were so many unanswered questions. Had they had children, at least a little girl? Why didn't someone talk of her? Had she grown up, or had she died? I think of that silence, still hiding the origins of those toys even today. Who and where was this little girl who was the first to play with them? Our visit finished with a glass of milk and a wonderful big cookie.

We loved Mrs. Loux, so on one of my visits back to Pennsylvania thirty or so years later I inquired about her. She was in a nursing home in Doylestown. Bill and I visited her because I wanted to reminisce one more time and thank her for the happiness she had brought to our childhood.

Aunt Elizabeth

My sister thought I was not only spoiled, but also excessively timid. She was two years older and I relied on her. I was afraid to go places by myself-until I was a sophomore in high school. That year I got a letter from my Aunt Elizabeth inviting me to Washington DC. She didn't invite anyone else, just me. How could I refuse? I don't remember the struggle, but I accepted. This meant taking the train alone, not one train, but four. I would have to change trains three times, first in Hatboro. That was easy. In downtown Philadelphia I had to walk down Market Street through City Hall where Willy Penn watched me from overhead, to change stations from the Reading to the Pennsylvania Line. That train took me the short distance to the huge station at 30th Street. Here fear of not finding the right platform was almost more than I could bear. What would I do if I got on the wrong one? Today I worry more about managing a suitcase!

I made it. My aunt was at the DC station to meet me. We got a taxi to her apartment. It was sweltering. She suggested that we sleep outside. But where was my bed? We dragged her single bed outside onto her patio. She explained that we would sleep head to foot. Her feet reached my face but my feet reached way beyond her face. I was so bushed that I slept like a baby, only waking up when the sun hit my eyes. There were people walking by on the sidewalk a few feet away looking over the low hedge at this lazy bones. I was beside myself with shame. My first thought was, had they seen both of us in that bed! Where was she anyway? Had I kicked her out?

That day we went sightseeing together. But first we had to return to the train station because, in my nervousness, I had grabbed my bag but left my purse on the train! We found it sitting on the shelf in the Lost and Found, intact. A cleaning man had turned it in. We went to the mall; saw the majestic Lincoln Memorial, the Washington Monument, maybe a museum. It was wonderful. We didn't sleep outside that night. I couldn't take another night of humiliation. In the morning she broke the news that she had to go to work and I would sightsee alone. That was not in the bargain. If she had told me, I would not have come.

She handed me a map and off she went. I don't know if I had ever read a map before. She expected the impossible. I chose as my first destination, the Folger Shakespearean Museum. Then I remember spending hours in the Mint. As I recall I met her for lunch, and then I was on my own again. I began to rather enjoy myself - not only the sight seeing, but the map reading as well. What would my sister think of me now?

A few days later I was to take that train trip in the return direction. Again I was filled with anxiety. When I heard the announcement that we had pulled into 30th Street Station, I had such a start that I grabbed my bag and only one handle of my purse. It opened up. The contents rolled over the train floor! Many of the other passengers came to my aid, and I was soon looking for the right platform for my next train.

As I, with both my suitcase and my purse intact, walked that ¾ of a mile from the tiny train station toward home, I told myself that I had accomplished the impossible. I imagined that now I could travel anywhere in the world on my own.

Today my sister says we've experienced roll reversals. She's the one who's afraid to travel alone.

Math Teachers

Hey, "Peggy I'll trade with you." It was my math homework buddy, Walter. He was holding the Science Award, and I, to my astonishment, the Math Award. It was just after our graduation ceremony from High School. These awards did not hold much honor, mind you. We were only 17 graduates.

Arithmetic had always been a mystery to me. In junior high in another school where we were much more numerous, I sat in the front row to the right. The math teacher was a frantic middle-aged man with slipping owl shaped glasses. He owned one black suit. I was never quite sure why he was trying to force us to understand something which either he had no idea how to convey to our disinterested faces, or he had never taught before.

I remember an argument he and I had in class. He maintained that 1 x 0 = 1. I maintained that if you didn't have any 1's, the answer was 0. Or if you had one zero, all you had was zero. Even if you had six zeros the answer is zero. The next day he admitted that he had been wrong. We were still amused by his needing to constantly catch his slipping glasses and by the frustrating little flicking motions of his chalk covered hands trying to flick the chalk dust off the blackness of his suit.

In 10th grade I moved to another school. What a change. The math teacher was in her 60's and had years of experience behind her. Geometry and Algebra were fascinating. It was like a new light in my head had finally reversed those nine years of negative reaction to math.

But the summer before my senior year she retired. I felt betrayed. Another middle-aged man with little round glasses and one grey suit took her place. I remember nothing today from that class except for one event. He had just returned some exam papers. We looked them over. I was puzzled by my grade, but waited till after class. "If there are no corrections why do I have a 99?" His answer, "Nobody's perfect. You have an upside down period."

I should have said, "Which one?"

He also taught Physics, my worst subject. We were to research the ins and outs of the water supply at our homes. My uncle had installed our artesian well so researching was easy. When I got my paper back, I found written in big red script: "What, no gold fish?"

Vivian and Her Brother

Vivian. What fun we had together. I met her sometime during my freshman year playing basketball at the University of Vermont. At UVM the pickings were slim and several of us girls played all three sports, field hockey in the fall, then basketball, and softball in the spring.

This was the era of MEN'S SPORTS, in capital letters. The women's athletic program was fun but only for the players. Nobody came to watch. No journalists came to us for interviews. There was no recognition, no award ceremony, and just plain fun. No one else cared except the women faculty members who were responsible to do whatever they could with the students who showed up to volunteer to play intramural sports. There were a few of us from my small dorm of 32 girls, Allen House. We would walk up together to the gym and play girls from other dorms. Vivian was the best player in every sport.

I had played softball on a recreational team during high school in Pennsylvania in the summers. A teammate's dad would go out of his way to pick me up because I was their pitcher. I had a wicked fastball. I used to practice with a tennis ball aiming at a little chalk circle on the side of the barn. I would spin that tennis ball with all the strength I had, and more or less hit that little circle pretty consistently. So my pitch was fast and accurate, and those country girls would strike out one after the other and complain that it wasn't fun any more because our team always won.

But when I got to college, country girls from Vermont were not at all intimidated by my fastball. In fact they loved it. I had never perfected any other pitch, not for lack of desire, but because I never had anyone to show me how. During my second year in college a new girl joined our dorm. She was tall and thin and had several evil pitches.

From then on I played somewhere else on the field.

I don't know at what point we were selected to represent UVM as a team. I remember traveling in a van to Brown, Skidmore College, University of New Hampshire and other schools in New England and eastern New York, mostly for field hockey and basketball. My most vivid memory was the arrival of the basketball team from McGill University in Montreal. They were good. While we Americans were still limited to two dribbles and had to stay in our designated half of the court, these Canadian girls played whole court and unlimited dribbles. I presume that our rules were meant to keep us acting more like ladies or to accommodate our inferior stamina! The solution was to play one half of the game American rules and one half Canadian.

Vivian and I soon discovered that we had other interests in common. We would attend the concert series or old movies or new art shows sponsored by the art museum. She joined my crowd of friends and we would find ways to get out of town to investigate the mountains or the lake as well as going to church on Sundays. We decided to room together during our senior year. I worked in a campus restaurant and was also house president.

Because my family lived in Pennsylvania, I wasn't able to go home for Thanksgiving or for any of the short holidays. Changing buses three times and then still having to find someone to pick me up in Trenton, New Jersey, took too many hours. So Viv's mom invited me to accompany her home to western Massachusetts and enjoy her family and meet many of her relatives who lived in the area. Her brother Fred had been in the Marines in China and had attended Virginia Tech. Doug had graduated from the University of Massachusetts. Her youngest brother was in the Army Medical Corps in Texas and later in France.

One day during our junior year Viv wanted me to read a letter from this youngest brother. She said that she didn't understand what he was talking about, but she thought I might. I went down to her room. Her bed was in an alcove and I sat leaning against two walls, reading this unbelievable letter. He explained that he had finally found what he had been searching for during his last years at the University of Massachusetts. He had become convinced that fraternity life with weekly drinking binges, attending classes sporadically couldn't continue. He was throwing his life away. What was the meaning of life and where could he find it?

So he quit college in the middle of his senior year and joined the army. Maybe God would become real on the battlefields of Korea. While he was in training as a medical technician in Texas, he attended a Southern Baptist youth retreat with other soldiers and went forward at an invitation to accept Christ. His life completely changed. His values changed, his desire for alcohol disappeared, replaced by a new passion and a new purpose in life. His letter recounted this remarkable experience to his sister.

I was enthralled. I did understand what he was talking about. I understood how Christ changes lives and gives new purpose and stability. I also thought right then and there, "I want to meet this guy."

Ophelia

First appearances are deceiving. At first glance she was only a square black box with a black hood sticking out the front and a rounded trunk lid sticking out the back, set on four spindly black wheels. When people first met her, they saw the dull black paint, the scratches, and her austere, frugal shape. But they also were a bit awestruck by her carriage; she just sat there with her large, bulging eyes looking straight ahead, proud as ever could be. Her past might have been sad and stodgy, parked in a dark, windowless garage, but now she was entering a new life.

The change came over her when she arrived on campus and we gave her a beautiful, delicate, almost ethereal name. Before she was called Plymouth Coupe, vintage 1933, but we named her Ophelia. Her spirits were now lifted with laughter and love. She endured with pride the astonished stares and whispers of passers by, or rather as she passed them by. We know because the three of us were inseparable. Vivian and I were roommates and both seniors at the University of Vermont. Ophelia and Vivian were the same age, 21, and belonged to each other. What fun the three of us had.

Viv, (on right) pretending I'm the mechanic

Her only weakness was that she had no rumble seat. She overcame that by letting our three laughing passengers climb into her trunk. What pedestrians first noticed, was the fast approaching sound of voices mixed with laughter, then as we sped by, six feet sticking out the opening, and six arms holding up that bouncing trunk lid.

But that is not the end of her story. Ophelia was sometimes called on to show her towing strength. Boys in their fancy sleek and shiny red convertibles would pull into the snow packed yard of our dorm to pick up their dates. "Could Vivian and Ophelia please come to see if they could pull us out?" She was a remarkable car with a remarkable driver. Never once did they let those boyfriends down.

Today all three of us are in retirement. At Viv's house Ophelia sits in a garage with windows. Her tires are flattened, her running boards are cracked, and some of her stuffing is loose. The engine refuses to carry anyone, only because she can't any more. But that pride is still there. You should have seen her on our last visit when Viv climbed into the driver's seat and I into the passenger's side. I'm sure her bones creaked but she didn't let us hear them. She acted as though she didn't mind at all as she opened her doors and welcomed us and sat staring straight ahead as she used to do, remembering the laughter and joy of past years. I'm sure she recognized our voices and heard the laughter again and felt the admiring stares of a whole family encircling her. She knew full well the part she had played in our lives.

Bill

He was much more handsome than I had imagined, my roommate Vivian's youngest brother Bill. When I met her other two brothers a couple of years before, Bill was away in the Army. When he came home he came to visit Vivian and another buddy up in northern Vermont.

This second visit was during my graduation from the University of Vermont. Even though Viv was in my class and should have been graduating, she lacked some credits. So why was he there? It must be because of me. I guess that I was not bad looking; but I had red hair, freckles and wore glasses, not exactly the campus beauty queen. We had a happy time during those few days all together with my family. Malcolm and Bruce were at their funniest and they had us laughing most of the time. Before we left campus Bill told me that he had never met a family like mine. What he really meant was as crazy as mine.

But more important than any of his many visible attributes, he was the man who had written those details of his dramatic conversion in that letter to his sister that I had read one and a half years earlier. He recounted how he had finally "found God" in the person of Jesus Christ. This new faith had given him a new life. Just reading of his trying to fill the void with alcohol, and of his denying the existence of God had been a thrilling experience for me. The frustration and desperation of living without a compass, with no sense of direction, with no goals, had ended when he had said yes to Christ. I had made a decision years earlier when I was probably around 10 years old that I needed a guide in my life. I had responded to an invitation in our little country Baptist church. After that step, my life focus had changed as well.

I never planned the kind of special guy I hoped to meet some day. There was, however that 'sous-entendu' that unexpressed understanding, that I would never even be interested in someone who was not dynamic in his desire to follow Christ. And here he was before me, much more than I could have imagined. At my graduation I was forced to assume that he was interested in me. Wonder of wonders.

I recently found a letter that I had never seen before among some boxes of papers. It was written by Vivian to Bill when he was overseas. Hidden among the paragraphs was quite a bit about me and what our friendship meant to her. She may have had a trick or two up her sleeve.

Wedding Bells

The first part of the summer of 1958 between his middler and senior year at Westminster Seminary near Philadelphia, Bill served as an intern at a church in Huntington, Massachusetts. He was to focus on the youth in town and also minister to the communities in the smaller villages on the top of the two neighboring mountains. These hilltop towns were built around beautiful old white clapboard church buildings. The church in Chester Hill was built in 1763. That church had weekly services but no regular minister. The church in Montgomery was closed. The town selectmen and some residents wanted to restore and refurbish their historic building built in 1810 and then open its doors for services.

Bill stayed with a family with five children. In addition to the tasks given him during those two months, he canvased the Montgomery community, visiting each home to get to know the residents. He learned everyone's name and even the ages of the children. He informed each resident that by mid-summer the church building would be reopened but he had to be away for ten days. He would be back after his honeymoon.

During this time back in Pennsylvania my family was working like crazy preparing the wedding. My mother adjusted my sister's wedding gown to fit me, made two of the bridesmaid's dresses, as well as my beautiful silk going away suit and her own silk dress. She also cooked the wedding rehearsal dinner; one of my sisters-in-law organized the reception, held on the lovely grounds of Westminster Seminary. Another sister-in-law did all of the bouquets and church flowers.

We decided to memorize our vows instead of repeating after the pastor - but he was to prompt us if we stumbled. Bill swept through his without a hitch. Just as I started, I saw the pastor close his book. I started strong and then stumbled. There was silence with no help forth coming. So it was Bill who had to prompt me!

August 2nd, 1958

After the beautiful, if somewhat embarrassing affair, we planned to head north toward a cabin on little Sugar River in New Hampshire. The next morning we stopped on the New Jersey Turnpike to fill the gas tank. Who should we run into at the same rest stop but Bill's family? Now what were the odds of that happening?

Where were we to live? Bill told me that when we returned to Massachusetts, we would live with the family with five children, three of whom were teenagers - after just one week into our married life. I wasn't sure I liked that. The reception at their house was quite different than either of us anticipated. After spending the evening together with the whole family, we went to bed. There was persistent rustling and giggling outside our bedroom door. Those five kids were up to something. They didn't want to miss our reaction when we climbed into bed and found the sheets not "short-sheeted" but "long-sheeted" folded back double down the middle of the bed! They were so much fun we grew to love them as our own family.

In early September we returned to our schools in Pennsylvania. I, in my third year teaching English at Philmont Christian Academy and Bill as a student at Westminster Seminary. Nine months later, after I resigned from teaching and Bill had graduated, we returned for a year and a half to those two churches in Massachusetts, until we left to prepare to sail overseas.

The closed church was beautifully restored. Two wood stoves still stood in the back with their stove pipes running the length of the sanctuary, vented out the front high above each side of the pulpit. These warm stovepipes would make the church usable during those New England winters. I was surprised that about 60 people attended that first Sunday. That was about capacity. As the congregation filed out after the service Bill addressed everyone by name, even the children. Everyone seemed to like him. One of the elders told me that they couldn't find anything to criticize. "He was perfect." How was I to respond to that?

We entertained together and we did some visiting together. I established a Sunday school. We ran a youth group together. I gave birth to Billy. I joined a group of town women who met each week for various artistic projects. And then another wonderful thing happened. A group of high school girls asked me if I could help start a girls' basketball team in the local high school. They had heard that I had played in high school and in college. I - me became their coach! When Bill was unable to babysit during practice, Billy sat in his little seat on the sidelines thoroughly entertained watching the ball fly by, with the girls running in front of him. I was incredulous that Bill's pastorate had created such an outlet for me.

We left the area in the middle of the second practice season. The Principal took over. The next spring a letter reached us in Tunis. Those courageous girls had won the Regional Championship!

Our First Home

In the fall of 1958 we returned to our schools in Pennsylvania. We had to decide where we would live. Should we live in a convenient apartment on the seminary campus? That would leave Mother and Daddy without a car, isolated out in the country on 'The Farm' where they were caring for my elderly aunt and uncle. My older siblings were married and had moved away. My youngest brother was away at school.

The best decision seemed obvious, live near them. Bill would now make that 30-mile trip to school every morning and evening with me since the seminary and the high school where I taught were close. On weekends we could transport my folks and my aunt and uncle if they were able, to church, shopping and on outings. We could live in the little clapboard cottage attached to the big main stone house. We had always called it "The End House."

There was one room downstairs with a little kitchen in the back with a sink and stove, but no room for a fridge. The only bedroom was under the eaves upstairs. We cleaned it up and bought second hand furniture. The $15.00 sofa was solid but very worn. My mother said that she would cover it. She would learn how as she went along. She and I went on a shopping spree, buying really solid upholstery material. I had always known that she was a genius. The results turned it into a beautiful brand new couch, with the cushions and armrests all corded.

I remember a little coffee table only because my naughty nephew used to come in and pull the scarf with everything on it off onto the floor. I always felt that he knew he could get a bigger reaction by being naughty than by being good. And he was right.

The outhouse was about 20 feet from the house out back. All the furnishing it required was an occasional roll of toilet paper. One snowy morning I was out there just before we were to drive those 30 miles to school. I lifted the little metal hook from the inside to open the door. The door wouldn't budge. I could see through the crack that the outside hook had swiveled up and hooked itself closed. Bill couldn't hear me and it was the dead of winter. Eventually he did come searching!

The Farm was sold in 1963. Bill and I were in North Africa. A short time ago we went to Wycombe to church and then drove out to Cherry Lane Farm hoping to find the owner at home. I was surprised when Mrs. Miller took us, not into the main 260-year-old house, which was now an official historic site and where she had lived for many years, but into our little 'End House'!

She explained that when her husband was alive they had lived in the big stone house, but now that she was alone she had moved out to live in this smaller extension. It had been 54 years since Bill and I had lived there! She had transformed it into Better Homes and Gardens beautiful. The plaster had been removed from one wall uncovering a beautiful old stone chimney. Three new windows looked out onto the side garden where the old enclosed staircase had been. An extension out the back provided room for the laundry and bathroom and staircase leading upstairs. The porch had been buttressed up and filled with lovely furniture. No more did the grazing animals do most of the mowing. Now, all of the yards on every side are manicured, with flower gardens bordering the lawns.

Out of curiosity, we went out back to find that old wooden outhouse. Only a bit of the cement remained. What were the Millers thinking when they removed that part of history? I guess the Historical Society may have decided that it wasn't worthy of being included as part of the official Historic Site!

CHAPTER TWO -
THE BIG ADVENTURE

Raising Cain - 1960-1961

During Bill's years at Westminster Seminary, he became fascinated with the theology of Islam and the way it had spread, replacing Christianity in the Middle East, but especially in North Africa. North Africa was known as the "The Land of the Vanished Church." The church fathers: Augustine, Cyprian, and Tertullian were North Africans. Despite intense persecution during Roman times, the church grew faster there than in any other area of the Empire. Many were martyred, thrown into the arenas, fed to the lions, because they refused to bow to the Emperor.

> Tertullian wrote: As often as you mow us down, the more numerous do we
> become: The blood of the martyrs is seed.
> Apologeticum 50

> Augustine wrote: Despite the fiercest opposition, the terror of the greatest
> persecutions, Christians have held to the belief that Christ
> has risen, that all men will rise in the age to come, and that
> the body will live forever.
> City of God 22:7

Bill read that during times of persecution, the church expanded. But with the Edict of Constantine in 313, Christianity became the state religion, and thus persecution ended. The churches expanded with political, economic and social conversions. Then divisions and heresies crept in and divided members. A few short centuries after the Muslim armies marched out of Saudi Arabia across North Africa in the late 600's Christianity had completely disappeared. In 1960 statistics stated that these countries were now more than 99% Muslim.

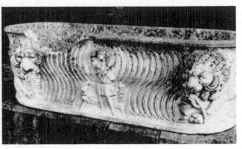

The Alpha and Omega Tipaza, Algeria   Coffin with Christ the Good Shepherd
Tipaza, Algeria

His growing interest coincided with hearing speakers from the North Africa Mission whose headquarters were nearby outside of Philadelphia. Our paths quite unexpectedly crossed with an excellent speaker representing North Africa at various venues in New York, Massachusetts, and Pennsylvania. Convinced that this was "our calling," we attended North Africa Mission's candidate school in September 1960 and were commissioned.

Four months later Bill resigned from pastoring the two country churches in western Massachusetts. Our assignment was to head to Tunisia to start language learning. But first we needed to raise some money for travel and equipment as well as $310 in regular monthly contributions. After several months of presenting North Africa and our financial needs in churches, thirty-nine individuals and nine churches helped us reach our goal.

Billy was an active and inquisitive one and a half year old toddler. I wonder if those months asking others to host us weren't harder on them than on us. I remember the glass trinkets on the lower shelves of one living room. They were just at his play level. They escaped unbroken.

Bill loved preparing and presenting messages. We were very much at home in smaller churches, but we were not used to the culture of the large churches with their big annual missions' conferences. We only attended one of these and felt quite lost amidst the experienced missionaries, their elaborate displays, and stories. One of the men from the Congo kept us and the packed church enthralled with his stories of exciting, scary moments, meaningful dreams and the numerous dangers he and his family had faced. We felt insignificant and inadequate.

We did have one moment in the limelight, however. One evening this same missionary opened his message with a little story of a different nature. He said, "I have always heard of a 'missionary call', but this was the first time I've actually seen one. And better than that, I've seen both halves of it, "Reddy and

Willing" (referring to my red hair and Bill's real name). Then he added, "Too bad they didn't name their son Abel."

When the conference was over, we recounted that incident to our American North Africa Mission Director, Dr. Frances Steele. He replied, "Well better Abel than Cain because you surely wouldn't want to raise Cain." Bill added, "Isn't it a Shem the way you're Hamming it up."

SS Independence - Scary Naples

SS Independence

Billy during a drill

On October 16 1961, Bill and Daddy drove our packed belongs from "The Farm" in Pennsylvania to the harbor in NYC. A fire backed up the traffic in northern New Jersey. They arrived at the port too late. The SS Independence was right there in front of them but on the other side of a locked gate. The guard had the keys, but he needed some fancy convincing. To Bill's horror my father passed him a ten dollar bill. We were starting our overseas career with a bribe!

Two days later we drove north from Pennsylvania again. About sixty of our family and friends came aboard ship to our farewell service and then waved goodbye from the pier. There was one item missing from our luggage. We hadn't brought the leash that the mission headquarters had suggested to keep Billy in tow, "so he wouldn't climb over the railing of the ship."

We enjoyed second class with pretty formal meals. Bill and Billy made good use of the pool. We played shuffleboard and admired the fall sunsets across the water. We passed the Azores and stopped in Casablanca, Gibraltar, Algeciras, La Palma, Messina, and visited Pompeii. In Taormina, Sicily, we visited an ancient Greek theater before debarking in Naples. We marveled at the setting with Mt. Etna in the background and the sea below, but we were most astounded by the acoustics. Billy ran down the seat rows from one side to the other, and we could speak to him in normal voices. That visit began our love and fascination with Roman and Greek ruins.

My first BIG scare happened, not aboard ship as others had feared, but during our layover in Naples. Someone had warned us to be wary of everything: "Don't drink any water." "Don't exchange money on the street." "Watch your luggage being transferred to the Italian line," etc. Happily we had never heard the expression, "See Naples and die." Was that a warning - or did it really mean once you have seen beautiful Naples you will be ready to die?

We found a hotel room near the port to wait for the transfer of our luggage to the Italian ferry to take us on to Tunis. Our room was several flights up with a narrow balcony and a wrought iron railing to about my waist. I was lying on the bed and looked up just in time to see Billy near the top leaning out. Pain shot through my body. I snuck up behind him, grabbed his clothes to avoid startling him into a nosedive to the street far below.

We were glad we had been warned to watch the luggage transfer. It seemed to us they planned to leave a case or two on the dock. Then we set sail again. We found our room down in the bottom of the Italian ferry and scattered the roaches to their hiding places as we walked in. We headed south to Sicily where we made one stop in Palermo and then, Tunis at last. Mr. Brown, our language supervisor, was there to meet us. He was from England and had already spent many years in North Africa. This long awaited day was the moment of new beginnings in this adventure with the Lord. We felt that we could overcome any obstacle with God's help and with friends to teach us.

Arrival in Tunis - November 1, 1961

Our unloaded luggage was waiting to be examined by the customs officials. They were off a short distance away joking and smoking together, ignoring us completely. Mr. Brown glanced over at them, picked up the chalk lying on the counter, put an 'X' on all of our pieces and told the porters to load them up. We had just passed through customs!

We settled into the servants' quarters just behind the Browns' house. The rooms: Bath, kitchen, living room, and two bedrooms were laid out in a straight line with a narrow tiled courtyard in front which ran the length of the house. The only windows were on the front side facing out onto this courtyard. A high wall with a door separated our courtyard from the courtyard at the back of the Brown's house. Mr. Brown apologized many times about our quarters and furnishings, but he also loved saying that "some missionaries who were long since retired had courted on that couch."

We loved the simplicity of our lives and Billy, very shortly after our arrival, began playing with a little boy named Bel Kacem. He and his family were homeless, so Mr. Brown had offered them the use of his garage. The two boys, two and three years old, were together most every day. No doubt Billy was quickly absorbing Arabic. Some young Christian men, a fellow from Finland and a Tunisian, also came to the house. Billy loved them. They toted him around on their shoulders and spoke French with him. He also waited for the Browns' nine-year-old daughter Carolyn to come home from school. We didn't know how much language he understood but our neighbors loved to see this tiny blond blue-eyed boy sitting on the little step at the gate, clapping his hands and yelling, "Yahia Bourguiba, Yahia, Bourguiba!" (Long live Bourguiba!) Everyday the President's cortege with its motorcycles and flags passed at the end of our street taking President Bourguiba to and from his office downtown to his palace out on the coast in Carthage. The adoring populace lined the street and shouted his praises. Billy got caught up in their excitement.

Billy and Bel Kacem

He loved these visitors

There were also moments of too great silence. That usually meant that he was investigating some distant corner of the Browns' yard with its fruit trees. It had always been our policy to turn our backs if he fell or hurt himself and pretend that we hadn't seen what had happened - unless he cried. This time the silence was pierced by cries of "Mommy, Mommy." I ran around the side of the Browns' house to find he had climbed into their apricot tree, fallen, but not all the way to the ground. One of his feet had wedged between two branches and he was hanging upside down. He was two and a half.

We didn't see him fall down the Browns' cement cellar stairs, but he remembers that to this day. We found him at the bottom pretty bruised and shaken up.

The extensive Parc Belvedere was nearby and within bike riding distance. We flew down the grand avenue Mohamed V on borrowed bikes; Billy perched on the bar between Bill's knees. Once on our way home, I was far out front. I turned around to see if they were coming just in time to see Billy fly through the air and both of Bill's legs shoot up. Billy had slid around on the unprotected bar. His foot had slipped into the spokes of the front wheel. He complained that his foot hurt him. Other than pain and bleeding, they both survived without further injury.

Saturday mornings they went to the market together. They were walking down Avenue Mohammed V one day when Billy asked,

"Daddy, do we love cows?" "Yes, we love cows."

"Daddy, do we love garbage collectors?" "Yes, Billy, we love garbage collectors."

"Daddy, do we love Bourguiba?" "Yes, Billy, we love Bourguiba."

And we, too, were learning to love our lives in Tunisia. We loved our new colleagues and the times we spent sharing and praying together.

Marine Corps Fitness

Mr. Brown, our language school supervisor chose a new school motto: "Marine Corps Fitness." We guessed that he wanted us to be able to cope with any hardship or inconvenience without complaint. He wanted us to be tough! We didn't quite understand how this fit our daily lives. Each day was simple and straightforward: Learn the language.

One day Mr. and Mrs. Brown locked themselves out of their house. He and Bill decided that, since all of the windows had iron grills over them, the best solution was to kick in the back kitchen door. Bill and he lined up beside each other. At the signal they were to kick as hard as they could. Maybe Bill kicked a little off "straight ahead" or maybe Mr. Brown didn't get his leg out quite straight ahead, but Mr. Brown received Bill's cordovan shoe with its hard, thick leather sole down the side of his ankle. He hobbled around for some time, moaning and taking full advantage of his injury. Even the neighbors in the high-rise buildings around swarmed to their windows to witness the ruckus. The door gave way. They slept in their own beds that night.

That week as Bill filled out his weekly report, recording how many hours he had spent exposed to the two new languages, he added, "And I kicked my boss!" That event made a lasting impression. Mr. Brown continued referring to Bill's abuse of his boss right up till the last time we saw him shortly before his death in southern England.

After two months of trying to get our feet on the ground, Mr. Brown decided that we should host some of the mission visitors especially those from the States. One was Ed Steele, brother of Dr. Francis Steele, our US Director. From the onset Ed had been a very strong supporter of the new American branch of the North Africa Mission founded in 1881, which previously had been uniquely British. So this was an important visit. He had come from the comforts of a pretty luxurious American home to stay with us in the servants' quarters. The rooms were laid out in a line with the bathroom at one end and the guest room at the other.

He probably would have made out okay but it was winter and we had no way to heat the house except with a tiny kerosene heater that we had to turn off at night as the flame consumed the oxygen from the air. We didn't like its trade name, "DEMON" very much. That night it snowed. And as snow has a way of doing, it blew a bit into his room through the inch high space between the door and the floor tiles. As if that wasn't enough, he had to go outside to get to the bathroom. Ed was a tall man and our only beds were like cots. No doubt his feet hung out the end. We shared all of the blankets we had but it certainly wasn't enough. We didn't even think of the fact that it would take half the night for his body heat to get the dampness out of that unused mattress.

The next day Mr. Brown told us that our guest had requested to move over to their house as he had caught a bad cold. Had Mr. Brown assigned him to our house on purpose in keeping with his slogan of "Marine Corps Fitness?" One thing is sure. He had not explained to our guest, that that slogan applied to him as well.

Your French Is the Worst

Bill was to spend 40 hours a week studying language. Since I had Billy and the household to run I was to spend 20 hours on French. I had a class in the morning and a visit on a borrowed bike to a French lady's house in the afternoon. But Bill, poor Bill, was to attend the morning French class and study Classical Arabic in the afternoon.

Mr. Brown, who had set up the schedule, eventually hired a 16 year-old tutor to help Bill with French. We're not sure if his evaluation of Bill's progress was the only help he gave, but it is the only thing that Bill remembers today. This sixteen-year-old told thirty-year-old Bill, "You have the worst French accent I have ever heard!" A few months later Mr. Brown decided that this same young man should help Bill with Arabic. Again he proved consistent in his pedagogical skills when he said, "And I thought your French was bad!"

Four months after our arrival in Tunis, Mr. Brown decided that Bill should preach at the French language church. Most of those four months he had spent studying Arabic. Traumatic! He opened his message in hesitant French with, "I feel like the Apostle Paul." And after a pause, "I stand before you in fear and trembling." A few minutes later he asked Mr. Brown if he could quit and his answer was, "Keep going!" When the message was over, Bill disappeared. I couldn't find him anywhere. When he did show up at home he said that he had completely broken down and for the first time in his adult life had cried like a baby.

Years later we met one of the Frenchmen who had been present at that traumatic event. He told us that when Bill opened his message saying, "I feel like the Apostle Paul," he had asked himself, "Who does this American think he is, comparing himself to the great Apostle?" But when Bill continued, saying, "I am standing before you in fear and trembling," he decided to listen. One of the other men present that day says that he still remembers the content of that message - 45 years later! But Bill wants to forget the whole experience.

Shadrach, Mechach and Abednego - July 1962

In the spring of 1962, five months after our arrival in Tunis, we heard that the language-training program was being transferred to Morocco. All of the new arrivals from the U.S. and the UK would be sailing directly to Casablanca. Some of the appointees studying in Tunis with us would stay and some would move to Casablanca. Bill and I were to move to Algiers. At Easter we heard that the front of our mission house in Algiers had been blown off by a car bomb planted in the street out front.

The "Accord d'Evian" had been signed in February ending the almost eight years of fighting in the Algerian War for Independence, but it didn't end the bloodshed. In fact it had escalated. The French residents who had run Algeria for 130 years were not going to give up easily. If they were being forced to leave, the least they could do was leave destruction in their wake. Bodies were being strung up from telephone poles during the night in downtown Algiers. Torture continued in the prisons. Pregnant women were slaughtered; olive groves, the mountain populations' primary source of income, were burned; the University of Algiers library was gutted. Our workers said that they were all right, but that it wasn't wise to send any one else into such an inferno. By the end of the war one tenth of Algeria's population had been killed!

So, we too were to leave for Casablanca. Friends came to see us off. Everyone wanted to kiss Billy goodbye, but he only permitted a young new Tunisian Christian, to kiss him. The temperature was 118 degrees. We boarded the steaming Tunis Air plane that had been sitting on the tarmac for hours. This was the first flight to fly all the way from Tunis to Casablanca through Algerian airspace. For years flights from Tunisia had been diverted to Marseille, France, and then headed south to Casablanca to avoid the dangers of the war in Algeria.

The ground crews had not done their job. The plane had been sitting on the tarmac with no cooling system. It was stifling. We expected that it would all cool down soon, but by the time I noticed that Billy's shorts and T-shirt were completely wet and Bill's shirt was only dry on the center strip of his collar, he was feeling sick, and the stewardess was calling for a doctor because other passengers had fainted. Mr. and Mrs. Brown and Carolyn were seated in front of us. I can remember leaning over the seat and telling them that now I understood how Shadrach, Meshach and Abednego felt. There were no drinks or food on board!

We landed in Bone, present day Annaba, Algeria. The opened doors let in what seemed to us, a cold freezing breeze. The cool air dried our sweaty clothes. In Algiers, soldiers wearing berets with their machine guns ready, milled through the airport.

It was July 10, 1962. We had only spent eight months and nine days in Tunisia.

Billy and Kinne

Casablanca, Morocco seemed very different from Tunis. First of all, we had to tell Billy that it was no longer a good idea to stand on our front balcony yelling, "Yahia Bourguiba!" Moroccan ladies lined up to cheer their King Hassan.

Billy and Kinne, Switzerland Summer 1974

I guess I thought that a three year old would be able to cope with memorizing some King James English so we started on the 23 Psalm. He recited accurately "The Lord is my Shepherd, I shall not want. He makes me to lie down in green pastures," then silence. Looking around the kitchen he replaced, "He restoreth my soul" with, "He stores me behind the stove…"

He was now playing with different children. Carolyn lived too far away. The other children in the building all spoke French so he was becoming quite fluent. One day Mr. Brown asked us if we were aware of how much French Billy was speaking. They had been tossing a ball back and forth and one of them didn't catch it. The ball had rolled under a chair. Billy said, "Elle est allée se coucher." (It has gone off to sleep.)

But his best English-speaking buddy was Kinne Rider who was nine months older. Why he called Billy, Bill Doll we never understood. When they were together they laughed and giggled cooking up their mischief. Tearing up books and throwing the pages out the window to be caught by the wind during naptime only happened once. At least they were not sitting on the windowsill with their feet hanging out over the ground two stories below. That was when he was with the concierge's son.

One time while Kinne was visiting, the three of us were sitting on the couch singing together when Billy stopped, "She's my mommy and you can't have her." His inexperience with sharing with a sibling came through again while in the bathtub together. Looking at some toys he said, "These are my toys and you can't take them home." Frustrated, Kinne retorted, "Yes, but I can take the bathtub and the water!"

Casa Robbers

I awoke with a start. What had startled me like that? There was a flickering light in the hall. Someone must have struck a match right outside our bedroom door. I was fully aware now. The first thing I thought of was of a friend in Morocco who had awakened in the night and started to get up to investigate a noise and was stabbed in the chest right in bed. The knife just missed his heart. I must not make any noise or move. But three-year-old Billy was in the room down the hall.

If I awakened Bill he would grunt or say out, "What's the matter?" How could I make sure Billy was safe? I awoke Bill with a gentle push and as I expected, he grunted. I pointed to the door. He flew out of bed and flung the door shut. I picked up the iron off the ironing board and Bill wielded his camera tripod. We heard through our open window, someone dropping to the gravel driveway, then the crunch of running footsteps.

We opened the bedroom door. I went down the hall to make sure that Billy was still asleep as Bill turned toward the living room. The front door of our apartment stood wide open. Then I went into the kitchen, checked to make sure all of our kitchen knives were in their place and stepped over a dark object on the floor. Our visitor had not run out the front door and down the steps to the entry door but had climbed out the kitchen window, down the exterior water pipes. I looked out. For the first time I realized they formed a sort of ladder from the driveway right up to our apartment.

When we were sure we were alone we turned on the lights. I picked up the dark object lying in the middle of the kitchen floor. It was my dress that the robber had dropped in his haste to get to the window. It had been on the chair by the bed. Had he actually been in our bedroom right next to the bed a few inches from where I was lying? Where else had he been? What else had he taken?

We began searching. Bill's jacket was missing from the armoire. Some jewelry was missing from the dresser drawer. The radio was missing from the living room.

The next morning we felt it was important to inform our neighbors. Our concierge warned us that Rule Number One is never let your intruder know that you know he's there. He might go to extremes to assure his escape unseen.

Change Again - February 1964

Our days in Morocco were also numbered as they had been in Tunisia. After one year and seven months in Casablanca we were again reassigned, this time to Algeria. We were the only ones of our language class making this change. We packed up and boarded the train for Oran in western Algeria in February 1964. The team of four that had been residing in Oran was down to one, a woman on her own. We novices were to fill in the gap to form a new team.

CHAPTER THREE - ALGERIA 1964-1982

Background

During the 19th and the first half of the 20th century the French controlled huge swathes of Africa. There were, however, distinct policy differences in the way France governed each area. Morocco and Tunisia were declared protectorates. But Algeria with its huge potential in natural resources of oil and natural gas, and its agriculturally rich land, along with the size of its European population, mostly French, was declared a province of France. Algeria, located across the Mediterranean in North Africa, was five times the size of France itself. The distance from Algiers to Tamanrasset in the Sahara is farther than from Algiers to London.

Algiers port and Casbah, 1830

The French colonial period in Algeria began in 1831. For security reasons the French adopted a policy of destroying much of the historic Casbah, with its winding streets and nooks and crannies known only to the immediate local population. Eventually the traditional coppersmith street, the leather-worker street, and others, disappeared. The teaching of Arabic was outlawed. French became the language of the state.

After almost eight years of horrific struggle, with torture and assassinations a common occurrence, Algeria gained independence from France in 1962. As it became increasingly clear that independence was inevitable, the French citizens, most of whom had lived in Algeria for many generations, left in droves loading the departing ships with only a small portion of their possessions. Abandoned apartments with their glass chandeliers and the hand carved furniture filled up with people from the countryside who, in some cases, brought their animals with them. We heard stories of animals kept in bathtubs clogging the sewer systems.

When we arrived in Oran, Algeria, in February 1964, just two years after the signing of the Accord d'Evian, we found a different atmosphere from both Tunisia and Morocco. The people were scarred. Bill met men on the street who wanted to talk and needed to share what they had lived through, of the torture they had experienced or had themselves inflicted. Who of their compatriots would or could listen to them? They told heart-wrenching stories of pregnant women losing their babies under horrific circumstances and of bodies hanging from telephone poles. A French Pastor said that he decided that he could no longer continue his ministry in Oran on the day that his son came home from French School and asked him how many Algerians he had killed the night before.

The Algerians were retrieving their homeland. The French or 'Pieds Noirs' who fled were leaving their homeland. They had lovingly referred to the capital, Algiers as 'Alger, La Blanche.' It was a beautiful city built on several hillsides surrounding a natural port. Winding roads wove back and forth up the hillsides around the French style villas or higher apartment buildings. Connecting these curves were steep staircases for pedestrians.

The new independent state chose to adopt a socialistic form of government. The apartment buildings in downtown Algiers, the capital, as well as those in other cities, and the vast farmlands in the countryside became 'bien d'état', property of the state. The huge date palm groves in the Sahara were taken over, too often by people with no experience in their care. The newspapers and radio broadcasts were full of the kind of rhetoric heard in Russia: the 'agricultural revolution,' 'the five-year plan.'

With the absence of new construction, combined with the huge birth rate, overcrowding became a serious problem. Not enough schools, untrained teachers, forced Arabization caused huge dropout statistics. Children were rotated in and out of school two hours in the morning and two in the afternoon.

As they left their classrooms other children filed in. A friend told us that she had passed classrooms where the children laid their heads on their desks while the teacher knitted. The government was obliged to hire from outside the country to fill professions left empty by the French departure. Hundreds of Arabic speaking teachers from the Middle East filled the schools. Doctors came from the Eastern block. They spoke no French or Arabic. Firemen and police were trained in Russia.

As Arabization swept the country, store names had to be changed. Street names were painted over and new names, usually a martyr from the War for Independence, replaced the French. Algeria was searching for a new identity. Throwing away the old had been costly in lives. One tenth of the Algerian population had died. The trauma affected the Algerian psyche. Successfully realigning itself with the East and socialism, and with the Arab Muslim World would take time.

Initiation - Oran

Our new team in Oran consisted of one British woman and us. She initiated these green horns to life outside of language school, introducing me to some of her friends. Soon, we were joined by a Swiss woman. The following letter I wrote two months after our arrival.

"The room we were ushered into was topsy-turvy with furniture, shoes, papers, and odds and ends strewn here and there about the floor. In the midst of the confusion sat five women completely oblivious to the noise of three young children who ran in and out, but very conscious of the intrusion of two foreigners. The girl we had come to visit was not among them and soon one of the children disappeared to find her. Shortly a young teenage girl, hair disheveled as though she had been sleeping, appeared. So this was Aisha, the girl who had completed more Bible Correspondence Courses than any other in Oran. She greeted us warmly and quickly tried to orient me to the situation. Four of the five women seated on the floor were neighbors. The fifth, the one with the baby on her lap, was her fathers' second wife. Aisha had four brothers and six half brothers and sisters.

She didn't wait for us to ask any questions, but went on to tell us how six months ago her father had married her, sight unseen to a young man, and after six unhappy months of living with his family, she had come home again. For two whole months she had not been allowed to step outside the door. She had been under age when her parents married her and next week her case would come up in court.

How in the midst of all of this had she read so carefully so much scripture and answered so accurately so many questions? She said she just read the scripture over and over until she understood. It soon became apparent that she understood a great deal. She chose the parable of the sower as a passage she thought especially beautiful.

We read other scripture with her before leaving and made plans to meet every Monday for study around God's Word. Visits like this, modified in some aspects, have now become part of my ministry here." Newsletter, April 1964.

An Exciting Visit

Never in my wildest dreams could I have imagined the news that reached us in the spring of 1965. Mother and Daddy were coming to Oran, Algeria. Life was more stable now after the horrors of the war and we had had a year to settle in. Billy was happy in a French preschool.

We had friends down the street, a British lady, and a Swiss lady, and in the other direction a Spanish pastor and his wife. They lived upstairs in an almost defunct Methodist Church. They had stayed behind when many Europeans left in the mad rush back to Europe at Independence. They were older than we were, which gave us a sense of security. Then we met a young man of Christian origin from Jordan. With his help we started an Arabic church service in the Methodist building.

Hugh and Helen Brown

We had no car or telephone and not much idea how we would give Mother and Daddy a good time. They would take a Mediterranean Cruise from New York, enjoy one stop in the Azores, and then leave the ship before even entering the Mediterranean Sea, disembarking in Morocco, where we had friends willing to receive them. Our friends put them on the train to Oujda, the closest Moroccan city to the Algerian border. A friend who had a van offered to drive us to the Oujda train station and then back across the border.

Their train arrived! One of the first things Mother said to me was, "Peggy, I have to go to the bathroom." She explained that when she saw a man come out of the little toilet at the end of their passenger car she reasoned, probably because of a misconception of women's place in society, that the facilities were only for men, so she returned to her seat - for a trip of seven or eight hours! We hunted around and found a little shed in the yard of the train station. I opened the door to a hole in the floor. My 70 year old mother was going to have to squat!

On Friday we attended the Arabic church service. On our way home, to my complete amazement, Mother told me that "nour" meant "light." The message was from First John. She had compared the frequency of Brahim's mentioning the word with the scripture passage in English. Then she asked me about other words he had used. I was surprised and proud.

Jump!

Our apartment building had a functioning elevator. The little box with double wooden doors ascended and descended inside a wrought iron security grill in the center of the building. The staircase curled around the shaft. The elevator worked pretty well most of the time, but there were occasions when it insisted on stopping between floors. Mother and I were laden with our groceries when the elevator chose to stop half way between the second and third floors. It obeyed none of my commands.

There was no one around to help. The only thing to do was jump. I opened the wooden door and then the grill door and proceeded to jump to the floor below. Mother handed me the groceries and I lowered them to the hall floor. I turned around to help her jump. There in front of me was a four feet opening between the floor of the elevator and the hall floor and a great void down the open shaft. Any misstep would be exceedingly consequential. I told her to sit down on the elevator floor. I grabbed her as she pushed toward me. My stomach turns over every time I remember.

A conference was scheduled in Algiers so we set out together. We were housed in Lilias Trotter's Dar Naama. It was a cold and rainy April, and this house of winding stairwells and twisting halls was damp, much colder than outside. Mother and Daddy must have suffered but never complained. After the conference we had an invitation to go up into the of mountains of Kabylia for a few days. When the sun was out it was splendid. The bus conductor spoke Arabic and French with the passengers until we got into the heights, and then he switched to Kabyle, one of the Berber dialects spoken in these mountains. This was the first time I had heard a person, perhaps with limited schooling, switch with ease among three languages. In Djemaa Saharidj we stayed in a house with a large fish, a Christian symbol from Roman or Byzantine times, carved into a foundation stone. It testified to the original population's Christian past.

Then our lives took an unexpected turn.

Coup d'Etat

The four of us were standing on our balcony watching the events unfold in the street one story below. A soldier was crouching on one knee atop a military tank positioned just a little distance to our right. He braced his machine gun ready to shoot, only turning when he sensed a movement or when a person came into view. A young boy came around the corner. When the boy saw the gun focused on him and heard the soldier yell, he started running for all he was worth, down the whole length of our street. There was no corner to duck into. Bill remarked, "That's the first time I have ever seen anyone run for his life."

During the night, I had been awakened several times by a loud unidentifiable noise. The only comparison I could think of was the sound of falling candlepins in a New England bowling alley. President Ben Bella was on a state visit to Oran. Today he was no longer president. The sounds I heard were shots reverberating off the walls of buildings along the narrow streets.

A woman came out on the balcony facing ours. She was hidden from the soldier's view. She called out to us in French, "Do you understand what that soldier is yelling?" He's telling you to get inside immediately." We hurried in from our vantage point.

Then we heard loud screams as a woman ran out onto another balcony across the street. She started to climb up onto the railing. Several family members ran out to grab her. She obviously intended to jump. What could have happened? The neighbor who had translated the soldier's Arabic, explained that this lady's husband had been standing in their second floor living room when a bullet fired from the street had entered their open balcony door, ricocheted off their marble fireplace, and hit her husband in the chest. He was killed instantly.

How naive we were! The same thing could have happened to us. We had actually been standing outside on our balcony, as though we were inviting tragedy. How could we have thought it was safe exposed like that, just because we were not Algerian, consequently immune?

President Ben Bella had come to power after deposing Algeria's first highly respected interim President, Ben Khedda. Now he, too, was deposed by this new President, Houary Boumedienne. We had had front row seats witnessing how one person greedy for power replaces another greedy person. 'Tout a coup,' all of the sudden, just like that, Algeria had a new President.

Visit Cut Short

Within days of our return to Oran from our one foray to the capital and into the mountains, I began feeling sick. I couldn't eat anything. I couldn't turn my head without losing what was in my empty stomach. My skin turned a deep yellow. My French doctor was having his own personal problems. During one of my visits to his office he recounted how he had been held up at gunpoint in his own house. When he finished his frightening story, he looked at me for the first time and said, "You don't look very good." He put me on a fat-free diet and said nothing else about a diagnosis. When I felt better I returned to my old routine of shopping, cooking, the usual household chores and taking Billy to and from school each day - exactly the opposite of what I should have been doing.

While I was bedridden, Bill and Daddy traveled to villages selling Bibles after Bill received official permission to sell 'Bilbes' (That is actually what the official document says.) around the western part of the country. When Bill was busy, Daddy went off by himself. We were amazed that he found his way around, met young people and made friends. Every night he came home with a new story. He took pictures of people and promised to send copies back. He bought an original oil painting on one of these outings. My only concern was that he be back home before nightfall.

Daddy had the brilliant idea that Billy would teach him French. He chose a few phrases and asked his five-year-old grandson to translate them and then help him memorize them. Daddy mispronounced and twisted them around, sometimes on purpose and sometimes not. Billy laughed till his stomach ached. On one of his walks to pick Billy up from school, Grandpa suggested they stop at a store on the way home. If Billy promised to do the negotiations in French, Grandpa would buy him a gift. They came home with a kite. That kite caused quite a stir a few years later.

Each month I had a relapse. A decision had to be made. I was too sick to remain in Oran, so I would have to return to the US. I was almost five foot eight and weighed 104 pounds. My skin was yellow and I often felt very weak. This turn of events was a big heartbreak for us all. We hadn't been able to give

Mother and Daddy the trip they had anticipated and now they were forced to cut this trip of a lifetime short. Mother decided to return to the US with us, and Daddy chose to continue his visit to Paris and the UK as planned. We flew on to Philadelphia while Daddy visited Paris.

But before we left the Oran airport, Bill and Daddy took out their cameras to take some last pictures. The police were jumpy after the coup d'état. They were everywhere in the airport. We had not yet learned that taking pictures in airports was generally forbidden throughout Africa. The police took Daddy and Bill away and unloaded both of their cameras. At least they gave the cameras back. Daddy never was able to fulfill his promise to mail his photos back to his young friends.

The drama for him continued. Now he was on his own. While I was in the hospital, we followed Daddy's adventures from his postcards, first from Paris and then England and Northern Ireland where he looked up lost relatives. At the airport in Paris on his way to London he arrived late at his departure gate. The desk clerk told him to run as fast as he could down the stairs and across the tarmac. The stairs were being towed away and the plane door was closed. He was then told to run back into the terminal; so back he went only to be told that he should try again. So he ran down the stairs again and out the door, across the tarmac just as the stairs came back into place, and the door reopened. But his hat blew off, so he ran after it. When he arrived at the top of the stairs, a loud cheer went up from the gallery viewing area. He turned around and raised his hat to say goodbye to his cheering section.

In Philadelphia there was a wheel chair waiting for me on the tarmac and I was taken straight to the hospital. This was the first time that we heard my diagnosis - hepatitis. After six weeks, five of which were spent in isolation, I was released. Four months had passed since I fell sick on the 13th of April. My American doctor was very strict. He told me that I would be feeling better, but I was to obey his orders. I was to drastically limit any activity. His military patients in Viet Nam, who had pulled rank on him and signed themselves out from his care, had died. He was taking no chances. It was two years before I fully regained my strength.

Mother stayed with us in Pennsylvania caring for Billy and cooking. Many days she could not come to the hospital because of her headaches. Unbeknownst to us, she was suffering from a brain tumor, which took her life within three years.

Billy and School

When Billy was four he attended an Arabic language pre-school in Morocco. He came home each day with this little hand-held blackboard and practiced writing the Arabic alphabet. This exciting adventure was interrupted just a few months later when we moved to Oran, Algeria. There he entered a French school where he sometimes served as interpreter for other children who couldn't speak French. After one year and four months in Oran, I fell sick. We left for the US for medical care.

His first grade teacher in Pennsylvania did not seem to appreciate his story telling skills and his over-active creative imagination which exposure to other cultures may have stimulated At least that's what I called it. One evening she telephoned to say, "Billy is a liar." When I asked why, she replied that he had told the class that he was a fireman and had fought a big fire. I could only imagine his embellishments. She did not appreciate this fantasyland he inhabited. I couldn't see her face when I told her that we actually had seen a huge and tragic fire the night before. But his version of the story had made him a fireman. I had to admit he must have been disruptive. But his other teachers had told us what an interesting child he was.

She added that he was always the first to see that it had begun to snow or that there was a squirrel in the tree outside the window. I kept my reasoning to myself. He had not seen snow for years and in Algeria there were no squirrels. Why shouldn't he be excited? I was too shocked to ask her what she thought I should to do about it.

So he failed Miss Johnson's first grade. I'm sure she was glad to see him leave. In 1966 we heard that Bill had been elected to serve as Regional Pastor. We were now to move again, from Oran to Algiers. This was our fifth city in as many years, and Billy's fourth school. When we sailed in 1966 he did not remember a word of French. We registered him for school but said nothing about his having failed American first grade. He entered our neighborhood French school at his age level on October 18, 1966. By Christmas, with a child's capacity of recall, he was fluent again and was able to read in French. I know there were windows in this classroom. There just weren't any squirrels or snow.

Dar Naama - House of Grace - Algiers

Dar Naama on rue Ali Khodja, El Biar, Algiers, had been the center of the Algiers Mission Band activity for sixty years by the time we arrived in 1966. Lilias Trotter and her friends had purchased it in 1906. It was a fascinating building with 57 rooms, we were told, marble stairways and tiled corridors, and had been a Turkish Pirate Captain's house, no doubt a safe haven during the 'War of the Barbary Pirates'. The once open-to-the-sky courtyard found in the center of the main house was encircled with white twisting pillars.

The second floor rooms, each open to an inside balcony overlooking the courtyard below, were interconnected so that the women could circulate without being seen by the men sitting below. It was a fascinating place, from its location on the very heights of El Biar, to the innumerable secrets hiding in its nooks and crannies. What episodes of history it had witnessed before 1905 we will never know. Lilas Trotter, who had brought her skills as a writer and artist to Algeria in 1886, and her friends from the Algiers Mission Band found it during a time when Lilias was suffering from the damp and cold of their house at 2 rue du Croissant in the Algiers' Casbah.

After spending some time confined to bed by her doctor in January of 1905 and realizing the consequences on their health living in the dampness and draftiness of a the Casbah house, which was completely drenched when rain poured into the center courtyard and which contained rooms with no fireplaces, they went up to spend a few days in a little hotel in El Biar. They wanted to purchase a home but so far had found nothing. On the last day as they walked along a ravine, they saw an old rambling house on the hill above them. Finding no one to welcome them, they entered through an open door on the lower side into an open courtyard with orange trees. This eventually became known as the "Orange Court."

Blanche A. L. Pigott quotes Lilias in her book entitled, *I Lilas Trotter* (pg. 110):

"A perfect rabbit warren of a place, bare and dilapidated, but oh! The possibilities of it, not for ourselves, but for the work. It seemed like a bit of a fairy-tale or a dream suddenly dropped down to earth, yet with a curious sense that it was no dream but a wonderful bit of God's unfoldings." By July 1905 the house was theirs and Blanche Hayworth, with her housekeeping skills set about to make it really theirs.

Perhaps the greatest legacy of that property are the thousands of hours of prayer that transpired there, for the country and the people of Algeria and for the establishment of the church of Jesus Christ. When we arrived in Algiers in 1966, we visited Lilias's prayer room which had been the original creamery, and as we remember it, below ground level. It was circular with tiled walls. Above a narrow circular marble bench was a strip of her beautiful calligraphy of scripture.

The smaller more homey open courtyard, referred to by Lilias, as the 'Orange Court' was down back behind the main house. For many years Si Embarek, who worked for the Algerian Bible Society, lived there with his family. This remarkable man had accepted Christ years earlier while helping translate the Algerian Arabic New Testament. Were the tiles on the walls evidence of the Barbary pirates' raiding ships more than a century before? In the center of this Orange Court was a well. Harold Stalley, whose wife Jesse, had been Lilias Trotter's secretary and had cared for Lilias in the last years of her life, told us that there was, down in this well, a secret passageway that tunneled underground for miles all the way to the port! He had climbed down to investigate, went a little ways, but found it collapsed.

Lilias' Algiers Mission Band eventually merged with the North Africa Mission. Maintenance of such a huge property was overwhelming so it was to be sold. An elderly Algerian Christian, who had experienced its vibrant role in the past history of missions in Algeria, told us he felt that its sale was a sacrilege.

I have one tile, one piece of pottery, and one Berber chest from Dar Naama. They are very precious and are in prominent places in our house in Durham.

Church of the Holy Trinity, Anglican

It was in the fall of 1968 when the British Embassy called with a great suggestion. "We have heard you have a church congregation and soon will have nowhere to meet. As you know we have an empty church building. Do you think we could get together?" The First Secretary at the Embassy was suggesting reopening the closed Anglican Church building. The English speaking Christian leaders in Algiers were to come together to discuss this exciting possibility.

At the time of that telephone call the English Protestant Service was meeting in the center court of Lilias Trotter's famous house, Dar Naama, with children's classes held in a few of the many empty rooms, and now that house was up for sale. Moving to the Anglican church building was a perfect solution. The British Ambassador, as the Queen's representative, would automatically become chairman of the Church Council.

The Anglicans were only a small minority, so a traditional Anglican service would not suit. The new Council wrote up a compromise order of worship. The pulpit would be shared. The congregation began to grow with British, Americans, Swedes, Danes, French, Canadians, Ghanians, Egyptians, and other African countries represented as well as a few Algerians from time to time. The American Chief of Mission and his wife were Catholic. They attended Mass on Thursday evening so they could be free to attend this Protestant Service on Friday. (The weekend was Thursday afternoon and Friday.) The church was often full with classes for children held in every available space. One year the choir sang a bit of the "Messiah."

Parents told us that they were obliged to attend because their children did not want to miss Sunday school. We ladies organized a women's weekly morning Bible Study. The biweekly evening Bible study was one of the highlights of our lives. Along with the fun and study we spent time praying for the growth of the Algerian Church. We actually had baptisms of locals in a homemade pool in a dug out flowerbed in the yard of one of these members.

The council asked Bill to preach for a six weeks. He laid out a plan to cover the basic Gospel in six messages. What a blessed time that was! There were conversions. One American teenager told us that she had accepted Christ her first week in Algeria while Bill was preaching on John 3:16. An Italian told us, "I came to Algiers for many reasons, job advancement, a good salary, adventure, but finding Christ was not among them." Another lent his pool for baptisms.

Eventually, there were changes of personnel at the Embassies. The Ambassador who had helped through the transition was posted elsewhere. New arrivals who knew little of the recent background history wanted to make the church a purely Anglican service with a salaried vicar. A lady complained that Bill did not serve communion according to the Anglican service requirements. I remember some of those communion services so full of meaning as Bill broke a loaf of bread symbolizing the body of Christ broken for us. The symbolism was so real it brought tears to our eyes.

And so it was very easy for us to move on to a new venture.

Eglise Evangélique Algérienne

The afternoon Arabic service for Algerians that had also been meeting in Dar Naama had to find a new locale as well. We decided to rotate to different homes. This group was also growing. Throughout the city, in addition to the Anglican English Service, the French Reformed Church, the French Catholic services, and the small Arabic group, there was a fledgling Protestant Service in French beginning to meet in downtown Algiers. When Bill completed those six weeks we left the English church to join this group meeting at 'La Bonne Nouvelle' (The Good News), a storefront that had once been a Christian bookstore. On weekdays it was a Reading-Resource Room for university students.

Eventually the afternoon Arabic groups merged into this French meeting. The resulting bilingual service became the major church for Algerians in the capital in the years that followed. Gradually new Kabyle songs, written by some of the young converts were added. The Kabyles are one of several groups of Berbers, a different ethnic group from the Arabic speakers. The Berbers are the original inhabitants of North Africa. St Augustine was a Berber born in Algeria.

By 1981 this group in Algiers numbered in the 60's with many baptized members. All leadership, trained elders, deacons, children's classes, church lending library, prayer meetings, Bible studies and worship, were in the hands of Algerian Christians. One of the wonderful features of this group was the span of ages. The Lord brought two older Christians who had a dynamic influence on the new converts. Some of the other older members were new converts. The majority were young people.

We foreigners involved in this service felt that it was necessary to model what a New Testament Church is. A Muslim is taught distorted ideas about Christ, the Trinity, the Bible and the Church. So services focused on basic Bible teaching and preaching with application to our lives. These were expanded with weekend seminars on the Dangers of Sorcery, Christian Marriage, How to Teach Children, What is the Church? What is an Elder? What are a Deacon's Responsibilities? Theology classes were taught in our living room on a semester system: Introduction to the Old Testament, Introduction to the New Testament, Acts, Romans, Doctrine, and Church History. Once a month the whole church met together in the woods for a picnic with singing and a brief devotional.

Baptisms were wonderful picnics on the beach. As the afternoon advanced and the other beach goers left for home, and as the sun turned the horizon and water into silver and then gold, the men and white robed women waded into the water as a public witness to their life changing faith and to commit the rest of their lives, come what may, to their Lord Jesus Christ.

There are three memories Bill and I both have which stand out above all the others: The wonderful love we witnessed and experienced in this tight-knit group, their love of prayer, and their drive to tell others how the Lord changes lives. These were the keys to church growth. We have often repeated that we learned how to pray, and how to worship the Lord from Algerians.

We are grateful we were able to witness this new church function for a whole year without any foreign leadership. Then the Lord, with the help of the Algerian government, took us out of Algeria in July 1982 and on to a new adventure.

God Answers and Uses Prayer

I believe that God answers prayer in several ways. We found group prayer an exhilarating experience overseas. We have often said that we learned to pray and worship from Algerian Christians. God hears the words of our requests and answers as He sees fit. But in addition, He is pleased with the passion of our hearts. Miracles happen when we pray with urgency. "The fervent prayers of righteous men are very effective."

God also uses the act of praying for good in the lives of those who pray. Praying, aware that we are talking to the God of the universe, expecting Him to move is an act of faith, but also a marvelous boost to faith. It also reinforces our love for each other. I personally feel clean and deeply happy after praying with others who have a common focus and desire a common goal. And then when we see God answer, we are often in awe of his love and power. It is similar to the reaction of our 6-year-old neighbor after I fixed him a special snack. It must have been different from what he expected. He said with his eyes fairly popping out of his head, "That's awesome. I've never seen anything like it!"

God uses passionate group prayer meetings in the lives of those who observe. Those who may have no belief in Christ at all or even those with religious convictions who have never witnessed the marvels of a group of Christians who pray expecting God to answer, are often profoundly affected. They may experience a wonderful boost to their faith or even a new conversion experience. Muslims become acutely aware that they don't know a God who can be trusted like that, a God who cares like that, and a God who hears like that. They want to learn more.

One day Bill pulled into our local gas station and spoke to the attendant in Arabic. He immediately asked Bill if he were a Catholic priest. Bill told him that he was a pastor who taught the Bible. The young man replied that he would like to study the Bible. He came to the house to study for some time before Bill invited him to our nascent church's Friday morning worship service. There he met some of the young believers and one of them invited him to the Wednesday prayer meeting. He asked Bill later why he hadn't invited him to a prayer meeting first because it was during that prayer meeting when one of the other young guys, addressing God directly, prayed for him. It was during that prayer that Christ entered his life. God used the experience of his witnessing real, convincing, intimate, believing prayer. Where several are together in Jesus' name, He is really there.

My Algerian next-door neighbor was a bit older than I was. She became one of my closest friends. We talked about Jesus together as well as the events of the day. One day she came to the door to say that her son was lost in the desert. What should she do? We prayed together; the son was found. I did not know all of the details, but what I do know is that she attributed our praying to his being found. This was the biggest step toward her accepting Christ.

When people asked me what was the secret to the early growth of the Church in Algeria during the 70's and 80's, my immediate answer was LOVE and PRAYER. The young converts really loved each other and loved to pray together. They had a wonderful example in a remarkable Algerian woman who was strong in faith and a lover of prayer. She organized prayer chains and all night prayer meetings. The youth followed her example. Like Daniel, she confessed the sins of her country and asked for forgiveness; she praised the Lord with heartfelt eloquence. I was filled with awe when she praised her creator. I had an overwhelming feeling that God Himself was pleased. She was a blessing to all who came across her path. Everyone could tell that she had an intimate relationship with God himself.

Another characteristic of the church in Algiers and no doubt in other cities as well, was a desire to see the church grow. Not just a desire but also a passion. Their faith put their goals into the realm of the possible, not the impossible. A university student was converted and immediately prayed for his family. I will never forget the day, after a trip to his hometown; he announced his brother's conversion. The next visit, his mother. When we left Algeria there were about twenty Christians in that city. A few years later a young women excitedly told us that there were 200 Christians in that same town.

The story of the church growth in Algeria is not over yet. There is now a church in every department or region, and in some areas, in every town. Prayer performs miracles. God's answers to passionate prayer are unstoppable and unlimited.

Come to My House

A speaker during our candidate school back in 1961 told us that we should be able to say in sincerity, "You want to know who Jesus is? Come to my house."

One of our desires was to always have an open home. Our apartment had a guest room with its own toilet and sink. It was easy to have a guest or two and we often did, whether they were young people from North America hitchhiking across North Africa, or locals visiting from another city, or anyone who needed a place to stay. On many occasions we had bedding laid out on the living room floor because the rooms were occupied. Guests for meals was almost the daily norm, invited or unannounced.

Some guests stayed for longer periods. An older Algerian lady who had no children to care for her, a young convert who needed to convince her older brother that she had a safe home so he wouldn't marry her off to one of his illiterate friends, a young woman with children whose husband was erratic and violent, a young couple who wanted to get married but had nowhere to live, and even a kleptomaniac. She found living right in our house quite profitable! Summer teams came to help us out, but I sometimes felt that I ended up serving them. Guests came and went as they did in the homes of our colleagues. We never ran out of money and as I recall only ran out of energy on a few occasions.

Each time Bill answered the phone with the phrase, "Oh, where are you? I knew that someone else had arrived unannounced and needed transport from the train station or the airport.

We can only hope that some did see Jesus in us. Some departed leaving God's blessing behind. The following two stories were the exception.

He Came from Texas

Some guests tested our patience. One day a Frenchman who was living in Algiers called to say that there was an American at the port with a rather large truck. He could not clear it through customs. Because of the language barrier, they were unable to communicate. He needed a place to stay.

Naturally we took him in. When he arrived we sat down to hear his story. He belonged to a church in Texas. One day a member had prophesied that the Lord wanted them to make a tent that would seat a good crowd of people as "a gift to Africa." The ladies set about hand sewing this immense tent. In the end it was so heavy they had to buy a large secondhand truck to transport it. That truck and that tent were stuck in the port.

When we asked his destination, his reply was, "The Lord will show us." It seemed obvious to us that his church may not have realized, and perhaps he still did not know that Africa is comprised of more than 50 countries each with its own importation regulations.

His story continued. Three men had driven the truck from Texas, put it on a cargo ship from the East Coast of the U.S. to Amsterdam. They drove south across France, but stopped to sightsee, so by the time they reloaded it onto a ferry in Marseille, "headed to Africa," the other two men had run out of time and left to go back home.

So what was the problem at the port? Customs officials and the State Police insisted that he wasn't equipped to cross the Sahara. He needed at least three drivers, several spare tires, tools for repairs and innumerable jerry cans of fuel and water. He had none of these and the tent filled all of the space available. Still he insisted, constantly repeating, "If God is in it, it's got to be good!"

What church could have conceived such a project? He showed us photos of longhaired, long skirted ladies sitting together sewing the tent, and an "untouched" and "un-doctored" photo of their founder, William Branham. He explained that the halo encircling his head in the photo was the sign of divine visitation on their prophet. He added that another proof of his importance was that Branham's name contained seven letters, the "perfect number in the Bible," whereas Billy Graham's only contained six!

The days dragged on so we insisted he come up with a plan, first of all deciding on a destination and then how to get there, since crossing the Sahara Desert was a closed option. I ended up calling a telephone number, given us by the Frenchman, of a French-speaking pastor somewhere in Central Africa. The humor of this ridiculous moment did not escape us! I had to yell into the phone that I was calling from Algiers, that he did not know me, that I did not know him, but we had a tent to give away! Did he want it? He seemed dumbfounded but finally said, "Well, I guess so."

Our houseguest then made plans to ship the truck and its tent back across the Mediterranean to Marseille and then ferry it again from the west coast of France to Senegal. Once in Africa he started driving east. I cannot remember the details recounted in a report letter we received. We do, however, have a vague recollection that he delivered the tent and truck to the first person he met who could use them.

I was so relieved that he was gone from our house. With him went that all consuming pressure and maybe some vague evil that I had been feeling. As the door closed, I went to bed and and stayed for several days until my strength began to return. That pastor in central Africa never saw his tent. Who knows, maybe he was relieved - almost as much as we were.

Moonies in Algiers!

A young American man walked into the University Reading Room while Bill was on duty. He had noticed English books in the window. After the usual chitchat, Bill learned that he had arrived in Algiers with another American guy, one girl and one Canadian guy. They were living in a cave on a hillside not many miles from our house. They said they were Christians. Bill invited them for a meal and then also suggested that they might want to meet our little church group.

As I washed their clothes in our bathtub, I was surprised by their expensive quality - way too expensive for one living in a cave! We saw them often but we did not realize the depth of our own naivety, as they revealed nothing about who they really were, or how they replenished their money supply, or how they filled their days or even their purpose in coming to Algiers.

Our little church welcomed them but only the Canadian could communicate with anyone. A French lady in the church said she understood two percent of what he said in his Canadian French. Then we made our biggest mistake. We asked American friends, who had a basement that included a sink and toilet, if they could take them in. When they agreed, we felt quite relieved that they were no longer living in that cave.

The story continues with considerable drama as we listened to our American friends tell of their growing suspicions of the group's claims to Christianity and of other mysteries surrounding them. None of us had ever heard of their sect. She finally asked for a copy of the letters that they were typing out on her typewriter. These letters were full of fantastic claims; it became clear that they were great liars and that it was only the young woman who went out on the streets to beg. The letter included reports of the sums of money received and even implied the services she offered. They gave glowing, lying reports of their speaking in the church. We were slowly discovering that they belonged to the Moonies. They were in Algiers to spread the teachings of their founder, a Korean, named Moon. One day our friend went down into her basement unannounced, and found all four of them together naked.

They went on their way the same day.

Across the Kitchen Table

The table in our kitchen in Algiers with her pale green vinyl top and strong white body and legs sat silently no matter what events surged around her. Her two extension leaves willingly lifted as needed, especially for a dinnertime late arrival. She listened without a word to news and advice, and complaints, and sorrows, and laughter, and sometimes discipline. "Billy, eat your peas!" Stop wiggling at least till I count to ten."

One afternoon when Billy was an early teen he came in from outside. Because we had guests he leaned over to whisper in my ear and I smelled cigarette smoke. I took him directly to the kitchen. I told him to sit ON the table. I took advantage of the opportunity to warn of drugs as well as cigarettes. I was well armed with illustrations of friends or family who smoked or took drugs till it destroyed their brains or killed them. He was not bored! He told me years later that after that speech he never had a lit cigarette in his mouth again.

One evening his young French friend Frederic stayed for supper. "What's this?" he asked as I placed a bowl of cream of potato soup on the table at his place. He disparagingly said, "I've never eaten white soup before!" Did that mean the French deprived themselves of cream of celery, potato, asparagus, or chicken soup, or even clam chowder?

One afternoon one of the young Algerian Christian women sat at that table. She couldn't tell me what was wrong. I hoped to help her through her agony.

"Are you pregnant?" I asked.

"Yes." she answered. Then she asked if we would be willing to meet the father.

A few days later we again sat at the table. She asked me what I thought of him. I had to be careful. It was too late to give a negative evaluation. They got married. After the birth of tiny Leila we made huge quantities of the traditional 'tamina' on that table, and I served it to each guest. As that cute little curly haired girl grew we placed her on piled up cushions so she too could join us for a meal around our table. My visiting father named her, "Earthquake."

Zohra sat at that table every morning for a month or more struggling to drink a doctor's remedy for high blood pressure. On her first doctor's visit he had told me that her blood pressure was so high that she shouldn't be alive. I was to boil orange tree leaves and have her drink the potion each morning with a clove or two of raw garlic. Pour little fragile wrinkled Zohra, her white hair turned henna orange, sat there straining to swallow this natural, cheap and extremely bitter cure. She had been faithful to the Lord down through the years. We loved and respected her so much. I hoped regular visits to a doctor would help get her strength back.

And then there were the large suppers where we would invite the whole group of our young Christian friends back to the house for waffles after a picnic in the woods or at the beach. Bill and I would hurry home to start preparing and as the group trailed in, many of the women gathered around the table to peel veggies for soup as I mixed the waffle batter. We only had one waffle iron so the men sat in a circle in the living room waiting as we served each in turn. The chatter around the table in the kitchen outdid that in the living room. I don't think anyone went away hungry.

The living room was a solid wall away from the kitchen. Bible studies or prayer groups took place there. I hated missing conversations as I prepared a snack or meal. Some of the young men and girls began gathering around the table in the kitchen, either one or several at a time. I loved having them there. The conversations were often more than trivial chitchat as they advised each other touching on marriage, their parents' search for their future spouse, or the housing crises, or the latest news on the street. Or even how a new Christian survives in a Muslim culture. They shared with me, as they shared with their mothers, knowing that I would then share with Bill.

These young people also kept us abreast of the latest Algerian jokes usually at the expense of some important political figure. They could make us laugh at even a sad story. They taught us so much.

All the while that little green vinyl topped table never said a word, but she knew she was really the rallying point, the epicenter of attention. She served us well for sixteen years.

Emotional Return to Algiers

The air wafting down the steps as we boarded our Air Algerie flight, heading back to Algiers after the summer months in the U.S., smelled of dirty socks and sweaty feet. We had spent the last two nights in England with some friends who were renting an Elizabethan style home. That peaceful relaxed atmosphere would be in sharp contrast to what lay ahead.

We enjoyed the flight across the channel and across France, but as we crossed the Mediterranean nearing Algiers, the stress of the possibility of a nasty reentry, either with the police or with customs, began to feel almost tangible. What was in our luggage that might get us into trouble? Vanilla? Popcorn? Personal items? Had we declared every single cent of foreign currency? Soon we would be at the mercy of a fickle customs officer. In some ways their actions were understandable. Compared to Western Europe, there was so little to buy in Algeria that anyone who had the opportunity and the money to travel out, would return with gifts for every member of his family as well as items to sell. We once saw a man carrying a car door over his shoulder, his arm through the opened window. Why shouldn't the customs official try to profit through this privileged opportunity to dig into luggage?

We were living in socialist Algeria where incompetence ran high and productivity ran low. We were back in push, push, push land. I still remember the smell of urine as we entered the airport. Usually once we were through all of the customs formalities and out in the parking area, that tension would dissipate and that wonderful feeling of returning home to our apartment and friends replaced it. But for some reason this return trip was different. My negative feelings persisted.

Within hours of our arrival we heard that our Algerian daughter, Rania, was ill. We dropped our luggage at home and headed to the clinic. Why were cats running down the hallways into the patients' rooms and out the open windows? We found her room and hugged her warmly and then began asking questions. She had had a miscarriage. Before the visit was finished I took off my shoe and began killing the ants that were making a trail up and down her sheets. I couldn't believe it when she asked me why I was doing that? Was I going crazy? Didn't she mind the ants on her bed?

The next morning we headed to the Monoprix. The name was left over from French Colonial times, but the store itself was owned and operated by the Algerian Government, as were most of the businesses in town. Almost all of the apartments and villas were government owned. We paid our rent to the local government office. Manufacturing was stifled and importation minimal. Algeria owned the third largest gas reserves in the world, but this potentially wealthy gas and oil producing nation with it's huge natural resources had chosen, at the time of independence, to align itself politically and philosophically with Russia and Eastern Europe. The doctors were often from one of these countries and could not communicate with their patients. Algeria had the third fastest growing population in the world, but construction was at a standstill.

Over half of the population was under sixteen years old. Young people could not find housing so were constantly postponing marriage. Some apartments housed four or more families, one in each room sharing the kitchen and bathroom. The buses were crowded beyond description and ran erratically. The stress felt by the population was palpable.

The crowded Monoprix was not full of buyers. It was just full of people. Many were standing in line waiting for one item or another. In a socialistic state you get paid whether you produce or not, so the sales clerks took their time. But on this particular day the line did not stretch out the door and down the sidewalk. When that happened you got in the line and then asked what everyone was waiting for. Eggs? Soap powder? Batteries? Sometimes the person before you in line did not know! Many carried a folded-up "Maybe Bag." Just maybe there would be a surprise item to buy. We joined the meat line, then the vegetable line. As we were leaving we passed by the soap counter. As I recall there were rows and rows of LUX soap bars. Just then a young man brushed past me taking a little extra time to rub against my breasts. I completely cracked. I lifted a clenched fist and hit him as hard as I could on his upper arm.

Bill saw what I had done. My own reaction was fright and shame. I lowered my head and slid further away only seeing the rows of Lux soap. As Bill pushed through the people to come up beside me, without raising my head, I asked him what had happened. He said the guy was really surprised and the ladies around had snickered.

I was so shocked and ashamed at my uncontrolled reaction that I decided to pull myself together then and there. The Lord delivered me from those negative feelings and with the help of our team prayer times, the meaningful group Bible studies, and the gradual but steady growth of the emerging national church, our focus was constantly redirected to the task at hand. We were very soon back on track. The joy and love we were experiencing far surpassed the pressures of life around us.

The deprivation was good for us. When we were able to buy flour or eggs, or come home with something in our "Maybe Bag," we experienced incredible joy- the same excitement our neighbors were experiencing. We were all in this together.

Bernard's Fedora

Summons to the police station arrived fairly frequently during our earlier years in Algiers. Certainly the authorities had the right to check up on foreigners and send them packing if they were breaking the law. However, several of our friends never knew what they were guilty of. Some could only imagine the reason, but others were absolutely sure that they had been expelled because some military leader or policeman wanted the house they were living in. That happened to our Danish artist friend. She and her husband were picked up within hours of the time they arrived back from vacation. The police took them right back to the airport with only their passports and we never saw them again. Soldiers immediately moved into their house.

Three years after our settling in Algiers, we received a telephone call from an American friend asking how I was. Then she asked how Bill was, how Billy was, and then how our dog was. We didn't have a dog. I knew immediately that she was informing us of some event that she didn't dare say on the phone. It was 1969. We found out later that the extensive fenced-in Methodist property with a few nice houses and a chapel had been raided during a youth retreat. All foreigners present were promptly expelled. The French pastor living in that compound and his Algerian wife were only permitted to take their passports out with them to France. Because one of their children, who was about ten years old, was not at home at the time, they had to leave without him.

The report in the newspaper the next day was completely fabricated, details skewed to hide the truth. A high ranking military officer soon moved into the principle house on this prime property and other military people filled the compound. A few months later this top military officer died. There were not too many tears shed. That property had served for worship, conferences, library research and other services. Before things calmed down, the Salvation Army, feeling expulsion was inevitable, decided to leave. With them went all the help they offered the poor. The Seventh Day Adventists who actually had a highly respected clinic and a church building toward the center of town were expelled. The Baptists also left.

One day Bill received a summons to appear at the police station. Seven hours later he was released, but was told to return the next morning. During the interrogation the Lord opened an opportunity for him to recount his testimony. He told the police that he had been a heavy drinker in college, that he had quit in the middle of his last year and joined the army because he felt that he might find God and get his life straightened out if he faced death on the front lines in Korea. He then recounted how he had found Jesus Christ and that it was Christ who had turned his life around. He had come to Algeria because of that experience. When these officers released him that afternoon they said that they wanted him to return the next morning to tell their superior officer the same story!

The next morning while Bill was at the station, two plainclothesmen came to the house. Were they there because they were following orders, or were they really investigating us personally, or were they still curious about Bill's faith experience?

There was no way I could refuse them entry even though I was home alone. They first asked to see any Christian literature we had. I led them into our guest room that was right next to the front door. There we had a cupboard with a few tracts. They were curious, but not really interested until one picked up a leaflet entitled, "Comment Fonder Un Foyer Heureux," "How to Establish a Happy Home." He read the title out loud and said, "Oh, I need that. May I have it?"

I was beginning to feel very relaxed about this kind of interrogation. As they were leaving I asked permission to ask them a question. "We have a trip to the desert planned for Thursday. Should we continue our plans to travel?" I didn't tell them Bill was Regional Pastor and one of his jobs was to visit our other workers. They said, "Don't cancel your trip."

And then they asked me a question. "Whose hat is that there on the bed?" I explained that we had a guest from France and he had left it there when he went out. Their reply was, "Don't tell him we were here." It was Bernard Collinson's fedora. He was our mission's Regional Director, visiting us to make sure that we were okay and to give us encouragement. I didn't tell the police who he was!

That night we praised the Lord with all of our colleagues including Bernard, telling how the Gospel had been shared in a place where we would not normally have chosen to go. We stayed on in Algiers another 12 years.

Peggy, It's the Bananas

"The Algerian ladies would really be happy to taste this," I said, as I smelled the hot slice of banana bread just offered me. My hostess was curious. "Why?" she asked.

"Well Algerians have not seen bananas for about six years. Algeria produces most of its own meat and vegetables and many citrus fruits but the government doesn't import bananas."

I was sitting with my friend Cindy and the wife of the pastor of the International Church in Rome. I had just flown in from Algiers and Cindy had met me at the airport. There were six Algerian women arriving throughout the afternoon and the next day from Oran and Algiers. They were delegates to a special prayer conference for Christian women from the Middle East and North Africa, to begin in a few days on the island of Cyprus. The invitation to bring delegates to this conference had reached us in Algiers at the same time as the rumor that the government had passed a new law stating that no Algerian female was allowed to travel without being accompanied by her husband or her father. It looked like we in Algeria would have to turn down the invitation.

But we didn't. The second barrier to overcome was the law making it necessary to assure the police that the ladies would be received and housed by someone in Europe. We could not state that the ladies were headed to Cyprus. That would only cause curiosity as to why they were traveling to such a highly unusual destination. I asked Cindy if she and friends in her church would make out 'certificats d'hébergements' with addresses in Rome. In addition we put a plan in place where the seven of us would leave on different flights on different days from different cities! Only one of the ladies had ever been out of Algeria before. The others had never been on a plane.

Cindy and a group of volunteers were to meet them and ferry them to various homes of people in the congregation. I accompanied the driver to the airport. The ladies who had already arrived returned to the airport to welcome the others. As I climbed into the front seat for the first trip, I saw out of the corner of my eye a whole branch of beautiful bananas carefully laid out on the back seat. They must have weighed 10 to 15 pounds.

When all seven of us were together in Rome, we praised the Lord for helping us accomplish the impossible. That first evening Cindy transported us to the ladies' first sightseeing destination, a huge supermarket. The next morning we headed to the airport for our flight to Athens.

There we had a five-hour layover before flying on to Cyprus. I couldn't believe that I was in Athens and I couldn't leave the airport to see the Parthenon! In desperation I decided to try the only solution I could think of. I walked up to a window where I thought I saw some policemen and turned on what I called my "dumb-blond-act." It was designed to conjure up a bit of sympathy and implied that they alone had the solution to my problem.

I greeted them and then continued in English, "I have a problem." "Yes? What is your problem?" His heavy accented answer sounded kind, and interested. I continued, "Ever since I was a little girl and studied about ancient Greece I have wanted to see the Parthenon. I am an American and I don't need a visa, but I'm traveling with six Algerian ladies who do. We have a five hour layover, and I would love to go into Athens."

I was thrilled and afraid at the same time by his answer. "You don't have a problem. Just bring their passports and I'll write you the document necessary for you to leave the airport." I trusted him! He proceeded to type with two fingers their names, nationalities, passport numbers on an old typewriter that jumped up and down with the letters not necessarily landing on the same line. He handed me the paper and slipped their passports into a drawer.

The leftover bananas in the bag at right

I told the ladies to check all of their hand luggage in the lockers and we were off on an adventure. We climbed onto a bus waiting at the curb; destination written in Greek, which I guessed, said 'Athens.' When we arrived in the heart of town, I was really scared. What do I do now? I didn't have a clue! I looked around and saw a travel agency on the corner. I left the ladies on the sidewalk, went in and asked where the Parthenon was. They told me to take Bus # 3 and handed me a map. If we made a mistake there might not be anyone who could understand me, and maybe the returning bus might take a different route. I got an idea of where we were on the map and off we went on foot. In retrospect, we should have taken the bus.

Those ladies were so slow walking in their high heels and one of them always stopped, slipping into the shops without saying a word. I would turn around and count one, two, three... where's Assia? Then I would go back and beg her to come out of the store. And on we stumbled. Their heels alone couldn't explain our slow progress. Finally, I said in frustration, "Can you please tell me why you are so slow."

"Peggy, it's the bananas!"

I was flabbergasted. They considered those bananas so precious that they hadn't left them behind in Rome, or even in the lockers at the Athens airport!

I said, "Okay. Sit on that bench over there and each one of you eat two bananas!

The Parthenon was looming up on the right behind some scrub trees. We left the sidewalk and climbed up a bank through the bushes and there it was ahead of us. A childhood dream had come true! I was enthralled and scared at the same time. It was time to head back. We couldn't find Assia. In retrospect I think I thrust my dream on them.

They were probably saying what is this Parthenon anyway? If they had had a choice they probably would have chosen to ramble through the shops. We made it back to the airport.

The conference was all in American English, but the delegates were from the Middle East and North Africa. An Egyptian was designated to translate into Arabic. Spoken Arabic varies from country to country and the Algerian delegation had been educated in French. For them Egyptian Arabic was almost an unknown. A Lebanese women volunteered to do the translation into French but after the first session the ladies asked if I would take over. So I spent the rest of the conference at the simultaneous translation desk. The speakers' voices came in my ears in English and out my mouth into a microphone in French. I enjoyed myself immensely and my reward was the confirmation from the ladies that they were understanding well.

Whatever happened to those uneaten bananas?

What's in a Name?

My pregnant Algerian friends loved and trusted Amel, their midwife, and always hoped that she would be on duty when their contractions began. One day I found two of my closest Algerian friends lying side by side. Amel had delivered their babies just one day apart. It made me happy to see them chatting and supporting each other.

But nurses get sick too. From time to time Amel suffered severe pains in her abdomen. Gallstone symptoms were common among women in Algeria. She would give herself a shot to relieve the pain. As these attacks became more and more severe, she decided that the next time she would give herself a shot, grab a taxi, and head straight to Emergency at Mustapha Hospital. Because upon arrival her pain had subsided, the doctor told her that she wasn't suffering enough to be treated in emergency. She asked the doctor to schedule her for gall bladder surgery, but he said that was out of his jurisdiction. She would have to schedule herself through the normal channels. She had already tried to do just that.

Before Independence, Mustapha Hospital was a star among French Hospitals including those in mainland France. Despite the third fastest population growth rate in the world, the socialist government had not maintained the medical facilities to keep up with this growth, much less increase the number of roads, bridges, schools and housing. Not only were the buses, apartments, and schools packed out, but so was the national hospital.

Amel knew that she would not get the care she needed unless she found someone who would use his influence on her behalf. Finally, she was registered. On the day of the actual surgery, she was sitting in a circle with a large number of other women chatting about their different illnesses, all-waiting to be called for their anesthesia. Each had her hospital issued papers in hand. One of these ladies leaned over and said, "I can't read. Would you tell me what is written here?" As Amel read her paper, the lady cried out, "That's not my name!" They went up to the nurse's desk. She returned to her seat grateful that she had been able to help someone avoid a tragic mistake.

She sat down, and then looked down at her own paper. There too was the name of a perfect stranger!

Was the woman who had distributed the papers that day illiterate? Stories were circulating of the hospital's hiring procedures. Staff got hired the same way Amel got registered for surgery - through what Algerians called "shoulders" or a 'piston,' an influential person, or backstairs influence. The illiterate man working in the hospital pharmacy, dispensing medicines was there because a relative had arranged it.

It was common procedure for women to be released from the hospital with their gallstones nicely preserved in a small glass jar. This was happy showoff proof that they had survived the hospital experience. Amel herself was grateful to the Lord for His help. Soon she was feeling better and back at work in her beloved delivery room.

The Tale of a Tail

The knock on the back garden gate was a surprise. It wasn't yet noon so I really wasn't expecting Bill, who was out shopping, or Billy and Clyde home so early. I stepped out of the kitchen into the garden, opened the gate and found two men dressed in suit coats and ties. I knew immediately they were police of one kind or other.

"Is there a man named Clyde Hiestand staying here?" I replied that he wasn't there right now, but they assured me that they knew where he was. They wanted his passport.

I left them standing on the sidewalk and went back into the house and into Clyde's bedroom. His suitcase was lying on the floor. I pretended to rifle through his things and then returned.

"His passport is not obvious, and it is impolite for me to go through his personal items," I said. "What has happened? What's going on? I'm concerned because our son is with him." Billy was eight years old. I was really more concerned for Clyde, but this sounded better.

They assured me that I had nothing to worry about because they would bring Billy home. And they left. Clyde's fate was not included. Bill arrived a short time later from the vegetable market. Shortly there was another knock, this time on the front courtyard door and in walked Billy with Clyde accompanied by two plainclothesmen. As Clyde walked into his bedroom he asked me to get him a drink of water. He came back out with his passport, drank the water and left with the men. Billy stayed behind.

"What in the world is going on? What happened?" we asked as we heard the gate close. Billy acted as mystified as we were, "I don't know, but I think it has to do with the kite."

What was wrong with that simple cloth kite? Billy's grandpa had bought it for him in Oran a few years previously. Then I remembered that the tail was red, white and blue, the colors of the French flag - or the American flag. Algeria's flag was red, white and green. Algeria had only been independent from France for 5 years so there might be some understandable resentment. I suggested to Bill that he go down to the police station with a pair of scissors and ask permission to cut off the blue section of the kite tail. He should explain that the kite was a gift from Billy's grandfather so he had a sentimental attachment to it. This way Bill might save the kite and be able to get a bit more information.

The police seemed to like the idea; in other words, they fell for it! They kept the blue section and Bill came back with the kite and remaining red and white tail. Can you believe it? We realized that this could not be a scary investigation if they could accept such a crazy proposal. Then Bill returned again to the police station with a checker set so that he and Clyde could fill in time waiting for the police to come back from lunch break. Imagine sitting in the State Police station, under investigation, and a friend arrives with a checker set! Later that afternoon Clyde came back to the house and we were able to put together the pieces of the mystery.

We were together spending our summer vacation in Cherchell, Algeria, on the Mediterranean Sea. The Caesars had spent their winters there back when the city was named Caesarea. During Roman times it was the capital of the Roman province of Mauretania. (Not present day Mauritania.) It was a wonderful town. The lighthouse, the port with fishermen sitting cross-legged mending their nets, the beautiful coastline with numerous beaches, coastal islands, Roman ruins-even one of the original Roman arches was still standing as one entered the city. To the south a range of the Atlas Mountains separated the rich, fertile coastal plain with its fruit trees and vineyards from the Sahara Desert.

It was a beautiful place for a vacation. We had invited Clyde who lived and worked in Constantine in eastern Algeria to spend his vacation with us. He had ridden his motorbike the 500 kilometers across the country to join us.

The day before the police visit he and Billy had cooked up a plan to go out to investigate the countryside, camp out for a night, and try out the kite that Grandpa had bought in Oran a few years before. We packed some blankets, a bit of food for several meals and off they went on Clyde's motorbike.

They rode along the coast investigating beaches, found an old WWII tank, and decided before nightfall to find a camping site along the main road. They needed to be hidden from view. The best place they could find was a fairly deep ditch in a field. This would not only hide them from the road but they could also pull the motorbike down out of sight. They must have slept pretty well because they were wakened, not by the rising sun, but by a mysterious roaring sound which got louder and louder. It was obvious that the cause was fast approaching. Rushing water! They had unknowingly chosen to sleep in an irrigation ditch. They both reacted soon enough to rescue the bike and jump out.

There was a nice rolling field on the other side of the road. The wind would be stronger up there and perhaps they could get Billy's kite to really sail. They ran along the crest of the hill with the kite soaring. Before long their success was interrupted by a gendarme jeep and dismounting state police on the road below signaling for them to pull in the kite and join them. The police seemed happy with their catch and loaded them into the back of the jeep and off to their headquarters.

Why? Clyde had heard their reasoning. That little hill where they had succeeded in flying the kite was positioned in such a way as to give a view, between two mountains, of the Mediterranean Sea. It was shortly after the Six Day War between several Arab States and Israel in the Middle East. It was rumored that the American Sixth Fleet was sailing through the Mediterranean to show some muscle. Some overzealous gendarmes suspected that Billy and Clyde were sending signals to those Americans. These were tense times. Algeria reasoned that if the U.S. could fight way off in Viet Nam, then they could also attack Algeria. There was so much war hype that the authorities had actually opened up the old bomb shelters in Algiers. To us this was all so fantastic that we hadn't taken it seriously - but obviously someone had.

An over-zealous young policeman had suspected our eight-year-old son of being a spy! The next morning Clyde went downtown to get some repairs finished on his bike. The repairman said, "We know who you are. You're that 'spy' that the 'gendarmes' picked up yesterday." Everyone in the shop laughed. The news was all over town.

Angel Unawares

Our little Renault R-4 was packed full with four adults and three children. We were again on vacation in Cherchell. Most afternoons we set out to find a new and different place to investigate. Today our destination was a white rock capping a steep hill about 20 miles away. We drove almost to the top, parked, then climbed to the very top of the rock and sat down facing the Mediterranean. A steep incline, then a shallow valley lay below stretching to the Roman ruins on the cliffs above the beach. The Mediterranean Sea stretched off to the horizon. Those Romans sure did pick beautiful spots to settle.

The grassy slope in front of us was pocked with holes. Billy and his two friends were used to inventing their own games. They were soon playing a new version of hide-and-seek, jumping in and out. The northern coast of Algeria had served as a landing area for allied troops during World War II, so we imagined that these were fox holes dug in the hillside as the troops moved inland. We had already found a WWII Army tank right on the beach. There were also remains from Algeria's almost eight-year fight for independence. It never occurred to us that we should examine the holes to see if there was any lurking danger before the children started their play.

We sat chatting together in the warm sunshine, eating cake and afternoon coffee before returning to our vacation house. When we climbed back down to the car, we told the kids to climb the rest of the way up over the crest and meet us on the road on the other side. We were sitting in the car waiting when I noticed a shepherd boy coming up the hill toward us as fast as he could run. Just then Billy and the two girls reached the driver's side of the car. Billy blurted out through his panting that as he came up over the top of the rock ahead of the girls, he spotted another large hole to his right. He was running down the hill and intended to jump in one more time before reaching the car.

He said, "I arrived right at the edge - but someone put his hand on my chest and kept me from jumping in." That familiar fear-pain shot through my body. Bill got out of the car and returned with the children to see this hole. When they came back he said, "I couldn't see the bottom. It was at least sixty feet down there."

No doubt the shepherd was running to warn us of the danger. Billy suffered from nightmares for a few nights. We praised the Lord for his Guardian Angels. Here was a tangible proof of God's love for him. God had saved his life, not for our pleasure alone. What did He still have in store for Billy?

Saltines and Socialism

We were standing on a crowded bus headed downtown. Most of the passengers were silent, living with their thoughts, but not my visitor from the US. She was chatting away, expressing her observations, assuming that no one would understand. Although her remarks were in no way offensive, the volume of her voice made us conspicuous. And it was highly possible that at least some of those around us were students and might well understand English. I was pretty sure that everyone was listening. She immediately lowered her voice at my signal and that was that.

A few days later she and I drove out to attend my weekly English language ladies' Bible study. The ladies were from Sweden, Denmark, France, Canada, England, Wales, Norway, Scotland, Italy, Egypt and the US. We drove out of the city, along the Mediterranean coast to a little settlement called Club des Pins (Club of the Pines). The houses stood on a small hill overlooking the beach. They were similar in style, but varied in position. Each had large, beautiful tiled fireplaces along one wall of the living room. The wall facing the sea and either side of the fireplace was glass from floor to ceiling. These beautiful houses were in stark contrast to the usual deprivations of a country bent on imposing its socialistic form of government.

Many different nationalities lived in Club des Pins with one thing in common. They were all employed by the nationalized state oil companies.

Foreign companies had signed contracts to help Algeria exploit its vast oil and gas reserves. Some of the ladies who attended the Bible studies were married to these highly qualified technicians from around the world.

That morning as the number of ladies began to swell to 18 we decided to have the leader conduct her prepared study and then we would break down into three groups for discussion and prayer. We had already formed fast friendships and shared our hearts with each other. Some were lonely or depressed; some were professional women with none of the language skills to hold jobs; some wanted to be back home; some knew that their husbands were unfaithful; some had children with health problems and were afraid. We cried with each other, sympathized and prayed for each other. We knew that the Lord cared and could help us through each day. Our motto was: "Share your cares, cry, and pass the toilet paper!" In this socialistic state there were no paper handkerchiefs or paper napkins to buy.

Our hostess this week was a lady from Houston, Texas. We usually had refreshments of some kind after the study. This week's refreshments were especially wonderful. Our hostess had recently received a package from the U.S. She had decided to add to the usual cookies or homemade cakes something from her package. To our delight she apportioned out two saltine crackers to each of us.

That summer I came back to the U.S. to settle Billy in a boarding school in North Carolina. On the return drive north from North Carolina I stopped to visit that American who had visited us in Algeria. Referring to that morning in Algiers she said, "Peggy, I will never forget that Bible study. Here we were in a beautiful house overlooking the blue Mediterranean with the beach only a few steps away, on a clear sunny morning and what do you ladies go crazy over? Two saltine crackers!"

Landmines and Geraniums

Our apartment building in Algiers had twenty-three apartments. Down back was an empty space where the residents parked their cars and where the children played away from the street. From our back balcony on the third floor we could watch the kids kicking a ball, having fist fights, throwing stones, and best of all, we could keep tabs on some of the disagreements if they got out of hand! At the far edge of this courtyard were the vestiges of a metal fence that had been torn from its moorings and lay flat on the ground. It had once stood to separate our courtyard from the courtyard of another apartment building. Now the kids from down there could easily come over to play in our larger space. I sensed that there was a rivalry between "them" and "us."

Many of the buildings in Algiers still had graffiti on the walls left over from the hatred of the seven-year-war for independence. Our staircase bore a huge OAS sign.

The Organisation de L'Armée Secrète had been made up of French colonialists who were determined that Algeria would not gain independence. In the last years they fought both the French government forces and the Algerian Resistance fighters. The family that had lived in our apartment just before us told of the day their children had found a trip wire in the courtyard leading to an unexploded device. A demolition crew removed it, but that story stayed in my memory.

One day I had a fun idea to occupy the children playing below with more constructive play from their usual pastimes. I gathered them around me. We were going to plant flowers where that trip wire had been. I had a lot of geraniums and other plants on my balcony. We dug enough holes for the lot and stepped back to survey our work. They were thrilled. And I was proud. Each one of these plants would be theirs to care for.

The next morning the children came to the door to announce that their plants were gone! The kids from "down there" had come over after dark, dug them up and planted them in their own courtyard. But they added that I was not to worry because they had gone over the fence and brought them back! So much for my idea of beautifying our grounds. I should have known.

Chakchouka

This was an Algerian ferry. That was obvious. You didn't have to notice the Algerian flag flapping in the wind or see the ship's name or even read the occasional Arabic instructions posted here and there. It was the music first and foremost that cried out that this ferry belonged to Algeria and not to France. Arabic music is in no way western. The instruments, often unknown to us in the west, produce sounds that can be very agreeable to the western ear or can irritate because of our lack of understanding of the nuances of the seemingly endless repetition.

From the time we boarded the car ferry in Algiers for the 24 hour sail across the Mediterranean to Marseille, France, Arab music was being piped all over the ship. We would soon be needing some calming music. We didn't know it when we boarded, but this was not going to be a pleasant, calm, smooth sea passage. We parked the loaded car in the hold, climbed the stairs to find our cabin and then went out to investigate the ship and meet some of our fellow passengers. Billy soon made friends with some of the Algerian crew and disappeared.

Before too long the ferry began to roll from side to side and slap from bow to stern against the rising white caps. Now Bill has never been a good sailor. He returned to his bunk first and I soon followed realizing that there was no way that we could eat the meals I had prepared, and no way that we would be able to keep what we had already eaten if we were not in a prostrate position.

Groaning was not one of our habits so we said little and silently moaned. At one of the roughest moments, I muttered to myself, "I got on this ship of my own free will and now I'm going to die."

Some time later Billy burst into the room. I asked him where he had been. His reply. "Oh, I made a friend. He is one of the crew and he showed me around the ship. We went to the kitchen and made Chakchouka." Now chakchouka is delicious - a mixture of tomatoes, peppers, onions, eggplant, olive oil, stewed together on which eggs are dropped, simmered in the vegetable juices and served hot with Algerian bread. My only thought was, who could possibly eat an egg at a moment like this? Chakchouka is also a word that means "a mixture, a crazy mess." Our stomachs were already chakchouka.

Just outside the port of Marseille is an area dubbed 'La Gueule du Lion' (The Lion's mouth) because the sea is more agitated there than even out in the open sea. Our misery only got worse. The Arab music played on, but just as the ferry pulled into the protected port and up to the dock, the rocking motion stopped.

So did the music. In its place we heard a choir singing in English from Handel's *Messiah*, "Hallelujah, Hallelujah, Hallelujah." Those Algerian crewmembers had a wonderful sense of humor.

The Circus Is Coming to Town

A circus was coming to town! They would set it up in the limited space on Place des Martyrs, just above the western extension of the port of Algiers. The Barbary pirates had sailed from this port for more than three centuries raiding ships as they passed through the Mediterranean Sea. The circus was to share the square with history itself. In the center of the circling city streets stood a large white mosque.

It was rumored that this mosque had been designed for the Dey of Algiers by a Christian architect who had been captured and taken as a slave off a passing European ship. When his workmen finished their masterpiece, he revealed his long held secret. He had designed this beautiful structure in the shape of a cross. This believable legend ends confirming this was his crowning work, but also the last of that Christian architect. The modified mosque stands there today, and for those of us who have heard the legend, it stands as a testimony to the bravery of a man committed to his own faith in Christ no matter the consequences.

Djamaa el Djedid, Place de Martyres, Algiers

The level land continues about 150 yards inland before the buildings climb up a fairly steep hill. Tucked behind a row of apartment buildings lies the Palace of the Princess, with its ornate arches, carved balcony railings, and colorful tiled walls. The Pasha presented it as a gift to his daughter, Khedidja. Built in 1517 and expanded through the centuries, it eventually became the home of Napoleon III and his wife Eugenie on their visits to Algiers. Nested against the climbing hillside was another mosque. Belying its origins, it looks more like a Catholic Cathedral with its double spires. The guide claims that it was first of all a mosque, modified into a cathedral during France's 130 years' occupation. At Independence it was restored back to a functioning mosque.

Looming up the hill behind climbs the famous Algiers Casbah with its narrow winding streets, walls so close together overhead that they nearly block out the sky. These houses served as hideouts for the pirates. With the natural port close by, they could easily raid ships of their goods, take slaves, and then escape to their homes with ease. Independent America fought its first war, The War of the Barbary Pirates, along these shores.

And now a gaudy, multi-colored circus with it's tents and banners, scantily dressed women and men acrobats, wild animals, tinny music and clowns, and all of the necessary paraphernalia would be plunked down in the middle the square, no doubt blocking traffic the whole week of their visit! We weren't the only ones excited about seeing something so out of keeping with our usual lives. Up to this point the only circus we had ever attended was on the television screen.

We arrived with Billy, were able to find a parking space on a side street, and joined the tail of a long queue. Now if you have ever lived in a crowded city in a developing country you will know that a line anywhere, whether to buy tickets to a circus, or to load onto a bus or train, or for check-in at the international airport, or even to buy bread does not in any way resemble a line. If you show even an inkling of patience you will not get in, or get on, or get up. So we were not at all suspicious of all of the pushing and yelling and brushing past. From past experience we knew enough strategies to succeed. But before Bill could react to an extra close movement behind him, his wallet had disappeared and was being passed from hand to hand and eventually into the maze of the streets of the Casbah.

These kids were as quick as the blink of an eye. After all they had had centuries of practice and experience behind them. Their great, great, great grandfathers were those Barbary Pirates!

The big tent did not disappoint us. It was well worth the wait and the crunch, if not the loss!

Farida and the Sorcerer

As we walked into our apartment in Algiers we found a piece of paper that had been slipped under the door. "Please come immediately. Something terrible had happened!" It was from a precious young friend. We had just brought Billy home for lunch and he needed to get back to school, so after feeding and sending him off we drove down to her house.

There was blood spattered on the walls of their living room. She and her sister talked through their hysteria. Farida's husband had lost his temper once again and had battered their mother who was already bedridden and dying of cancer. A quantity of the blood was from her sister's broken nose. The reason for this outburst was unclear, but we were learning fast that he was unable to control his fits of anger.

Up until the time of Farida's marriage these three women had been living alone with no male family member to protect them or to advocate on their behalf. That is not an enviable situation for women in the Muslim World. Before we met them, Farida's father had worked for the French police during the war for independence. To the Algerian freedom fighters he was considered a traitor. One morning as he was hoisting the French flag in front of the local city hall a shot rang out and he fell to the ground dead. A Swiss lady took pity on the girls and eventually introduced them to us.

By the time that her mother died and her sister had married and moved to France, Farida felt that we had become her family. Down through the years she often found refuge in our house and lived with us even with two of her children.

One day several months before this incident she had brought a young man to introduce him to us. He was as handsome as she was pretty. But he was also a very proud individual, trained as a fireman in France and I suspected was in his element breaking down doors and forcing his way into buildings. We were wary, but they married anyway. He moved in with her family until the incident of beating her mother. She got a police injunction against him and moved in with us. He would not leave her alone. An investigating policeman told us that this was a clear case of someone who couldn't live with his wife or live without her.

One evening he arrived at the door and we let him in. When she begged me to not force her to go out with him, he turned violent. She ran through the apartment into our bedroom and I locked the door and stood in front of it. As Bill went to get the help of a neighbor, he turned on me twisting my arm and throwing me to the floor. The neighbor was able to calm him down and eventually convinced him to leave the house. I unlocked the bedroom. She had not hidden in the room. She had to be on the balcony. But she was not there either. Had she jumped three stories below? I was frantic. I discovered her cowering in the corner of our next-door neighbor's balcony. In horrific fear she had climbed around the separation wall over that empty space three stories down.

We were sure then that she was no longer safe at our house. We found two foreign families who agreed to keep her hidden for a while. When we hadn't seen him for months, she moved back in with us and started a job as a telephone operator. One morning our phone rang. It was one of her colleagues who said that she had not arrived at work that morning.

As the day wore on we still had no idea what had happened or where she might be. Bill and I sat down and pleaded with the Lord to protect her. Mid afternoon the phone rang again. She had turned up at work and was coming straight home. She would explain the whole story when she arrived.

But she didn't come!

Sometime late evening she walked in exhausted. She began telling us first of all why she hadn't been able to come home earlier in the afternoon. Fidel Castro was visiting Algiers on a state visit. Boumedienne, Algeria's president, had ordered all of the offices downtown closed so that their personnel would be out on the street. At the same time, all buses and taxis were ordered to stop running. In that way he could assure that there would be a cheering section along the streets to welcome this visiting head of state!

We listened with incredulous ears as the other story unfolded. That husband of hers would stop at nothing to get his unwilling wife back in his clutches. He had met her as she got off the bus in the morning. He was not alone.

The man with him was carrying a canvas bag. As she descended the steps this man stared at her as though their eyes were locked. Despite her protests, her husband announced that they were going to a cafe for coffee. As they sat down the other man again locked eyes with her and she felt that she was losing her self-control. They left the restaurant together and headed not toward her job, but toward her husband's father's house. She kept asking herself why she was following them and yet she had no control over her actions.

His whole family was waiting for her. As they sat down the man opened his bag and began arranging its contents. She realized at that point that he was a sorcerer. He lit a fire in his little clay container full of charcoal, sprinkled some powder, and laid out some strange smelling stones. She was told to circle the fire seven times. I asked her why she had obeyed him. She replied that she was so outnumbered, one against ten others. As she sat down she started to sob. Then she shouted out that sorcery was against the law, and that she was against it too, because she was a Christian. She added, "Even the Minister of Religious Affairs is a Christian!" That misstatement broke our tension and we laughed. The Minister of Religious Affairs is the most powerful Muslim Imam in the country. She meant to say Minister of Finance.

The sorcerer began to show signs of confusion and then fear, and finally he blurted out, "I have no power over this woman. She has been to a sorcerer who is stronger than I am."

The Lord Jesus had heard our prayers. He knew where she was and what her needs were. He had protected her. That other sorcerer was Jesus! An Algerian sorcerer had, in effect recognized that Jesus was more powerful! Amen and Amen.

Sorcery

During our first years in Algeria we met a young women who, a few years previously, had married a believer, but was already a widow. Friends explained to us that her husband's family had slowly poisoned him with mind-altering drugs because he had left Islam. He was guilty of apostasy, a crime worthy of death. Gradually we learned of several different forms of sorcery prevalent in the Algerian society.

In addition to expressions in Arabic that ward off the evil eye, Fatima's hand appears frequently in jewelry, doorknockers, and wall hangings. This symbol of the Prophet Muhammad's precious daughter's hand is considered a talisman against evil. It is also referred to as 'khamsa,' the Arabic word for 'five' referring to five lifted fingers. Some people claim that these fingers also represent the five pillars of Islam.

Men, but most commonly women, pray to dead saints, as well as to living saints, called Marabouts. Their response to your request to find a good husband or succeed in your exams and so on, might involve the ritual of sacrificing a chicken or a sheep facing toward Mecca, and putting its blood under your pillow or secretly under the pillow of someone else to attain your request. Amulets containing Koranic verses were commonly pinned to a baby's clothes to protect from the evil eye. It was never a good idea to admire an object or compliment a baby's appearance because that drew the attention of the evil eye. There were practices that resulted in severance of relationships or even in your enemy's illness or death.

I was visiting in a young lady's home when a neighbor brought in some hot steaming homemade bread. They did not share it with me. I asked if they would save it for their evening meal. Their reply startled me. "Oh no. We won't ever touch that bread. She may have hexed it or put some poison in it to do us evil."

Sometimes we found molten lead forms on the ground around our apartment building. Our neighbors explained that it had been used to either determine the future or to bring evil on a neighbor. On one occasion Bill came home from work with all of the symptoms of a heart attack. The doctor's diagnosis, "There is nothing physically wrong with you." The next morning he found a yellow sulfur powder spread along the walls of the University Reading Room where he had been on duty the day before.

After the visit of a particularly contentious family who were unsuccessfully asking us to comply with their wishes, I found four drugged roaches under a throw rug in our living room. It had never occurred to me that they would press their case to such extremes.

Lilias Trotter, in some of her writings from the early twentieth century and using the image of the north wind, refers to the battles she and her band of workers faced. The new converts suffered, not only from severance of family ties, or from loss of inheritance rights and other physical suffering, but also from pressure of another dimension: mind altering drugs, placed in their food or drink, sometimes resulting in premature death, or the use of spells and hypnotism. This is similar to what our adopted daughter Farida had experienced in a previous story.

So in the church in Algiers, in addition to the weekly Bible studies and prayer meetings we felt it necessary to not only teach theology and church history, but also, to set aside whole weekends dedicated to subjects like Christian marriage, How to teach children, and The dangers of sorcery and how to combat it. When our speaker asked the twenty or thirty Algerians in the room how many had had direct contact with some form of sorcery, every hand was raised.

Facing these evil practices and evil spirits with group prayer, putting a prayer guard around the nationals, and ourselves proved to be the only effective antidote.

Hidden Treasure

"Why do you have a picture like that hanging on your living room wall?" our Algerian guest asked. I hunted for an answer. "It's there in your honor. Don't you see that those are your pajamas on that clothes line?"

We had to admit that our decision to hang it there was crazy. It dominated the room, this huge black and white photo of dirty crowded white houses, pressed against each other, climbing up the hill of the old walled city. The Algiers Casbah was famous as the hideout of the Barbary Pirates. Laundry was hanging on the lines and bedding lay sunning where it had been flung over the walls surrounding the flat roofs. The photo was about five feet long and more than two feet high.

Some French photographer had mounted it on a strong wooden frame and then left it behind when he had fled the country, joining thousands of other Frenchmen fleeing to France when it became clear that Algeria had won its War for Independence. A neighbor and I had found it in the basement of an apartment building crammed in among the furniture stored there since the end of the war in 1962. Fifteen undisturbed years were enough to infest the beautifully carved armoires and chests with woodworm and grime.

Our new acquisition stuck out of the back of our Renault-4 car as we drove through the city up to our apartment. It was filthy. I took it out onto our balcony to dust it and then I laid it out on our hall floor and wiped it with a damp cloth. It was still too dirty. It was worth nothing as it was, so if I ruined it what had I lost? I slid the end into the bathtub. I rubbed it with soap and then hosed it down. It still had little black spots. So when it was completely dry, I again laid it on the hall floor and with a piece of white chalk, I tried to cover all of the little dark spots. I cannot honestly say that it was beautiful in any way. But it was certainly unique and became a great conversation piece giving us many moments of laughter.

My partner in crime and grime was a neighbor, the wife of a French diplomat. I first met her when I came home one noon hour and found her sitting in our living room with her two little girls, (one of whom was not yet potty trained and wore no diapers). I was returning from our weekly ladies' Bible study and was reliving the blessings I had just experienced with those ladies. I could not keep my joy to myself. As I poured out how the Lord had answered prayer and how we had cried together, and how the Lord seemed so real to us, she began to ask questions and finally she said, "I need that!" She became a regular at the studies and we became very close friends.

One morning she called to say, "We're going antiquing today." I protested that my day was already planned - and then we drove to the Casbah. It was she who had taken me to the basement full of old furniture where I found that photo. As the Casbah came into view, she said, referring to the dirty walls, "I think the Casbah needs a chalk treatment!"

She had an eye for hidden treasures. She told me some code phrases that we could use with each other to hide our evaluation of a find from the dealer. We would dig around in the piles of junk chatting to each other but never disparaging any item so as not to hurt the dealer's feelings. She was an accomplished bargainer succeeding in making purchases for a song. She confided in me that when her husband retired she was going to open an antique shop in France.

That afternoon she called asking me to come over to see her transformed antique purchase. The chest we had found that morning had been covered in filth with torn leather hanging from every side. She had cut off the leather with a razor blade. As she washed it, polished the brass trim, oiled the beautiful wood, she uncovered the brass inscription *Alger 1876* on the lid! We found some wonderful treasures together but my greatest treasure was knowing her. What fun we had. The Bible study ladies enriched the rest of her time in Algiers until her husband was moved to a new posting.

Daddy's Visit

Anything for a laugh

For quite a while Daddy seemed lost after Mother died. I can only imagine how lonely he must have felt. He eventually saw that it was necessary to give up his apartment in western New York. He spent time with Bruce in California, with Edith in Canada before living out his years with David and Coral in North Carolina. He also decided to come back to Algeria to visit us, this time to Algiers. His visa would last three months. He seemed to adjust easily to the cultural differences. Bill was preaching in the Anglican Church during that period and we had many international friends there. They took an interest in him and enjoyed his jokes. The church was a typical Anglican style old stone building with high arched ceilings and stain glass windows. Daddy warned the congregants that when they had a guest speaker, they should be sure to warn him to speak clearly and loudly because…. "in this church the agnostics are bad."

Our friends asked him how he succeeded in making so many Algerian friends with no language skills. He replied, "Well I just speak in signs and wonders. I make signs, and everyone wonders what I'm talking about!"

Shortly after his visit began in the 1970's, I became curious as to why the Algerian children who lived in our apartment building would run away when Daddy was around outside. One day I overheard one of the mothers threaten her son that if he didn't behave, Monsieur Brown would give him a shot. This was a common threat used to control children when they were out in public. I spoke to that neighbor explaining that that wasn't fair to my father because he loved children. Shortly after that, I glanced down off our back balcony and saw Daddy with his suit coat and fedora walking into the courtyard with several little girls holding on to his fingers on each side. He spoke no Arabic and no French. How had he managed to win their confidence?

When the three months of his visa were expired we sent him to friends in Marseille. They had five children. He loved being there but we had to have him return to us after a rather long extended stay in France and a visit to Germany. As we drove him from the airport to the house, he made an interesting and profound observation. "There's that old feeling again." He had sensed, without any concrete experience of his own, the oppression of a restrictive regime, that atmosphere of repression and fear, which hangs over a country where human rights are abused. Algeria's socialist government had two standards: one for the privileged and prominent and one for the others, especially those who lived outside the capital.

The populace counter-reacted with jokes which commented on their daily lives: "In Algeria there are two groups of people: Les AlgeROIS" (those who lived in Algiers are kings) "et les AlgeRIENS." (Algerians in general were worth nothing). A popular New Year's card had a cartoon attached to each wish. "I wish you prosperity, wealth, health, etc. and to not have to stand in line like last year."

Before returning home to the U.S., Daddy visited Paris, spent considerable time in England staying with friends he had met in the Anglican Church, and perhaps traveling to other parts of Great Britain. Every time we came home to the U.S. we visited him, once in California with Bruce, in Canada with Edith and several times in Franklin, NC with David. He died in August 1983 at the age of 88.

Peggy and the Ambassador

We had arrived too early and were being scolded by the Ghanian Ambassador to Algeria. He told us that no one, absolutely no one, arrived at an official reception early. We were surprised and shocked, and responded with silence, then apologies. After a bit of reflection, he decided that he really couldn't leave us standing outside on his doorstep and ushered us into the empty reception room and then disappeared to finish preparing for this celebration of Ghana's independence.

I couldn't tell him that our invitation card said 6:00pm. It was already 6:20.

There was no one else in the room, except the friend who had arrived with us, so I whispered to Bill that the Ambassador's secretary had obviously made a serious mistake in filling out our invitation. Her second mistake was not checking them over before mailing them. During the years that Bill served first on the rotation of preachers and then as interim vicar at the Anglican Church where we got to know the British Ambassador and other Embassy personnel, we received invitations to several Commonwealth nations' celebrations as well as the annual Queen's Birthday Party.

I was standing alone at the far end of the reception room admiring a lovely fireplace when the next guests arrived. Two men walked straight toward me. One of them stretched out his hand, I thought to shake mine, when instead he picked up my extended right hand, put it to his lips and kissed it. We began small talk, with him asking me questions through an interpreter. I wasn't too sure who he was or what language he was speaking or why I was being celebrated until a man walked over, saying some incomprehensible words. They excused themselves with little bows and actually backed away.

I soon found out that this hyper polite gentleman was the Russian Ambassador. He had mistaken me for the Ghanian Ambassador's wife!

It was the height of the cold war. Had I inadvertently accomplished a diplomatic coup? Could this be considered some kind of significant international success? Would he have treated the American Ambassador's wife the same way? Was he embarrassed because he didn't think twice about mistaking this very light skinned American lady for a Ghanian? But alas, no harm or benefit came of it that I know of. It was only me, after all. I was surprised and flattered, and proud that I had held my own during this strange conversation. And I have one more story to tell.

Sea, Snow and Sand

I once read in a travel brochure that in Morocco it was possible to swim in the morning, ski at noon, and be in the desert at night. We had already planned a trip that just might prove that claim true for Algeria as well. Bill needed to head south to Tolga, an oasis town in the Sahara to visit an elderly French lady who was under his pastoral care.

We waited till Billy's next mid-semester break. We chose to avoid the main routes and take an entirely different road that we had found on our map. It climbed into the Atlas Mountains where it reached a river at the very crest and then continued south beside the river, dropping down the other side of the mountain range. As long as we kept heading south we figured that this little road would then intersect in the Sahara with an east-west road, which connected two fairly important cities. We could easily reach that road before nightfall.

The gas tank was full. I had packed enough food. We felt happy and excited as we left the coast behind. Even before we reached the crest, we ran into snow. We finally arrived at the point where the road met the river. Water had flowed from the mountain heights for millennia and had cut a deep channel through the rocks into the mountainside. From the road the view of the river and the cliffs that rose above us was unbelievable. Up on the side of the highest cliff, nearly facing the road were rows of dark holes obviously cut by humans. What were they for? And how could anyone even get up there? We figured that they looked like storage areas or even dwellings. Perhaps that was where some mountain dwellers had stored grain and other valuables or even hid themselves from an approaching enemy. We had to stop to investigate. Bill parked the car right in the snow on the road. There were no other cars to worry about.

We climbed down the hillside to the river. The water cut through rock leaving a stone archway overhead. The immense rocks under our feet were white and yellow and greenish, worn smooth through the centuries. The shallow water was crystal clear flowing over those multicolored rocks. Everything was beautiful. We walked along the river bed a short distance and on the way back one of us spotted a plaque, written in French, fastened to the cliff. It read, "This is the farthest point south that Roman Legions ever reached."

It was getting late so we returned up the hill to the car. It was stuck in the snow. With a bit of effort with both Billy and Bill pushing, we were soon on our way again heading south down the mountain. As we descended, the snow disappeared and the river beside us became smaller and smaller. So did the road. It ended right into the dry rocky riverbed. Was that little line on our map a lie, or had we misinterpreted it? Maybe we should put up a sign, "This is the farthest point south that this road has ever reached!"

The rocks rolled here and there under our tires and we bumped and slid from side to side. We were driving a Renault-4, one of the cheapest and lightest cars on the market - the exact opposite of a sturdy four-wheel drive. We crept along. The sun was now hanging over the horizon. At least we knew that it was setting in the west. I kept thinking that as long as this rocky creek bed meandered south we would be okay.

Suddenly the rocks stopped. We pulled out onto a level area. The ground was flat in every direction, ahead, to the left and to the right as far as the eye could see. Not a tree or a person or any sign of life anywhere. The sun was dropping faster. Easy driving. I saw a mysterious glint of light ahead. That little black spot off in the distance grew into a square, then into a house with a man standing outside. We drove up beside him and asked directions. As we pulled away, I said, "I know what that glint of light was that I saw." There was no fire, no light in the house. The man we had been talking to had all gold teeth; every single visible tooth was shiny gold. Had the last rays of the setting sun just for an instant reflected off that mouth? We laughed releasing the tension of the last several hours.

That Moroccan brochure could also describe Algeria! We had been on the coast in the morning, STUCK in the snow at noon and LOST in the desert at night.

Held Hostage

The dirty laundry lay sorted all over the floor. It would take most of the morning for me to get all of those sheets washed and out on the line. At 10:30 the phone rang. It was a Belgian friend saying that she was working as a translator for ABC television, but had discovered her English was not adequate. Could I come and help? The ABC-TV news media with their crew and equipment had just arrived in Algiers, and had been assigned an office alongside all of the other American and Algerian networks at the RADIO - TELEVISION ALGERIENNE (RTA) headquarters in Algiers. I arrived to take her place at about 12:30. The next few days were some of the most exciting of our 16 years living in Algiers. Before it was over I had been offered a job with the news media.

Algerians were proud that their country was acting as the neutral negotiator between Iran and the US in what was known around the world as the "Hostage Crises." On November 4, 1979 a group of Islamist students and militants had raided the American Embassy in Teheran and held the American diplomats and Embassy staff hostage. It was now January 1981. After 441 days in captivity, the crisis was drawing to a close. The Algerian negotiators had accomplished the impossible. The 53 hostages were to be released.

Algeria was uniquely qualified to serve as the U.S.'s intermediary with Iran. Algeria was, like Iran, an Islamic nation with a revolutionary tradition. When official diplomatic ties between the U.S. and Iran were cut off, the Iranians asked Algeria to represent their interests in Washington, so it was only natural that they also ask Algeria to negotiate a hostage deal. Algeria chose three envoys, the Algerian Ambassador to Washington, Redha Malek, the Algerian Ambassador to Teheran, Abdelmalek Ghraieb, and the Central Bank Governor, Mohammed Seghir Mostaphi. All three had played significant roles in Algeria's fight for independence from France. These men shuttled tirelessly for weeks in their attempt to convince Teheran that they should release the hostages still being held at the American Embassy. They worked under the tutelage of the minister of Foreign Affairs, Mohammed Ben Yahia.

The American Ambassador to Algeria, Ulrich Haynes, was also uniquely qualified to accomplish his role in the negotiations, interviews and history making. (He was a tennis buddy and personal friend, of our son, Billy.) He was not a professional diplomat but was a political appointee of Jimmy Carter's and had once been a businessman in Iran. Many months before the hostage crises started, he was aware of the deteriorating relations between Washington and Teheran and had decided that it was no longer safe to maintain a business there. He had withdrawn his company's assets and personnel before risking complete loss.

As the crises reached it's successful conclusion, on his last day in office, President Jimmy Carter conveyed a message to Algerian President, Bendjedid Chadli, expressing "an immense debt of gratitude." "We would certainly not have concluded this accord, if we had not had the assistance of your government." Other US officials expressed their admiration of the "tireless" work and "the imagination and understanding of the Algerian delegation throughout the ten weeks of ceaseless negotiations."

It was on Saturday January 17th, as the logistics of the hostages' release were still being hammered out, that I entered the ABC office at the RTA in Algiers. In gratitude to the whole nation of Algeria, it had been decided that the freed hostages would first set foot on Algerian soil before being sent to the doctors waiting for them in Frankfurt. In a well-calculated slap in the face to Jimmy Carter, the hostages would not leave Iranian air space until Ronald Reagan had been sworn in as President in Washington on Tuesday, January 20th, 1981.

The room assigned to ABC was very small. As I was being initiated and introduced around the room, I tried to understand the phone system, retain names and understand their jobs and learn what was expected of me. Basically they needed someone who could do the negotiations, telephone calls, errands into the city, purchases and other jobs as they unfolded that required the use of French. It was a bit daunting but basically I was thrilled. The excitement swirled around us, in the elevators, in the hallways where Algerians as well as all the other American anchormen, photographers, producers, and correspondents of the other networks were running to verify and then broadcast breaking news.

The photographers were gathered around the American Embassy and the Ministry of Foreign Affairs and the airport. They recorded any movement, arrival or departure of a dignitary. The networks had hired Algerians on motorcycles as deliverymen. In the rush to send the latest video recording to the RTA to be aired before the other networks, they could speed through the traffic much faster than a taxi. One of my jobs was to take the elevator down to the street level, find ABC's motorcycle man or taxi driver, retrieve the tape or message and get it back upstairs to be aired before the other networks received theirs. I remember enjoying chatting with these drivers several times a day. I once overheard one of them say, "It's easy to see that she's Algerian. You can tell by the way she acts and the way she talks to us."

Another time I was delighted to hear one of them yell to a taxi driver of another broadcasting company, "You get away from her. She belongs to us!"

The ABC producer said that they needed to be ready to broadcast at the moment the 'window opened on the satellite'. When there were serious technical problems, I got so tense I started to pace the hall. One of the broadcasters told me not to worry so much; that it had always worked out! The little office had a huge picture window that looked out over the city and the port. The anchor always stood there at the time of the live broadcast with the gleaming lights of the city behind him. My favorite city made a beautiful backdrop.

The most fascinating technology was a mysterious series of four boxes less then a foot square, piled on top of each other. I got to use it quite often. It was our telephone. We could talk to New York, London, the airport, the Aurassi Hotel and Frankfurt. Voices were so clear. But we still needed to go through the local phone operator. On one occasion after considerable persistence, I finally got through to London and asked for Peter Jennings. I can't remember if I actually spoke to him myself.

As the 20th of January approached, news was still coming in, in spurts. ABC New York informed us what the other networks were reporting, and we confirmed that it often turned out to be unreliable rumor. Each time a plane landed at the airport, everyone would jump. The cameramen at the airport were transmitting to the RTA live. We were transfixed to the screen. I was so proud of Algeria, our adopted country!

Toward evening a plane with Iranian markings landed. Three men in long black coats came down the stairs and into the airport. Someone yelled, "Peggy, go find out who those men are!" I guess the fact that I was not a real journalist was very obvious, because I then asked where they thought I could find out that Information. "On the third floor!" I ran as fast as I could entering any open door on the third floor to ask the Algerians to identify those three mysterious men. Some said they didn't know, and some told me they were some agricultural experts! Imagine Iranian Agricultural experts arriving at such a moment as this! I didn't get the same answer twice. Their arrival went unreported.

Meanwhile, the hostages waited on the runway in Teheran for four hours before taking off at 5:25. The calculations were precise. They were not to leave Iranian air space until Carter was no longer president.

The plane landed 444 days after the American Embassy in Tehran had been forcefully entered. The first passengers off the plane were the three Algerian negotiators. The hostages were accompanied by a man carrying a sub-machine gun on his back. As soon as his feet touched the ground, his gun was confiscated by the Algerian authorities. Warren Christopher, Ben Yahia, Ambassador and Mrs. Haynes and other Embassy families were there to greet them. All Algerians were watching their television screens.

In the ensuing interviews in the VIP lounge one woman hostage said, "I can't tell you how much your prayers and letters meant to us. Only the Lord knows how much they helped. We couldn't write to you but your letters got to us." Then she started to cry. I wonder what she would have added had she known that the Algerian Church had stayed up all night praying for them. Several other hostages spoke with gratitude for the role Algeria had played in their release. They were served refreshment, and listened to a speech by Warren Christopher and Ben Yahia. Christopher lauded Ben Yahia, adding that he hadn't slept for three nights. They then flew off to the waiting doctors in Frankfurt.

I got home at 3:45 am and had to return by 8:30am. Billy, working as an interpreter for ABC Radio had been at the airport. We sat in his bedroom sharing our evening's experiences before going to bed for 3 hours of sleep.

The next two days I spent cataloguing the mountain of videos some of which only had a minute or two of recording on them and helping close down the headquarters. American customs charged not by the number of videos but by the number of recorded minutes! What a job. And Saturday Bill actually drove the last ABC employee and his equipment to the airport, after spending all morning helping him.

We set out the next morning for Tolga in the Sahara. Madame Lull had asked us to come because Mounia's father had locked her in the house forbidding her to continue her schooling. Could we please come to help negotiate her release? We were back in our own world far from the glitter and glamour of American television.

Billy and ABC Radio

Very soon after I arrived at the Radio Television building, I was asked if I knew of another translator-interpreter. Their counterparts in ABC Radio needed help. They were headquartered at the Aurassi Hotel across town. Bill was busy delivering tents and blankets to the earthquake victims in Al Asnam, many miles away across the country. Billy, on his winter break in his senior year at the University of Massachusetts, was working at Mitsui, a Japanese trading company as a translator. ABC hired him immediately.

When the American networks arrived in Algiers, they had drawn straws to see which company would be allowed into restricted areas in the event that the Algerian government only permitted one to enter. ABC had drawn the longest straw.

Billy seemed to be needed everywhere. On the day of the actual release he was asked to be the simultaneous interpreter from French to English at a news conference called by the Algerian government to announce the latest breaking news. When he realized that this would be broadcast live across the US, his adrenaline really started flowing. The lounge at the Aurassi Hotel was filled with correspondents from all over the world. He prepared himself by pacing off the big room, getting a feel for the huge lounge, drinking lots of water and finally felt primed. The phone line was open to New York. They were set to start. Then someone interrupted. The news conference had been cancelled! We suspected that Iran had decided it was too early to announce the release. The hostages were not to be allowed out of Iranian air space as long as Carter was still officially president.

Billy continued living his own drama. The Police refused to let the ABC radio crew designated to cover the arrival of the Air Algerie plane bringing the hostages into the reception area. Billy managed with some pretty fast thinking and some quiet, calming, flattering words. The police finally let them through. He said later that he just did what his dad would have done. Instead of saying "Why?" He just said, "Oh?"

But the hostage story did not end there. Some months later we received an audiotape from Billy, who was back on the University of Massachusetts campus. It was a recording of an ABC national radio broadcast with the voice of the ABC radio correspondent speaking of her experiences as a reporter in Algiers. It went something like this.

"When I came back from Algiers, people asked, 'What was the most exciting experience during your time in Algiers?' You would think I would have said, The moment the first hostage put his foot on free soil, or.., or…. But I can tell you that for me, the most exciting event was meeting a young man named Billy Call. Billy grew up in Algiers. His father is a famous translator/interpreter. If it had not been

for Billy's knowledge of the culture and language, we never would have succeeded in reporting the events. It was he who got us entrance into the airport, and it was he who spotted the plane in the distance before anyone else. He is an aspiring Air Force pilot."

When I arrived back in the U.S. for Billy's graduation a few months later, an Algerian Christian was traveling with us. He wanted to attend Billy's graduation and to spend several months for English exposure. We stopped in New York City and visited the ABC Radio Headquarters. That reporter and the others could not have been more felicitous, taking us out for lunch.

And ABC was selected as having the best and most accurate Hostage Crises coverage!

The Queen Is Coming to Town

We ladies were walking through the British Ambassador's Residence with the First Secretary's wife. She was explaining some of the details of the massive preparations for the Queen's impending visit. The Ambassador was single, so he needed a stand-in to carry out the duties that would have fallen to his wife. "Then we step over here and I explain that this piece of furniture belonged to Eugenie when she and Napoleon spent time here in Algiers." We continued on through the house. The conversation as well as all of the queen's movements were choreographed in detail ahead of time.

We ladies were also receiving detailed instructions. I had volunteered to help transport some of the queen's Britannia crew on a trip up the coast so they could enjoy a meal in one of the fancy homes in Club des Pins and then enjoy the beach. The day arrived. The Britannia sailed into Algiers harbor. There followed a continuous string of official events. Algerian dignitaries were received on the Britannia; the Queen and her cortege attended state dinners in the ancient palaces of Algiers. I was to participate in two events. Bill could have too, but he did not seem interested.

The Queen, as the Head of the Anglican Church would be making an official visit to the Anglican Church building in Algiers. A very small congregation was in place when she and Philip arrived with their attendants. They greeted the church council who were lined up at the door and then were to proceed down the aisle. The Queen soon realized that Prince Philip was not beside her. She was used to that. Up front and right on cue she pulled a drawstring hanging on the wall. A little black curtain flew back uncovering a brass plaque commemorating her visit. Then she walked over to a group of small children seated on a blanket spread out on the floor. Each one stood up, curtsied or bowed, and handed Her Majesty a red rose. It was beautiful.

Queen Elizabeth II in Algiers

On her way back up the aisle accompanied by the Vicar, she began shaking hands with the people whom the young vicar chose to present to her. She shook the hand of the British subject to my right and the lady to my left, skipping me. I was not a member of the Commonwealth!

As she left the hall we heard that there had been a bit of a commotion at the back of the sanctuary. Philip, instead of keeping pace with the Queen, had chosen to greet a pew of nuns dressed in their black garb sitting in the back, blurting out, "What regiment do you belong to?" He was living up to his reputation of often jumping protocol - of being his own man. On the way out into the warm sunshine I saw that she had signed the large guest book. Written diagonally across the whole page in beautiful script was, *ELIZABETH E.R.* My camera was not worthy of the event and my pictures are quite blurry.

A day later with my special permission badge I drove down into the port. I pulled up beside the Britannia and three young sailors climbed into the car. We were to wait in line and all drive up the coast together. All of the sudden we heard a loud cracking sound beside us between our car and the Britannia. One driver had not followed instructions. He had just driven over the mast of one of the crew's sailing equipment. The fellow sitting next to me said, "There goes John's mast." As we drove out they introduced themselves. "I'm Swampy Marsh, and he's Chalky White." I looked at him askance. He explained, "Well, we do this with all of the crew, if the last name permits it."

I ate lunch with the Queen's valet. The British women plagued him with questions. "What's your most important duty?" He replied, "The first thing I do as the Queen returns from an event and enters her stateroom is hand her a cup of hot tea." "And what's the first thing she does?" "She kicks off her shoes. When she is on deck waving goodbye to her hosts as the Britannia pulls out of port, she is standing in her stocking feet."

She is human after all.

Nicky Cruz in Algeria!

The light haired young man standing at our apartment door in Algiers was a complete stranger. He wanted to see Bill. He was looking for a church. We had lived in Algeria for sixteen years and had never had an Algerian make such a request on his first visit. Up to that moment, he had met only with disappointment at the few remaining Catholic churches that had been constructed before Algerian independence from France. Some of these buildings had no congregations. Others had been transformed into mosques. He had been summarily turned away from others. Finally he found one priest who suggested he might visit the French Reformed Church that still had a ministry basically to foreign Protestants but also to a few Algerians. His heart fell as the Reformed pastor's wife told him that their church was probably not what he was looking for either. She then suggested that he come to see Bill.

I promised him that Bill would be waiting for him if he came back the next morning. He told me later that he was encouraged because my hair wasn't very short and I was wearing a cross!

Kabylia

Bill was waiting when he arrived right on time the following morning. I can still see them on their knees and elbows on our living room floor studying a large map of Algeria. Bill wanted to be able to picture exactly where he lived in the mountains east of Algiers as his personal story began to unfold.

His family had been living near Lille in northeastern France. When his mother decided to come back to Algeria to their small village in the mountains east of the capital, Abdel had decided to accompany her. As they were leaving, his older brother handed him an audiocassette. In his village he looked up one of his childhood buddies. Together they climbed up to the roof to listen to that cassette.

It turned into a life changing moment. It was a recording of Nicky Cruz, the main character in David Wilkerson's book, *The Cross and the Switchblade*, giving his testimony in a church in France. His English was translated sentence by sentence into French. *The Cross and the Switchblade*, written in the 1960's, is the story of a pastor who received a call from God to leave his rural Pennsylvania pastorate to minister to the gangs in the ghettos of New York City. He wanted to help young men who were on trial for murder. Nicky Cruz is the main character in this true story.

Nicky's powerful testimony of how Jesus delivered him from a life of crime and radically changed him touched their prepared hearts. Both of them accepted Christ that night. They soon realized that the most likely place to find other Christians would be in the capital, Algiers.

He had not yet found a place for fellowship. We invited him to our small church group that met in a store front on one of the main streets in downtown Algiers. The majority of those who attended were young men, some university students. The group was growing stronger all the time. Good teaching, love for each other and a love of prayer were the main ingredients of this enthusiastic group. During that week I spoke to some of the other young men telling them that there would be a visitor at the Friday Worship Service and requested that they be sure to welcome him. That Friday, when the service was over I asked our guest if this was what he had been seeking. Tears welled up in his eyes. He felt at home and from then on, when he was in town, came regularly.

The Soccer Team

There was no stopping this young man who had been so touched by God in that dramatic conversion experience. It was as though he had to tell the world about Christ. Our role became one of facilitating his vision. He seemed to have no fear, to the extent that some years later, he was showing the Jesus film in the village cafes. This film on the life of Christ was dubbed into Kabyle, becoming the first film these villagers had ever seen in their own Berber language. Jesus spoke Kabyle!

The next summer he planned a week's camping in the mountains. He told us that choosing the location was easy as there was only one place flat enough to set up tents. It was the place where the local village teams congregated to play soccer. We gathered equipment, pots and pans, burners, basins, and a twelve man tent which could double for sleeping, cooking, and for meeting in case of rain, to what he could gather from other friends. His plan was to invite all of the young fellows from the few house churches around the country.

When we returned to Algeria at the end of the summer, we heard wonderful stories of how the Lord had met with them. Abdel told us that one day the Lord sent a wind, a wind so strong it folded our heavy tent poles. As they struggled to right the tent, one of the soccer teams came over to give them a hand. Abdel invited the team to join them, explaining they were reading the Bible, singing and praying. That whole soccer team was converted that night - eleven young men added to the kingdom!

Somehow the police were alerted. The gendarmes arrived probably suspecting some political, subversive activity. The people living in these mountains are of Berber descent, a different ethnic group from the Arabic speaking population. They have their own culture and speak their own language. The Berbers had protested the suppression of the teaching of their language in the university and in the educational system in general. They were proud of the fact that they were the original inhabitants of Algeria and of all North Africa before the Arabs had swept out of Saudi Arabia in the eighth century, bringing Islam.

The government was careful to watch any suspicious activity. When the gendarmes saw that the group was comprised of a mixture of ethnicities, Berbers as well as Arabic speakers from other cities, they decided to leave them alone, at least for the moment. A few months later we had our first opportunity to meet this soccer team. They wanted to get together again for intensive study. They requested the use of a large house by the sea, which had been used for summer children's camps and church conferences. We offered to prepare the property. An American friend offered to do the shopping and cooking so that they would be free to spend more time studying and relaxing. They asked Bill to lead them in some of their Bible studies. I cleaned and dusted and counted out the blankets and dishes.

Some months later, the foreigner who had been at their conference, doing the cooking got notice that he was being expelled from the country. Within a short time five more of us, including Bill and me, were expelled from Algeria. It was early summer, 1982. The police refused to give us a reason for the expulsion orders. We tried to discover what we six, with our differing nationalities and professions, could possibly have in common. The only conclusion we reached was that all six of us had had contact with that soccer team gathered for the camp up in the mountains or in the house by the sea.

The Greatest Consolation

We felt that this government order had wiped us off the scene. We would never be able see our friends again. Where was the good in that? Time and hindsight opened our eyes. The Algiers Assembly was on its feet and didn't need foreign leadership. All of the elders and deacons were Algerian. There was a nucleus of strong baptized believers. For a whole year Bill and I and some other foreigners attended meetings, but all responsibility was in their hands. Hard as it was to accept, it was God's time for us to leave.

Out of North Africa

Years earlier we were sitting with a Swiss friend on a stone wall along the sea coast where we were house sitting during our summer vacation. She was explaining the tension of her most recent police interrogation. She was shaken thinking expulsion might be imminent. I was blessed by her absolute conviction, "I know that I will be here as long as the Lord permits." Her insecure future was secure in His loving hands.

Her statement stayed with me for years. In the early years of our living in Algeria, Bill was summoned to police headquarters on the average of twice a year. Many of our friends were being expelled, sometimes for no obvious reason or for trumped up charges. When would our turn come?

Late spring 1982 a young American, who had been living with us and had just landed a post teaching chemistry at a new university, broke the news that he had been called in to the central police headquarters and told that he only had a few hours to leave the country. No reason given. Instead of packing up, he went to the American Embassy where he was told not to leave till they told him to. The American officials wanted to investigate. He told us that the police had mentioned other names on the expulsion order. Our names were not among them.

So we traveled back to the U.S. for our scheduled "home assignment." Within a few days as he was preparing his own departure, he called us and said that the police were coming to our door every day looking for us. We should return immediately. We called Billy who was in the Air Force in western Texas telling him that we needed to return to Algiers immediately. He did not like the idea and asked us to come see him first. So we flew from Massachusetts to

Texas. We stayed up most of the night talking. The next morning we left, flying from Lubbock, through Dallas to JFK, to Brussels.

The trans-Atlantic flight was full of Belgian teenagers flying home after a year in American high schools. They had boarded with large size MacDonald's beverage cups, full of "coke." They were a happy lot and mine was the last empty seat squeezed in among them. The PA system was busy, "The plane cannot take off until you are all seated," was repeated several times. I dozed and woke to find one of them with his feet in my lap. By the time we landed in Brussels after two nights of not sleeping I was unstable on my feet. The airport swirled before my eyes.

We were met in Brussels by a friend whose family had been expelled from Morocco. He took us to his home. We knew that we could not continue on to Algiers in the state we were in. I asked him not to wake me for any meals. All I wanted was to sleep. Spending the night and next day with that family was a tremendous blessing to us. They knew just how we felt and how we were going to feel. We did not really know if we would even get back into the country. If that happened, we could not say goodbye to the best friends we'd ever had. We would never be able to see them again. We would lose our library, our photographs and other precious items. Our apartment was full of 16 years of memories.

We cleared police controls, then customs and caught a taxi to our apartment. We had made it! Some of the summons piled on the table were for Bill, but we were surprised that some were for me. It was Sunday evening. I persuaded Bill that he should not go to the police station until Monday afternoon. That would give us more time to take care of sorting through our stuff.

Monday afternoon Bill was ushered into an office. The policeman asked him where I was. Bill promised to bring me in the next day. Meanwhile I was separating items to keep and those to dispose of. Tuesday morning we both went together as promised. We were told we had 24 hours to leave. I asked if we couldn't please wait till Thursday. His reply, "No, Thursday and Friday are holidays and we wouldn't be able to escort you to the airport." Bill asked why we were being expelled. He said, "You know why." But we didn't. Bill quoted an Arabic proverb, 'El ma, mahou safi.' The water is not very clear!" There was no way to find out what we were accused of. So there was no way to defend ourselves, no way to refute the accusations against us.

Bill headed to Sabena Airlines office and found out that there was no flight out on Wednesday. He went back to the police and told them that Sabena had no flight out the next day. The policeman replied "Then be here at 8:00 Saturday morning." We had been able to stretch those 24 hours into five days. I headed to the bank to clear out our account. They told me there was no cash available.

It's no fun being expelled. You feel as though you are living in an unreal world. Something significant is being ripped up inside you and something you love dearly is being torn away outside you. I held onto hope that it was not true, that it was all a hoax, or that the policeman was going to say he'd made a mistake. But for us it was true. It was really happening. If it hadn't been for the fast moving events and work to be done and the myriads of people who came to help, sadness would have overwhelmed me.

By this time we had informed some friends, and then let the grapevine do its work. The young people started arriving at all hours. One of our precious friends, who had lived with us, came across the country to stay and help with disposing of items. Other young Christians came to help. I handed out tasks. The vicar of the Anglican Church offered to take precious items to his home and then out of the country in his van the next summer. We were able to say our goodbyes on Friday morning at the Algerian church service for the last time. The Algerians had been in charge of the little Assembly for over a year with elected and functioning elders and deacons. They were a loving group. They knew that the church's foundation was prayer. They would carry on.

Then the most traumatic day of our lives arrived in this July of 1982. Farida's love and courage astounded us. She accompanied us to the police station. It was not wise for her to be associated with us. We have not seen her since.

We were put into a police car. Instead of driving on the highway to the airport, the driver returned up the hill to Hydra where we had lived for 16 years, where we knew all of our neighbors, where Billy had grown up and where we had hosted hundreds of Bible studies and conferences. As we drove up, tears filled my eyes. I still could not believe that it was really happening. It has since been a puzzle to me why I could not let go and accept God's will for us, and trust that He had kept us there as long as He wanted, trust Him with our future, trust Him to open a new door with new joys and new satisfactions. But despite my self-pity, my inability to trust Him at that moment, that is exactly what He did. He opened a new and very exciting door for us.

Friends met us in Marseille. She asked me how I felt. Without hesitation I replied, "Worse than when my mother died." She replied, "Well you have to realize that this is a death experience."

They took us to an empty apartment. It would have been more therapeutic for us to have been with people with whom we could describe how we felt, describe the intense pain that we were suffering. We needed to talk. But we stayed alone for several days.

That was thirty-two years ago. The tears are streaming down my face even as I write this. It was 16 years later, while we were living in Tunisia, that we understood some of the details of why we were expelled. At the end of this chapter are three stories, which happened in Tunisia of unexpected contact with the church in Algeria. Today they are experiencing miracles every day!

Within seven months Bill had found a job in Mauritania in West Africa where there were no other Christian workers and no known national Christians living inside the country.

We Haven't Killed You!

It has always been our dream to make a visit back to Algeria. But once you have been expelled, the possibility of success is very remote. You cannot reason with a sovereign state, especially if you don't know what you have been accused of.

Eight years after our expulsion, while we were living in Mauritania, Bill got an invitation to speak at an church retreat in Tunisia. We transited through Paris. While there we spoke with friends in Algiers by phone. They suggested that if we were thinking of a return visit, this was a good time to try. Evidently there was so much chaos that no one would notice our entry. They were wrong.

I procured our visas at the Algerian Embassy in Tunis while Bill was in conference, and we planned a very simple three-day trip. We got through police controls and customs without a hitch. We were ecstatic. Algerian friends were there to meet us and whisked us off to visit families across the city. A reunion of English speaking friends had already been organized at the Anglican church and then another with the local church body. We had finished three visits when our friend who had organized the day said that we had time for one more before he had to get his car parked for the night.

We headed up the hill to our old apartment building. Our name was still on the mailbox! The same graffiti still decorated the hall stair wall. A neighbor who was retired from the police saw us in the hall and came out with open arms to hug us, inviting us for a meal. We climbed the stairs and knocked on another neighbor's door. We chatted with him, and then I asked to see his wife. She did not greet us. She simply said, "The police have been here looking for you." Anxiety and fear erased our joy and excitement. We turned and ran down the stairs to tell our chauffeur friend what had happened. We urged him to leave to avoid implication in our dilemma.

He calmed us immediately by saying, "You have done nothing wrong. There is no reason to be afraid. I will simply take you back to where you are staying. Then we will see where this is going to lead." We insisted that he drop us off a few blocks from the house so he would not be implicated. As we suspected, the police were waiting for us.

"The commissaire at the airport wants to speak to you. It's not serious, but you'd better bring your bags," one of them said. We crowded into the police cruiser guarded by three plainclothes men. As though we might try to escape! They dumped us at the airport and told us to sit on two orange plastic chairs. One of them had the seat half broken off. When I saw one of our escorting policeman leaving the airport, I ran after him. Too late. Had they just abandoned us? What did they expect us to do? I went over to talk to an official to see if there was some mistake. He asked if we had neglected to get visas. I told him that all of our papers were in order.

He came back a bit later and led us to the First Class Lounge. There were flight crews sleeping fully clothed on the padded benches. We found an empty space and lay down covering ourselves with our coats. In the morning a policeman gave us some vouchers for breakfast and lunch and then told us to stay upstairs until they called us. We were to return back to Tunis on Tunis Air late that afternoon. We were given no explanation of what we were guilty of. I wanted to ask why we had been issued visas if this was to be the end of it, but I held my tongue.

As flight time approached someone finally came to get us. We were taken down to a large waiting area, then told to sit and wait. We could see our plane on the runway. The other passengers were processed. I was afraid that we might be forgotten, so I got up to find the police headquarters in hopes of recuperating our tickets and passports. A man stopped me and asked what I wanted.

I replied, "Our plane is on the runway and someone has our tickets and passports." He asked, "Are you an American? We're going to escort you onto that plane." I had not expected that.

"You don't have to humiliate us any more than you already have." I said, "You just watch. Give us our passports and tickets and we are going to walk through that little gate, across that waiting room, out that door, across the tarmac and right up those stairs onto that plane." Tears welled up in my eyes.

He said, "Why are you crying? Oh, I know. You've never been through this before." I certainly wasn't going to tell him we had. And then his next words were really consoling! "You really shouldn't cry. We haven't killed you." I was stunned. Had he been trained in Russia? I must have impressed him with my logic. He retrieved our passports and tickets, and handed them to us. We were heartbroken once again as we walked out, across the tarmac and up those stairs. But at least we were unaccompanied.

What choice did we have? Who in this airport security police force would believe that we were ignorant of the accusation against us, that we were innocent? They were simply obeying orders.

Why We Were Expelled from Algeria

One of the advantages of moving from Mauritania to Tunis was its proximity to Algiers. Algerian Christians passed through and stopped for a visit. Three young men had just rung the doorbell of our apartment in Tunis. It was obvious that they were Algerians.

"Do you remember us?" one of them asked. "No, I'm afraid I don't. It's been about 16 years since we've been in Algeria," I answered.

"We're the reason you were expelled!" One of them said.

"If you're the reason we were expelled, then praise the Lord," I replied.

They introduced themselves. "Two of us were members of that village soccer team that accepted Christ one evening, back in 1981. We are pastors today! You know when we accepted Jesus into our lives, there was not one Christian woman in all of Kabylia - not even the shadow of one! Today we three are married and we each have two children. Two of us are pastors today."

Their enthusiasm in recounting this goodness conveyed their gratitude to Almighty God. Right from the time of their conversions they had witnessed God moving in powerful ways. Our own suspicions as to why the police took action against us were being confirmed. But how did the police link us to that soccer team? Why were two husbands expelled and not their wives and yet both Bill and I were expelled?

Evidently one of the new football player converts had decided to write down the names of foreign Christians as he met them and keep the paper in his new Bible. Part of the key to the mystery that we had lived with all of these years was simple. There were six names on that piece of paper when the police confiscated that Bible! All six of us received expulsion orders. Bill had led some Bible studies. I had the helped prepare the house for that retreat. Another had helped them get on a bus, and another had collected the tent equipment from their camp out.

There still remains a mystery today. What did the police think that list represented? Because those guys were all Berber, did they think that we were involved in a subversive resistance movement? From wielding a dust cloth to subversive activity! Now that is a stretch! But that expulsion order was also the key to our moving to Mauritania.

Away for Two weeks

One day two young Algerian visitors to Tunis were relating their experiences around our dinner table. As more and more people were accepting Christ, they felt they needed a strategy for continued growth. They decided to imitate Jesus himself. They would take Jesus' words at face value. Their first stage was to preach in the area where they lived which was in the mountainous region of Kabylia. The second stage would be to establish a church in every town and village in Algeria. The third was to go to areas outside of Algeria where the people had never heard the Gospel."

They continued, "Christ sent his disciples out two by two, so we divided ourselves into teams of two. We two traveled together. We chose a village, climbed up the rocky mountain slope above the village and prayed, releasing that town for Christ." Bill and I were sitting on the edge of our seats.

"After imploring God for the people in the village just below and convinced that God had heard us, we climbed down to talk to as many as we could. The village was completely open to the Gospel! It was as though the Devil had gone on vacation!"

In answer to our question as to how many villages had been touched and how many now have a worshiping group of converts; one of them cited a number, and then hesitated. They looked at each other. One of them said, "Yes, but that could have changed. We've been away for two weeks."

It Takes Time - Healings

One afternoon at a conference, I joined a group of young men who were sitting in the hotel lobby. I knew the Tunisian well, but learned that the other two were Algerian. I pestered them with questions. One of them was a pastor. As I urged him on, he told the history of God's working in his little town, about the growth of his church. He told us stories relating the marvels they were experiencing. Because they were all new converts, they had no one who knew hymns or could lead the worship. Somehow he acquired a guitar and left it lying around in his home. He never coaxed, but watched as his children became curious and started to experiment. Now his own teenage children lead the music and serve as a magnet to bring others to Christ.

The Tunisian interrupted, "Do you two know each other?"

The pastor responded, "No, I've never seen her before, but I can tell she loves me."

I was surprised, but I knew it was true. How could I not love him? I felt so privileged to talk with him. He had totally given himself to the Lord in the country we loved so much, where we had spent 18 marvelous years. He was an example of a man of faith, the kind that sets no limits on what God can do. I was sitting there hearing of God's blessing first hand; blessing that would eventually encompass other regions of Algeria. I was also in awe because I had the privilege of hearing how God was answering the prayers of hundreds, or even thousands, from the past who had longed to see this day. God was in the process of making the impossible, possible.

Our experience was similar to Jesus' words to his disciples after the seventy returned rejoicing that they had witnessed miracles. *"How privileged you are to see what you have seen. Many a prophet and king of old has longed to see and hear what you have seen and heard!"* (Living Bible, Luke 19: 23,24)

When he mentioned that his worship service lasted from two to three hours, the educated Tunisian chimed in, "You can't have a service that long! Nobody has an attention span that long!" The pastor did not say a word.

Later the same day he stopped Bill and me in the lobby. "I just want to tell you," referring to the length of his church services, "that when you're praying over people for healing, it takes time."

Today we hear of at least one church in every village in Kabylia, as well as at least one church in all of the other regions of Algeria. Their planned strategy in obedience to Christ's words, "Go into all the world and preach..." is being accomplished. They have nothing to fear because Christ had added to that command, "and I am with you even to the ends of the earth."

CHAPTER FOUR - MAURITANIA 1983 -1997

Background

Life in a desert thrusts you into the barebones of living. The luxuries, the trappings of modern, western life are not vying for your attention. Your main preoccupation is survival, which depends on success in the constant hunt for water and new grazing lands. The isolation of nomadic tent life develops a unique culture, a pride, and a set of values different from the rest of the world. It fosters a spirit of independence and at the same time interdependence and respect for and obligation to the immediate community or tribe.

Typical day in the 1980's

Moses and his people, and some of the Old Testament prophets found that the desert was where God spoke to them. Jesus was tempted, and prayed in the desert. The Apostle Paul went into the desert after his conversion. Mohammed was born and nurtured in the desert. An incredible something about that calm, quiet, mystic atmosphere inspires deep soul reflection and nurtures a poetic spirit.

The Islamic Republic of Mauritania is 85% desert, and over 99% Muslim. The dunes stretch east from the border with Mali and run literally into the Atlantic. The winds dump tons of dune sand into the Atlantic each year. During the years of French governing of the huge area called French West Africa, there was only one population which the French were unable to control: the nomads or "White Moors" of the western limits of the Sahara.

Founding of Nouakchott

At the time of Independence in 1960 the French divided French West Africa into several new countries. The land north of the Senegal River would be named Mauritania. Each country needed a new capital city, but where could or should one put a capital in the desert? They chose a barren spot where there was a small agglomeration, about 500 inhabitants, not far from the coast, not among the Black ethnic peoples from along the river, and not in the midst of the Moor Arabic speaking population. It was to be called Nouakchott. No one today seems to know where that name came from, or what it means. I once ran across an early document from the 1950's sent back to Paris from one of these French planners. It was a progress report. It said, in words to this effect: "We have chosen the location for the new capital of the new country of Mauritania. There is no natural port, no water supply, no natural source of energy and no manpower. You can see the challenge that lies ahead of us!" They set up generators and imported fuel. Eventually the city began to appear. They built an airport, a hospital, a post office, and some apartment blocks - all in the land of nowhere. A lovely tent shaped Catholic church appeared across from the French Embassy. Other Muslim countries arrived to build mosques. As

118

this new country became recognized, embassies appeared. The U.S. was first to recognize the country, so the Embassy staff vehicles bore the number 1.

The French realized that for survival, this new country needed more advanced education than the traditional desert 'Mahadras' provided, where the Marabout (an educated religious leader from the highest caste) taught Islam, Arabic, and Islamic Culture. He accepted a cow or camel as a year's payment from the young boy who boarded under his care. Girls did not normally attend school. Gradually, children began to attend local elementary schools in a few larger towns. Since distances were huge and there were no connecting roads, the French sent a plane to pick up select students for study in the only completed secondary boarding school down by the Senegal River. Our proprietor, a medical doctor, was on one of those first flights. Imagine, going to high school all the way across the country by plane!

The desert nomadic parents, however, realized that inherent in this progress, was the loss of their culture, their values and their pride, so they forbade their children to attend. Consequently in the early years only black students attended high school.

Fifteen years of drought dealt a final blow to resistance to change. The drought decimated the wealth and livelihood of traditional desert life. People fled to the few desert towns and to the capital. When we arrived in early 1983 the country was 23 years old and in its 12th or 13th year of drought. The concept of wealth measured in animal possession and the complicated tribal structures was dying before our eyes. The pride inherent in the caste system and other values was slower to die, but they were not impermeable to city life and education. White Moor children were studying beside children from a lower caste, even ex-slave children!

Years later one of my students told me that it was his uncle who finally persuaded his father to let him continue his studies. He traveled first by camel, then donkey to the just completed east-west road. There he was able to catch a 'bush taxi' to Nouakchott and eventually to the university. There the powers-that-be put him in the English Department!

Because of the drought there was a general leveling of the caste structure, from the privileged Marabouts and Warrior classes to the Craftsmen, Entertainers, Shepherds, down to the Servants and eventually to the recently freed Slaves. In Nouakchott families who were experiencing extreme poverty built shelters from discarded trash. Whole new neighborhoods sprang up. Everything was recycled. Animals foraged through the streets and filled their stomachs with rags and paper. How could this desert life change from gentle, and soft, and silent, to extremely tumultuous?

As we began to better understand this traumatic upheaval and observe the amazing resilience of the population, we read a newspaper headline that asked the question: "How is it that Two Million Poets Could Become Two Million Shop Keepers?"

Air Conditioning

Bill and I moved to the Sahara Desert in the spring of 1983 - Bill in February and I in April. In this case 'Spring' refers to a time of year rather than a 'spring is in the air' kind of feeling. There was still snow on the ground as I left Philadelphia. There surely would be no sign of spring at my destination. I flew first to Paris, and then had a layover with friends in Marseille. The flight from Marseille to Nouakchott would take about four hours.

I sat down next to a Frenchman and we began to chat. Suddenly, as we left Moroccan airspace everything outside the plane changed. Those fluffy white clouds were no longer fluffy and no longer white. There was a pall of orange grey with occasional bright orange flowing past the windows. My likable neighbor helped me understand that that was sand. Sand in the sky!

Bill introduced me to the city: Sand roads, sand on the leaves of the few trees, sand piling here and there against buildings, sand on every parked car, sand in everyone's hair, sand in your mouth, and of course sand in your lungs. On occasion there were little tornadoes of lifting, fast-swirling sand. No wonder both men and women's faces were half covered with ends of turbans and melahfas. People went about their business, as did the goats, camels and cows which roamed everywhere foraging in the trash, snatching a stay piece of paper, or cloth or plastic bottle.

Of course the sand didn't stay outside where it had free reign, but insisted on finding some creep-in space around windows, onto balconies, under doors and even through keyholes. Our third floor balcony doubled as the center of our apartment. We had to go outside through the balcony to pass from the kitchen to any of the rooms. And this balcony was open in the direction of the prevailing desert winds. Meal preparation included sweeping off the table with the broom, then washing it before we sat down. We kept our dishes in plastic bags.

The sand compounded with the mosquitoes and flies was what I call "a complete experience." Mauritanians had a saying, 'Dheban fi nahar wa namous fi leel' (Flies in the daytime and mosquitoes at night.) Then add in the heat. It was 105 degrees the day I arrived. Fortunately perspiration evaporated instantly, so the sand did not stick to your skin unless, of course, you used body lotion. We lived on the top floor of a cement block building with sun exposure on two sides and on the roof all day. By nightfall as the temperatures outside began to drop, the air inside was stifling. The wind that had lifted and flung the sand all day took a rest at night, but the mosquitoes were now at their peak. And they needed to eat.

What was the solution if we had to keep the unscreened windows closed? The little beasties were as persistent as the sand in finding a way in. We tried some poisonous mosquito-chasing product but worrying about its effects on our health didn't help us sleep.

Then we came up with an ingenious solution - our own air-conditioning set-up. It would work the nights that we had electricity. The little fan that a friend had given me in Marseille blew away some of the mosquitoes and cooled the evaporating moisture of the wet washcloth on my stomach!

My main consolation through all of this adjustment was thinking of the people who still lived around the country in tents. For them there was no escape.

Early Impressions - Nouakchott

First impressions:

Intense heat. Sand in the air. Unpaved streets. No traffic lights. Several different ethnic groups. Flies and mosquitoes. Beige colored sky. Tree leaves covered with sand. The colorful long flowing robes contrasted with the monotone beige background. Men with turbans and women with melahfas partially covering their faces. Black women dressed in colorful dresses with matching scarves dramatically twisted around their heads. Roaming unbridled foraging animals. Extreme poverty. Crippling drought. Overweight Arabic-speaking women.

Nouakchott on the dunes - Courtesy of Jon Shadid

Crowded ramshackle taxis with pieces of clothing flowing out around the doors on both sides. Large flat slabs of salt piled up for sale just outside the outdoor market. Women street vendors selling tiny piles of vegetables along the sandy roads. Ladies selling cooked couscous in the streets in the evening. Fishermen's boats arriving morning and night in the fishing village loaded with a fresh catch. Fresh camel's milk. Brilliant stars at night. Catholic Church in the shape of a large white tent. The Saharan sand merging with the beach sand. The desert touching the deep blue sea. Dunes pressed against the walls of houses. Wealth and poverty on the same street. Men drinking tea with its foamy head outside during Ramadan. Sand plows working incessantly to clear the paved roads. Men and women with blue skin from clothing dyed blue/black. Rock lined circles designating prayer areas outside the corner shops.

New sounds and smells:

Buzzing flies and mosquitoes. No sound of rain. Trees with a unique smell, especially if there was moisture on the leaves. Strong smells of spices and dirt in the food market making me cough. Vendors dipping vegetables into buckets of dark dirty water to keep them fresh. Neighbors reciting Koranic formulas thousands of times a day between the stated prayer times. A different Arabic, with a different lilt. Languages we'd never heard before. The rhythmic pounding as women, sitting in the sand along the street, using wooden bowling-pin-shaped beaters in place of an iron to remove the wrinkles from men's damask flowing robes. Electricity about three nights a week. The hum of gasoline generators. Electricity in different neighborhoods at different times. Running water flowing when the city's generators were running. No ringing phones. The soft evening air after the wind dies down and the blowing sand settles. The smell and lure of the sea coast where the sky changes from beige to blue out over the water. Deep silence at night. Camels and tents enclosed inside the walls surrounding large new villas.

Observations not necessarily visible to the eye:

Female circumcision. Tribal society. Caste society. Friction between races. A highly publicized news of a thief's hand chopped off just after our arrival. News report and photos of ceremonial destruction of a sugary syrup - mistaken for alcohol. Slavery outlawed but still practiced. Political parties designated by color so illiterates could participate. An estimated 17% literacy rate. Forced feeding of little girls. Contact from city to city only by national radio broadcasts. No electricity or phones outside the larger cities. Lights and radios and TV's running on car batteries in the desert. No road between the political capital and the economic capital, both on the coast.

Pleas for international aide: Countries abandon their efforts to build a port on the straight sandy beach. Chinese engineers succeed in building a quay for ocean sailing vessels - an engineering marvel. Attending the first game at the new Chinese built stadium seating 3,000. Chinese hospitals in the interior. The Brazilian paved east-west road 'Road of Hope" all the way to the Malian border. Catholic Relief Services, Lutherans and other NGO'S respond to pleas for help. The Saudi Islamic institute built of imported marble. The plan to staff it with Wahhabi preaching professors. It eventually houses classes for the two-year-old university. Powdered milk called "Kennedy."

Effects on us:

Challenge to understand the culture. Illness because the open spaces serve as a public toilet. Learning patience while building up a resistance to germs carried in the blowing sand. Boiling and filtering drinking water. Soaking veggies in bleach for 20 minutes. Battling boils and carbuncles. Wonderful friendships. Satisfying jobs. Cutting back on the sweet tea offered us because staph infections thrive on sugar. Household help, called "boys," to keep the house relatively clean. No other Christian workers for two years. Praying not only for survival but also for positive attitudes and a flourishing spirit. Gratitude to God for Christian friends especially a family from Togo, an American couple, a Peace Corps volunteer, an American Embassy employee, a lady from Mauritius and a French family who were our first friends. Frequent intestinal problems but never ever succumbing to giardia, or incurable amoebas. Eating from a common dish using only the right hand. No bread with any meal. No pastries or cakes in the local cuisine. Finally adjusting to the heat and the constant perspiration. Shaking the clothes to remove the sand and ants before bringing them into the house from the line. Frequent robberies. Sitting on the dunes eating breakfast while watching the sun rise and singing, "From the rising of the sun to the going down of the same, the Lord's name is to be praised." The changing beauty of the dunes as the sun moves across the sky. Tiny plants hidden here and there. Fascinating detailed footprints of tiny desert creatures. Looking for prehistoric artifacts on the desert floor. Rain after 15 years of drought. The desert becoming a greenish carpet for a brief period followed by a locust holocaust which cleaned out almost all green plants across the country. A year later finding several dead locusts inside pictures frames hanging on our living room wall. The ever-present mosquitoes!

As the years passed:

Our sand filled yard blooming with flowers. Temperatures there two degrees centigrade cooler than outside the wall. Rewards of teaching highly motivated students. Many graduates fluent and qualified to teach. English Department the largest at the university. Camels and tents enclosed inside the walls of large new luxurious villas. World Vision's arrival. Smaller NGO's working with the poor. Lives saved through vaccination campaigns and through emergency feeding centers for the malnourished. God showing his power in healing hearts and bodies. English language bookstore open for ten years. Our own lives enriched by hardships and joys. Fulfilling a life-long dream of painting. Bill's teaching, pastoring and counseling. Unforgettable experiences and priceless friendships. Praise the Lord. Small groups of worshiping believers. God's faithfulness.

It's All Bill's Fault

Here I was in a stressful situation from which there was no escape. We had only been in Mauritania for two months and I was interviewing for a job that I didn't want. I would turn 51 in a few weeks. Trying to understand a new culture, barely surviving in the heat, blowing sand and mosquitoes, I was not ready to add anything else. Bill had been out job hunting before his job at a local lycée came to a close. He found an opening that he didn't feel qualified for at the two-year old university that shared teachers with the slightly older Teacher Training College. He was, however, sure that this was the job for me.

I had no intention of taking a full time job. I had only four years of teaching high school English in the U.S. under my belt and that was 24 years previously. Teaching English to foreign learners is an entirely different kettle of fish. I told the Lord that if He wanted me to accept this job, He would have to make it impossible for me to turn it down.

I questioned the director about what the post consisted of and then I told her that I was not qualified. I couldn't teach comparative literature. African novelists had not even begun to write and publish novels until after I had completed my studies. The fourth year students were returning from their third year studying in a teacher training school in Scotland and were highly qualified in linguistics and pedagogics. I was sure that they knew more than I did about teaching English. After all, they had learned English as a third or fourth language and knew what was involved. I told her again that I wasn't qualified.

Her reaction? "That sounds very good, because a teacher who is not proud of her qualifications makes a better teacher." I guess that was the answer I didn't want to hear. She said to come back in the fall before classes started to find out more details. She was not sure just when that might be.

I started to panic. I couldn't control my tears. What in the world was I supposed to do? How could I prepare when I didn't know what courses I would be teaching? There were no resources in country and even the key to the English teachers' office was lost. I soon realized that much of this new experience with tension and emotional instability was due in part to my age changes and lack of sleep.

The sleeplessness persisted. I was becoming an emotional wreck. One evening a group of English speaking friends were together at our apartment for a Bible study. Bill was leading the discussion on John 17. My eyes fell on verse 11. Through my tears I read "the power of your name, the name that you gave me." What seemed strange was that this was Jesus praying for us, using the expression, "protect them by the power of your name." I had never thought of God the Father's name as being powerful before. Whether my interpretation was correct or not, that night and the nights following as I lay in bed sweating and swatting mosquitoes, I began invoking the name of God, MY FATHER. Although I may not have mouthed the words, I was, in effect asking for Him to calm my spirit. I fell asleep.

The other foreign teachers had already left for the summer. The only solution was to go to France and hunt for books. We borrowed an empty apartment in Aix-en-Provence and for weeks I studied the class notes of a friend who had his Masters Degree in teaching English as a foreign language. I copied them into a form that would benefit me. Then Bill was invited to speak at a conference in England. When the conference was over we concocted a plan. We used a map of the underground to visit the bookstores in London that sold books for foreign learners. Surely God could help me choose the books that would prove most useful for those as yet unknown courses. We took the underground from one bookstore to another, and I prayed.

We returned to Nouakchott in September and found no one on the campus. I took a taxi every few days to see what was going on. Finally, in October I heard that there would be an English Department organizational meeting the coming Thursday. I met three Mauritanian men, one Pakistani woman, and one Canadian woman, both of whom were married to Mauritanians. Classes were being assigned. I was given 12 hours. They would start on Saturday, two days later! How could I survive with one day to prepare? So I said, "I don't have to do that." The head of the department was shocked and asked why. I told him that I had no contract. He got up, and left the room. When he came back he told me to go see the director. She asked me a few questions and then handed me the best contract available, with furnished apartment and passage paid to the U.S. every two years. I guess I figured that was good enough reason to accept the courses assigned to me.

On Saturday I had a one and a half hour class, Introduction to Literature. I got the students to identify the arts and then we discussed their value, especially literature, in any society. I had had too little time to think the subject through for myself. I hardly knew what I was talking about. It was very clear that I was the one facing the steepest learning curve. I needed to learn about their level of English, about their culture, what their cultural sensitivities were, about their learning styles, how much material was necessary to fill two hour classes, as well as what material would help them the most. This was going to be a two way street. All of us faced a huge challenge, but their teacher had the most to learn.

I was pleased with the way that first class worked out, even though perhaps the value for most of the students was minimal. At least they were speaking, thinking and hearing authentic American. The next day, Sunday, I arrived prepared for seven class hours. I taught every minute of all seven hours.

And then I found out that the first week should have been designated as 'une prise de contact'. The other teachers kept the students for about 10 minutes, just long enough to meet them and explain what they could expect from the class. No one had thought to tell me that I wasn't expected to present any material until a week later. How could I have done that when I didn't know myself what material I was going to teach in the next hour, let alone the whole semester? But I guess my teaching right away and filling those hours served a purpose. The students saw that I was serious, and it also served to set a determination in me that if these young people had grown up in outlying towns or even in the desert, with little exposure to modern life, and had succeeded in getting accepted in this new experiment of a university, then I was going to do everything in my power to help them succeed.

Bill had gotten me into this, and he was the one who could get me through it. The books we had selected in London served as wonderful resources. Since the students had no books, and most didn't even own a dictionary, I felt it necessary to provide them with handouts, especially in grammar and literature. How could we discuss literature if they hadn't read the short story or essay or poem? There were no photocopiers available. This was the era of the mimeograph. Bill typed stencils hours on end, correcting mistakes with a little flask of corrector fluid. Neither of us were typists. It was essential that I choose the shortest essays, and short stories.

But then what was I to do with *Huckleberry Finn*, a whole novel? The solution was handing out selected passages that illustrated several of the dialects that Twain had mastered. After one of those classes some students asked me why I had cried in class. I hadn't cried, but tears had welled up in my eyes. One of the passages between Huck and the escaping slave Jim, was so real because we also were in a country that had only recently legally freed thousands of slaves. Most, however, were still serving as slaves. They had nowhere to go to make a livelihood.

The students did succeed. After the second year many of them went out to teach with impressive skills in speaking and writing. The teachers worked as a team, became good friends, and I felt well accepted. The British Government supplied scholarships to a teacher training school in Edinburgh for the best students after their second year. The Scottish teachers once asked me what methods we were using. How could we account for such success because the

Mauritanian students were head and shoulders more advanced than all of the students arriving from the other developing countries. The credit goes to those highly motivated students and our teamwork. Those three Mauritanians and the two other foreign ladies were excellent teachers and wanted the students to succeed as much as I did.

Several months into my first year as I was arriving for class I looked up and saw my waiting students lined along a railing. I was so glad to see them that I consciously said to myself, "Be careful. You can't kiss them. They are not part of the church in Algiers."

During my third year Bill was organizing feeding centers for malnourished children out in the far reaches of the desert and was gone 15 days each month. I missed him very much, but one day I realized that if something tragic happened to him, I felt so rewarded and happy that I would stay on right there in Nouakchott by myself.

Two years later I was asked to be head of the department. God, my FATHER had turned my insecurity and anxiety into satisfaction and even joy.

Twenty-Fifth Anniversary - Spent on the Fly

In 1983 our 25th wedding anniversary fell on August 2 the same date as it had on all of the others before it. But it was the first time that we had spent one in Dakar, Senegal. The circumstances of this overnight kept us from concentrating on that marvelous event 25 years previously. A celebration was not in the forefront of our minds. We had only lived in Nouakchott for five months and were now on our way out to Marseille desperate to get some books for my prospective job at the university. We had to fly south to get north.

This was our first initiation to sub-Saharan Africa. As we came through the airport doors to the outside, we were bombarded and pushed by men offering taxis, every kind of help, shopping, sightseeing tours, handouts, money, you name it. It was nearly impossible to get to the street. We didn't want any of these men to know how much we needed help. We picked out a not-so-fancy hotel and were quoted a price for a room. We went into bargaining mode. We asked if they had anything cheaper. We were testing the waters hoping that they would just lower that quote. But to our dismay they did have a cheaper room, and sent us downstairs into the basement to a stifling little hole in the wall where we promptly opened the little windows.

We decided to celebrate our anniversary by buying some ice cream - maybe a sundae. The French still had a significant presence in independent Senegal so there must be ice cream somewhere.

We walked the streets, up and down, arriving at what looked like a busy part of town; not one cafe sold ice cream. We asked everyone and followed no one. Rule number one in some African cities, not only because you could be taken advantage of, but because we didn't know how to pick and choose someone worthy of the name 'guide.'

When we returned to our room it was cooler, but the mosquitos found those open windows and were there ahead of us. We had forgotten that we were in malaria territory and hadn't taken any anti-malarial meds. It only takes one bite by one infected female mosquito. I wish I could say that we never made that mistake again. But both times we escaped unscathed.

When we got to France, we didn't remember that we hadn't had that ice cream. Anyway the 2nd of August was past.

Fish and Flies Associates, Inc.

From a letter to friends in the U.S. in February 1984, just one year after Bill's arrival in Mauritania:

Bill is feeling much better. Those big sores or boils are all gone. [He had several on his face causing his beard to fall out and his eye to swell shut. At one point there were twelve under his left arm spreading over his chest.] *His skin has lost that grayish look and is getting some pink color. He certainly acts as though he feels better. We are thankful.*

He has just made an appointment with the new Mauritanian Ambassador to the United Nations to set up English classes. This is in addition to his class with the Mauritanian employees at USAID. They will meet together five days a week until June. Now to answer your question: What do you do for entertainment?

As you perhaps realize, there is nowhere to go except to the beach or to visit friends. We have been to see one movie, a French film, a sort of soap opera, only because it was filmed in Mauritania. "Fort Saganne" was named after the only French Fort, which is still standing in the desert. It turned out to be a romance more than the history of the fort.

There is no forest to go to relax in. Last Friday (Thursday/Friday is the weekend), we planned a picnic after church with a few new friends. The idea was to eat at the beach and then do some fishing. It was our understanding that if the weather was not cooperating, that is, if the sand was blowing, we would eat our lunch at our house first. At ten o'clock the wind was kicking up a storm but one of the ladies still wanted to go, so we went, letting the best fisherwoman choose the best spot.

She chose a section of the 200 mile long beach near the artisan fishing port where the unsold fish get cleaned and dried. The heads and insides are thrown onto a huge pile. Not only is the odor more then a normal nose can stand but the flies swarm in black droves. As soon as we arrived those flies decided that they had had enough of their fish head diet and chose instead to join us to eat shrimp, avocados, sandwiches and cake. It was quite a new experience. Once in a lifetime is enough.

The wind had picked up enough to make that feature very unpleasant as well. Our friends were having a wonderful time standing out in the water oblivious of the misery of those of us on the beach. The sun on my head was more then I could stand so I headed back to the car and made the terrible mistake of opening the car door to get in and then leaving it open for a bit, to let some heat out. All of the flies joined me. They were very active, noisy, and happy.

One of the ladies had given Bill a section of line wound around a cork holder - the same equipment she herself was using. No rod. Bill finished his hand at fishing with one fish about 5 inches long. Our friend fished merrily away. When she had pulled in number 18, she decided that that was maybe enough and we could go home.

I think that Bill's parting remark, perhaps covering some humiliation, summed up the value of our attempt at entertainment when he said, 'Well, we've seen more flies than we ever have in our lives!'

I Don't Know Why I Swallowed a Fly

It was really the heat and the flies together that aggravated the most. I was standing in front of my class, periodically wiping with the back of my hand the sweat as it dripped from my nose - windows wide open. The flies were buzzing around. I felt one go into my mouth but where he went after that I didn't know. I reflected for only an instant and thought it worth my while to find out. I had seen some of the students spit out of the windows especially during the fast month of Ramadan when they didn't want to swallow their saliva, so I went over to the window. Making some vulgar scraping noises in my throat I tried to bring it up and out. If I succeeded I could spit it out onto the sand two stories below as they did. Hard as I tried, it didn't work. As I stepped back in front of the class I said, "That's the first time I ever swallowed a fly."

A student said, "The first time?!"

Sixty Miles for Lunch

We were heading east in a Land Rover, destination Boutilimit. Brahim, the World Vision driver, and Bill were enjoying a full view of the road ahead. The three of us ladies were in the back seat seeing only the view from the side windows. Not that the view out the front was much better. The wind was blowing hard from the left, and the sand was swirling across the road covering the paving making it necessary to make a calculated guess on occasion as to where the road actually was. The advantage to the front seat position was that Brahim, who kept his window open, only had the blowing sand flowing around the back of his neck but we had the full effect hitting us in our faces.

The World Vision director was busy setting up new projects when he heard that he was to receive and entertain two guests from the home office in the U.S. He asked us to take them to Boutilimit, a town about 60 miles to the east, (the Atlantic Ocean was to the west) have lunch, and return in the afternoon. There were several problems with this. First, we didn't think to say, "No." Secondly, he was new in the country and had never been to Boutilimit and thirdly, we were relatively new in the country and had never been to Boutilimit. So we would just have to rely on Brahim. Since Brahim was so important, it followed that if he wanted to keep his window open, so be it.

We looked across the terrain on the left, high dunes, and on the right, dunes of lowered heights, not a tree or shrub in sight in any direction. A surge of a new sense of responsibility enveloped me. It was my job to give these ladies a good time. I was their guide, their only source of information. My presence was their security in this somewhat scary situation. I had to keep talking. But what could I say? It looked and felt as though we were driving straight into the fiery furnace. I started a running commentary off the top of my head. I pointed out in detail the different colored sands of which I knew nothing. I had taken an Introduction to Geology course in college, but it wasn't much help here. I was chuckling inside as they craned their necks to take it all in.

I probably eventually explained the drought that was now in its thirteenth year, the rapid uncontrolled expansion of the Sahara, the disappearance of the Sahel grasslands, the wells that had dried up, the animal carcasses that littered the landscape, and the mass exodus to Nouakchott, the capital. It had been founded on a site with 500 people, some living in tents, 25 years before at Independence and was now boiling with 300,000 from an influx of families and their surviving animals.

At one point I turned to look at these new friends and said, "You should see your glasses. They are half full of sand." They shot back, "You should see yours!"

We arrived in Boutilimit. Brahim chose our restaurant. We walked into a cement block building with nothing but a dirty reed mat on the floor. We sat down on it, ordered our food from the three choices. Ours contained almost as much sand as couscous. Brahim ordered his favorite, a michoui, roast goat, which he tore off with greasy fingers. We had heard that white Moors didn't eat vegetables or fish, but this was the first time I had actually witnessed someone eat a full meal of only meat and mint tea.

As we stepped out into the dull thick air and sand-filled sky, we looked around and saw nothing else to investigate. We decided to drive back as quickly as we could. Boutilimit was not exactly a tourist's paradise. We had completed our mission with some doubts as to our success as guides. But wasn't World Vision there to help a suffering people? We had given these two women an unforgettable once-in-a-lifetime, frightening experience, and certainly a deeper understanding of the role World Vision might play as they continued their relief and development efforts.

I don't recall that we ever thought that God had actually forsaken this land. We were just beginning His new adventure. We were expectant and waiting to see what God had in store. He had answered our prayers in sending in World Vision, a Christian relief and development organization. Other Christians began to arrive. Bill had already started teaching an English class of Mauritanians at USAID and had a second class of one man, Mauritania's new Ambassador to the United Nations. I was enjoying my job teaching at the university.

Some years later as the weather began to change, the winds subsided, the blowing sand settled, and an occasional rainfall watered the earth, one of the national converts said, "Remember how we prayed for this country? One of those requests was for a change in the weather. Just look how God has answered."

Lost on the Beach

The wind blew the sand everywhere. We had not been out of the house for days except to go to and from work. And I was sick of it. Selfishly, I insisted that we could at least go to the beach where there was less sand in the air.

We didn't need a four-wheel drive to go the six kilometers. We just couldn't drive over the dunes to actually get close to the water. We turned north along the packed sand road that followed the coast, parked the car and climbed over the dunes that separated the piste from the beach. Ah, this was what I was looking for: a little exercise, the breaking waves, and a view of the sky. Way out over the water the sandy orange sky turned to a hazy blue.

We headed north walking barefoot along the edge of the water examining shells and other sea life. When we decided to return home, we turned and meandered back down along the water. We soon realized that we had no idea how far we had walked. How could we gage where we should turn to climb back over the dunes to the car? There were no natural landmarks, no trees, no rocks, just sand. We were new here and had not thought of piling up shells or even drawing lines in the sand.

We didn't start to worry until we tried to get ourselves back over the dunes to the hardened piste. Visibility was almost nil. The wind kept changing directions. We thought that we were walking in a straight line but instead we kept arriving back on the ocean side. We learned then and there that sand dunes do not lie on the ground in straight lines, and the wind blows in strange patterns. We finally found the packed sand road but not the car. We had no idea if the car was north or south. Finally a four-wheel drive packed to the roof with camping gear came toward us from the north. It looked as though the driver might pass right on without stopping. Maybe they too had had a scary time and wanted to get to safety. We flagged them down and asked the driver if he had seen a white car. His negative answer assured us it had to be south. We just hadn't walked far enough.

We found it, but I felt quite rebuked by my stubborn insistence that we get out of our apartment for some amusement. Our adrenaline had been pumped, but not only by amusement! We did learn a lesson. In a country like this, with weather like this, you prepare for any eventuality.

Tidjikja for Christmas

The crowd was pushing in on us. We assumed that the din of men yelling instructions and the crowd milling around us was normal as departure time approached. Cases of evaporated milk, and bags of sugar and tea and other essentials were being passed from hand to hand over our heads. It was Tuesday and we were waiting to board the once-a-week flight from Nouakchott to Tidjikja, a city out in the center of Mauritania's chunk of the Sahara Desert.

I don't suppose most people would have thought that this building was fancy enough for an international airport. It was a rectangular building of cement block with windows on one long side looking out onto the runway, with four support pillars down the middle. But there were flights in and out by some pretty impressive airlines: Air France, Sabena, Royal Air Maroc and Air Afrique, Air Senegal, as well as Air Mauritanie. I always assumed that all disembarking passengers passed through the airport, but in those early days there wasn't much to keep them from just walking from the plane, out across the sand to the road. It wasn't a busy airport but it served as lifeline to the rest of the world.

I'm afraid that we used to chuckle at the green, folded paper airplane logo painted on the tail of Air Mauritania's jets. The pilots, however, were well trained and the planes well maintained. Those two Fokker jets were able to assure flights to Casablanca, the Canary Islands, Bamako and Dakar and more, as well as connecting the major cities inside the country.

Today we were "in line" for an internal flight. But as usual there was no line, just ladies in their colorful wrap around covering, pushing forward with the even more aggressive men. I don't think the thought passed my mind that these other would-be passengers knew something we didn't. Then someone told us that a carton of airline tickets had been stolen from the Air Mauritania office in town. There was no way for the officials to know who had paid for their tickets and who hadn't.

We gradually worked our way forward trying not to give way to a foot slipped in ahead or an elbow coming in on one side or the other. Our experiences getting on busses way back in Algeria stood us in good stead. We flung our suitcases up on the counter as we had watched others do, not for inspection, but for check-in. Ours were mostly full of fruit and other impossible-to-find commodities out in the desert towns.

We were on our way to Tidjikja to spend Christmas with a small team of World Vision young people. The feeding center for the undernourished children project had recently opened and most of the foreign team members came and went every six months. That didn't give them time to adjust to the climate, sand storms, or customs before they were ready to leave. Those who stayed longer needed to constantly adjust to new team members. The new director, working in Nouakchott, who had set up the project, thought that our presence might bring a bit of stability or even a homey feeling of Christmas with those goodies in our bags.

If a traveler was hard up for money, or if he wanted an exciting experience, there were two options of transport to Tidjikja other than by plane - an 18 hour overland trip by four-wheel-drive Land Rover, or even cheaper, by truck. Most of the truck's passengers were relegated to riding on the top of the commodities loaded in the back.

The Land Rovers were usually well filled as well. If there were already four passengers in the back seat, four passengers also sat in the front seat, one to the left of the driver and two others to his right. The last half of the way there was no road, just a rocky, rutty piste, and frequent waits for pit stops, motor repairs, and Muslim prayers.

I'm not too sure why we accepted to take on this extra burden, even if it only involved a plane trip. I was teaching at the university. Bill also had a teaching schedule but had begun helping World Vision with some of their new projects of flood relief. But, in the end, this trip did give me a fuller understanding of the origins of some of my students as well as a very upset digestive system.

I had a lot to learn. We gradually began to understand some of the tribes, their locations and how they ranked in the levels of respect due them by other Mauritanians. Some of my students were from our destination Tidjikja, the center of one of the most important tribes. One of these young men was bright and obviously very sure of himself. It was he who warned me in class that under no circumstances was I to introduce the subject of music. That was the concern of the Griots, a caste of people much lower down the status scale. He also advised me at another time when there was a brief reference to farming, "Only Blacks work the soil." After his second year he won a scholarship to study in Scotland. He returned for his senior year, and then the Ministry of Education sent him off to teach English in a high school. The last I heard of his whereabouts was several years ago. He was posted to the Mauritanian Embassy in Washington, DC!

So here we had arrived in the land of this very proud tribe. The houses were beige, some large and some small and some very small. Some had an outside staircase that reached a little room constructed on the roof. It was easy to see your neighbor climb to the toilet! But then he could see you too. We got our water from a dirty barrel. Most cooking was done outside on inefficient wood burning contraptions - another reason there were no trees. Peace Corps young people were feverishly building wood-saving stoves around town. Most everyone "lived on the floor'" with no furniture.

The children came in droves to the feeding centers. On occasion, fairly well dressed and healthy looking women came carrying babies in various stages of malnutrition. Sometimes mothers were sent away angry because their child weighed in at the borderline and no free food was allocated to her. The team offered nutrition advice, but there was so little available in the market. Could the majority of these families even afford what was being recommended?

It was obvious that the pride that permeated my university student originated in a by-gone era. Tidjikja had once been a thriving city strategically located on the camel caravan routes between North Africa and sub-Saharan Africa. Those important trade routes no longer existed because there was no need, but also from lack of water. The 14 years of drought were beginning to accomplish what only an earth shaking event could - the leveling of wealth, the shifting of values, and eventually the first throws of the breakdown of class distinctions in this tribal, caste society. A man's wealth had been measured in the number of animals, camels or cows, or slaves, he possessed. No rain meant no grasses or grains to feed them. They were worthless.

The Return Trip

Tidjikja Airport

Soon it was Tuesday again. The plane from Nouakchott arrived, and returned on Tuesdays. Its arrival was one of the week's main attractions. Crowds flocked to the airport, by foot, or on donkey carts. These colorfully dressed people chatting and laughing, with the beige rocky landscape serving as backdrop, was like a scene from a movie. The drama climaxed as that immense green and white Fokker jet from the capital came into view through the sand-filled sky, circled to chase any wandering goats and landed perfectly on that packed gravel runway.

The airport building here was considerably smaller than in the capital, my memory says about 15 feet by 15 feet. We walked in the open door on one side, then out the other, across some loose sand, onto the runway, around the plane's nose to the stairway.

There was already a crowd there before us. No doubt some of these people were holders of those stolen tickets. The policeman standing on the first step would need to be armed to maintain order. And armed he was - with a bullwhip! Each time the crowd surged forward, he raised his arm and the whip whistled through the air. The retreating crowd formed a semi-circle. We had developed a strategy years earlier when we were faced with getting through crowds. Bill would send me into the fray and he would remain behind with the hand luggage. I was a better pusher then he was. Although he was stronger, he was much politer.

As soon as the arm holding the bullwhip dropped, the crowd surged forward. Each time he swung, I gained a little ground toward those steps. When there was only one row of men between me and the policeman, he reached down and grabbed my arm and started pulling. There was no way I could get my feet to follow that arm, so he let go and raised his bullwhip again; the crowd withdrew forming another semicircle just to the extent of the flying whip. He grabbed my arm and I jumped onto the bottom step, the first one to board the plane!

I carefully took my seat on the left side. The right side was for smokers. The plane filled quickly. People tried to take the seat that I had reserved for Bill before he finally got on, and even after he got on. They were used to putting three passengers plus children in two seats. We held our ground. Hard as I tried, and in the interest of everyone's safety, I couldn't conjure up enough sympathy for this habitual overcrowding.

But you can understand how they felt. The only alternative was that bumpy, backbreaking 18-hour overland trip or the weeklong wait for the next Tuesday flight.

Teargas

The phone rang. Bill answered and heard an anxious voice say, "Where's Peggy?" It was the American Embassy.

"She's supervising exams at the university."

"You'd better go get her."

So Bill went to get a taxi. That put both of us in the chaos of "the danger zone."

It wasn't the first time I had whiffed tear gas. Several years before when I was teaching a course on the second floor of the Saudi built Islamic Institute which housed the overflow of the university classes, I assumed that since the room was full and the students were attentive, that we had nothing to fear from the milling students outside with their calls for justice. I just carried on. The soldiers arrived, threw their tear gas canisters to disperse the crowd and to arrest the perpetrators. The weakened vestiges of the gas rose to our open windows hardly even irritating our nostrils.

But this demonstration today was very different. The whole main campus was in an uproar. A greater number of students were demonstrating for what they felt was a greater cause. The United States was threatening to attack Iraq, a sister Arab nation. A short time before this moment the Iraqi Embassy, in a show of solidarity with Mauritania, had invited all Mauritanian children who had the first name of Saddam for a special party with prizes. Mauritania and Iraq were great friends. The Peace Corps Volunteers and extra American Embassy staff had already been evacuated to neighboring countries. Non-essential staff from other embassies also left.

The deadline set by George Bush Senior for Iraq to pull its forces out of Kuwait was closing in. It was January 15, 1991. The First Iraq War started two days later. Bush had made it clear that the bombing would start just after midnight if Saddam Hussein did not comply by ordering his troops home. One of the minor consequences for us of his chosen deadline was that the University of Nouakchott was in the middle of the fall semester's final exams. Two of the Peace Corps volunteers were teachers. The Peace Corps office had telephoned me a few days earlier informing me that the volunteers were being evacuated and asked if I would be willing to supervise their exams. I agreed. We had no intention of leaving.

Why should we? We had survived a coup d'état in 1965 when the President of Algeria was overthrown. A tank was in the street in front of our house. Our neighbor was killed by a stray bullet. But we were untouched. We had also stayed in Algeria during the Six Day War in 1967 between Israel and several Arab countries. The American Embassy had actually called us at 4:30 a.m. telling us to leave, but we had decided that we were not in danger. And, we had remained in Mauritania during an earlier coup d'état. We felt very far away from Kuwait.

So here I was on the campus in an amphitheater that seated about 100. I did not know any of the students. The exams that I had supervised the day before had proceeded without incident despite the rowdy milling students outside. I don't remember experiencing much fear at all. I guess I was naive, only able to see the students and my responsibility to them. I knew I was respected and even liked. I sympathized with their need to make their anger known.

But in reality we were not in a position to weigh the consequences of the invisible deliberations of government officials, nor were we able to judge the ability of the government forces to protect any foreigner. Nor were we sure of the sympathies of the general population. I suppose that with an illiteracy rate of around 70%, rabble-rousers could easily excite the majority to violence. I did take the precaution of informing the 'Directeur d'Etudes' where I was on campus and requested that if the situation got too agitated would he please send someone to escort me out of the classroom area through a locked gate into the administrative section which was only about twenty feet away from where I was standing in Amphitheater Four.

I arrived early and greeted the eight students waiting for the classroom door to be unlocked. Other students came and tried to get the eight to leave. We entered. I said nothing. I stood down front with my arms folded saying nothing. Gradually more students came in especially when they saw that I was writing on the board. I still said nothing and didn't look at anyone. As more students arrived and were debating what to do, I simply said twice, "It's easier to take an exam sitting down."

As the room became calmer, I added, "You don't know me and I don't know you, but I am not new here and I can only function if the room is quiet." As I handed out the exam papers still not looking directly at anyone, I said, "This exam will last for one hour and a half. Read all the way through to the end before writing anything." The room calmed immediately. There was dead silence. It was unbelievable. I had no idea if they had understood me or not, but they had understood that this teacher meant business.

I answered individual questions. About twenty minutes later the noise outside began to increase. The amazing quiet continued in the room. Then we heard two shots. Four students stood up and those around them said "Sit down!" Tears welled up in my eyes. We had no idea if the shots had hit someone. At one point students came in the door to cause a disturbance, and some of the exam takers chased them out. I watched about six students cheating but I could not risk upsetting the calm. As they left I spoke to them privately and told them that it was too late now, I had seen them cheating. Some students left taking their exams with them, others handed them to me. Some papers had no identification on them.

When every student had left, I exited the door that led smack into the main campus. I heard a haranguing female voice in the main lecture hall. I couldn't see how large her audience was. My goal was to get to the car as soon as I could. All of the sudden I sensed that there were two men walking beside me, one on either side. As I turned to see who they were, I was grateful beyond words. I knew them both well. They were two upperclassmen who came to our house for discussions and cookies. I was immediately touched and grateful that they had appeared at that very moment. They said that they had come to the campus because they had heard I was there, and to escort me through the soldiers to the street to my tear gas filled car. Bill was waiting. We drove straight home.

The American Embassy was working hard to keep all of us Americans who were scattered throughout the city abreast of the latest developments. We learned that the Mauritanian government had just informed our Embassy that they would not be able to assure the safety of foreigners who chose to stay. More Embassy personnel were evacuated. French citizens who needed to stay in country had moved inside the iron gates of the French Embassy.

We made arrangements for two friends to guard our house 24/7. We were evacuated two days later to southern France on a plane that departed at midnight. The bombing had started by the time we landed in Marseille. Bill returned to Nouakchott ahead of me several weeks later and started clearing out unnecessary papers and other items just in case calm did not return. But life slowly resumed its normal pace. Rumor had it that Saddam Hussein's wife had come for safety to Nouakchott and that at least some of Iraq's commercial airplanes had spent the duration of the war lined up on the runway of the Nouakchott airport.

Healing in His Wings

There was still tension in the air in Nouakchott even after the hostilities of the first Gulf War had ended. We were evacuated to France on January 17, 1991 but were both back in our house several weeks later. We wanted very much to visit some of our Mauritanian friends, but we did not want to bring attention to them or to ourselves by being seen in this rather poor section of town.

After dark we drove in a circuitous route, parked, wrapped our turbans around our heads, walked up a deserted alley and knocked on their back door. The two sisters and the children were delighted to see us. We caught up on their experiences during the war. Their house had been searched because a neighbor told the police she was storing arms! All the police could find was a bag of rice! Tensions were high. Was Saddam's wife really in Nouakchott? Iraqi commercial airplanes were lined up on the runway at the airport.

But the biggest concern of the evening was that the younger sister had been sick for about three weeks. She had an appointment at the psychiatric hospital the next morning. She was simply unable to sleep. She described how tired she was and that the doctors had not been able to help her.

She was lying on a mattress couch in their living room. Her older sister was sitting a little ways away and the children were all there with us. Bill and I moved to sit on the floor so that we were next to the couch. I asked her to sit up and drink a full glass of water. As she lay back down I reached over and put my hand on her shoulder. Bill placed his hand on my shoulder and her sister and we began to pray. As Bill was praying I felt a surge pass through my body from his hand. By the time we finished praying she was fast asleep.

Two days later we found a note in our yard. She had slept through the whole night. Would we come and pray again the next night. The piece of paper had been slid under our gate the day before. We had not seen it and had not gone back to pray at their house the evening before. The next time we saw her she was delighted to tell us that she was feeling better and had not kept that psychiatric appointment. She had slept well every night since. Our faith was strengthened as we praised the Lord together. We praised him too for the strong conviction we had had that we should go to see them that evening despite the possible trouble it could cause.

Keep us, Lord, from missing the opportunity to see you work in simple yet marvelous ways.

A Great Friendship

She was fairly robust. She covered that plumpness with a beautiful long, about six foot piece of fairly sheer material which she tied at each shoulder, and then wrapped up over her head. The hanging remainder was flung back over her left shoulder. A lot of frustrating persistence was often necessary to keep that sliding cloth in place, to keep her head covered. I admired the lovely flow of these colorful garments against the beige of the desert sand that enveloped the city. They seemed to exemplify a spirit of freedom, beauty and courage to survive, in such austere circumstances. They also stood in stark contrast to the women's garb of the Middle East where women wore a combination of several headscarves pinned so tight to cover every single hair. For me these scarves represented a view of life and of Islam radically different from that of my friend's culture.

She was beautiful as well, with smooth radiant skin, high cheekbones, and straight white teeth. Even when she was poor it seemed that she could walk anywhere and display elegance. She feared nothing. At least it seemed that way. She had doubted Islam and probably had accepted Christ before we became friends. As time went on, Christ became very real to her and she began telling her relatives and friends.

How she came into my life is a long story but we became very close. When people saw us together they would sometimes ask if I were her mother or if she were my daughter. She always responded with a yes. Once at the airport a lady asked me which one of us was traveling. And then added, "She is going to miss you very much."

Her husband was very shy. The first time he came to our house he couldn't eat. He sat with his head down looking at his hands. Every once in a while he slid the fork over the plate but nothing reached his mouth. But when he studied the Bible with Bill, he opened up and began to discuss. One day when he and Bill were together in the living room, she and I went back to our office/guest room. We lay on the two beds that were placed along two adjoining walls. We lay head to head and began to giggle about those two men in the living room. How in the world had God gone to all of that trouble to bring us four together? It was a silly, happy time I will never forget. Gradually her husband's shyness disappeared and he became a pretty impressive preacher with good insights.

When they both found jobs they were able to move to nicer quarters. She was busy and I was teaching, so she suggested that we eat lunch together every

Saturday at her house. We all sat on the floor around the bowl of 'chib-ou-jen' rice and fish smothered with veggies, eating with our right hands. One Saturday we found two spoons laid out on the plastic tablecloth. I guess that was a commentary on the pain our ineptitude was causing. Those veggies or balls of rice needed to jump into our mouths with a flick of the thumb, nothing dropping. We were more than willing to oblige.

We lounged on the low couches after the meal as we waited for the three glasses of tea. Making sure that half the quantity is foam turns the process into an entertainment. The third glass is the cue for the guest to leave, but here together there was no protocol. By then anyway, Bill and her husband were both fast asleep.

The real question was how was it that we two, she from a nomadic Saharan culture could adapt so quickly to being the closest friend of a middle-aged lady from Pennsylvania? We didn't communicate with each other in either one of our mother tongues. And how was it that this American lady could admire her as something very, very extraordinary, could trust her implicitly, respect her opinion in things cultural and love her with all her heart? I cannot think of any real reason other than our common focus and common love for Christ.

And then we retired from her country. As the years pass we have grown apart, but that love is still there hidden in my heart, and I know we will meet again.

A Wish

I used to wish that the gap in my two front teeth would close-until we lived in West Africa. The standards of beauty were different there. Rotund women were the most desirable. They were so hefty that they often had difficulty walking or climbing stairs. Fortunately tents don't have stairs. Slightly buckteeth with a space between the two front teeth was also desirable, and common. Tooth brushes sold and used right on the street, in the office or even in school were comprised of about four inches of stick broken off from some tree, often carved with geometric designs. Some people held this stick with all five fingers wrapped around it, the arm twisted so that the little finger and the back of the palm moved up and down on the lips. This "brush" produced the whitest teeth imaginable, giving most people a gleaming smile. There was no shame in spitting onto the sand or floor the tiny splinters as they broke off.

My attitude toward my teeth changed slightly. Still I was unaware of some of the other standards of beauty until I was in the dentist's office with my friend who was waiting to have a wisdom tooth removed. She was dressed in her wrap around melahfa, head and legs covered. I was dressed in western clothes, a fairly long skirt and blouse, with my head uncovered. I had not paid attention to the only other patients in the waiting room, two ladies sitting facing us, also covered from head to ankle. It soon became obvious that they were curious about us. How could two ladies, dressed so differently and obviously so different, possibly be so intimate in their conversation?

"Is she your mother?" One of them asked.

My friend replied, "Yes."

"She is so beautiful. Look at her teeth!"

"And look at her legs!" The other added. I pulled my longish skirt down. "They are so pretty"

"But her hair! Just look at her hair. It looks like a horse's tail!" I guess it was straight and bit straggly and fading red. Horses in this country had their tails died with henna leaving them a bright orangey color.

I tried very hard not to laugh. After all they had flattered me. Twice.

Air Mauritania

We were waiting on the tarmac seated in an Air Mauritania jet in Nouadhibou, the port city in the north of Mauritania. We had just flown down from Casablanca on our way south returning to Nouakchott. The incessant moving around of the other passengers was not like any thing we had ever experienced before. We were not bored. An exciting live movie was unfolding around us. These passengers were not returning from vacation. They were would-be merchants transporting goods from outside the country.

As soon as the plane had touched ground and before arriving to a full stop, the disembarking passengers began gathering their packages from under the seats, from over head and from the aisles, and started moving toward the door. They didn't need to unclip their seat belts because they had never fastened them. As they descended to the tarmac the passengers from the rear surged forward and claimed the empty seats. A few sat down. The others left some bags here and there on the seats and then they too descended to the tarmac with still other bundles in hand.

The plane had a bit of a grubby look. It made this flight often. All of the luggage stuffed here and there must have added to the wear and tear. There was no water in the rest rooms. A supply of water would have added more weight and the plane could not have accommodated all of the extra luggage. The announcements had been duly read over the PA system but I doubt that the flight attendant cared if her instructions were comprehensible or not. We had been served a pretty tasty lunch which had come aboard in Morocco. It was much better than the one I'd received on the flight from Nouakchott. That consisted of a drink of soda with no fizz, and a sandwich made of a slab of baguette with a folded piece of chicken skin tucked inside. But Mauritanians were great mint tea makers and my little half filled, foam covered tea was delicious.

There were no seat assignments. From past flights we knew that the non-smoking section was the whole left side of the plane, so we had carefully chosen those seats, not realizing at the time that this would give us an excellent view of what was transpiring outside. We had been so preoccupied analyzing the movements inside the plane, that we hadn't seen the crowd of greeters on the ground below our window. Little groups of friends were forming and bundles were being exchanged with laughter and hugs. It was a colorful sight, the ladies dressed in their multicolored wrap around melahfas and men in either white or blue flowing boubous.

Were friends greeting friends that they did not see very often? Yes, but these were also business transactions, Mauritania style. Friends or relatives who can afford to fly out of the country either to Morocco or the Canaries, bring back what they know is not available at home. They distribute it in a completely down to earth simple fashion to be resold. Many people make their living this way. No custom's fees, no inspection, and everyone is happy with the arrangement. I am sure that our eyes missed the essentials to the process. We didn't see money handed from one to the other, or find the answer to the important question, who needed to be paid off?

But before the plane continued its flight, two big burly men, obviously from the recently freed slave caste, boarded the plane, moved to the back and lifted to their shoulders the burlap bales that had been wedged into the two back rows. They made a total of four trips carrying them off the plane. Why these bales weren't in the cargo hold I'm not sure. Maybe it was easier to avoid passing through the airport in view of waiting custom officials. Having them already in your possession made it easier to go directly from the runway tarmac to the waiting vehicles. In due time many of the passengers boarded again to finish their flight to the capital.

I was glad that we had chosen Air Mauritania over classy Royal Air Morocco. The cost was the same. If we had flown RAM, we would have missed this live movie.

I Know You!

The World Vision Director invited us for dinner. He had a special guest visiting World Vision projects from a Lions' Club in California. Maybe his Lions' Club would help finance a project. The director thought that it would be good for us to meet him, since Bill was involved in setting up the feeding centers out in the remote settlements in the Sahara.

All of the sudden the guest interrupted the conversation. Looking straight across the table at Bill he said, "I know you." We were all startled. "Give me a run down of your life so we can see where in the past our lives crossed."

Bill started, "I grew up in Massachusetts, was in the pre-med program at the University of Massachusetts in Amherst and began to drink heavily, so I quit during my senior year and joined the army in January 1953 during the Korean War.

The mystery was not yet solved. Bill continued, after boot training in Virginia, I was sent to San Antonio, TX, to Laboratory Technician School." Everyone in the room was listening intently so as not to miss the "Eureka Moment."

The guest interrupted, "I too, was in the army in San Antonio but not on the same base. Go on."

Bill added "I attended a youth retreat sponsored by Trinity Baptist Church. It was during that retreat that I found what I had been searching for - Christ. The young people returned to the church afterwards, some to be baptized. I was asked to give my testimony and tell why I wanted to be baptized."

The guest cried out, "I was there at that retreat and I still remember what you said!" He recounted some of the details. The fact that the guest recognized Bill after all those years and then was able to remember so much was unusual. But even more surprising was that they had reconnected halfway around the world, in the Sahara Desert. How many years had transpired? About 34.

A Saharan Joke

The student was from a nomadic family. The study year was over and he was on his way home for the summer from school in the capital city. He arrived up north near Ouadan by ramshackle taxi, hired a camel, and rode to the place where his family's encampment had been when he left them. They were nowhere to be found. Off in the distance he saw a tent with a few animals tied outside. He rode over hoping they might help him.

He introduced himself and asked if they had any idea where his family might be. The reply: "They were here several weeks ago but decided to move on." The man lifted his arm and pointing his finger across the vast Sahara said, "I suggest that you go in that direction. Then on Tuesday, turn right."

'Leblouh' among the Moors

"I'm not fat," she said, as she compared herself with the people milling through the airport. "Just look at them."

But in contrast to these foreigners around us, Miriem had had no choice about being overweight. It had been forced upon her as a child because the highest castes in her White Moor culture believed that fat was beautiful. Fat girls found good husbands. Girls of her status were expected to fill two roles: make tea, and bear children. Slaves did everything else.

One of our first observations on our arrival in Mauritania was the number of very thin men and very hefty women. The women walked slowly swaying from side to side. We labeled it the 'Nouakchott Waddle.' Their melahfas covered them from head to ankle, except for the face and forearm, but this loosely fitting wrap around covering did not hide their size. Often it slipped aside showing a massive arm or a leg where a dimple replaced the anklebone. Walking long distances was impossible. We sometimes found ourselves stopping to stare as one climbed awkwardly into a taxi, leaving the ends of her long flowing robe outside where it flapped in the breeze.

Within a couple of years of our arrival in Nouakchott we were at the airport to pick up a friend arriving from Tidjikja. A few passengers deplaned, but there seemed to be a hold-up. A very large woman came out to the platform at the top of the stairs. She looked down, took hold of the railing, and slowly placed one foot over the top step, held it a while, then drew it back. She turned around and tried the same process backwards. That didn't work either. After some puzzling moments someone helped her sit down and she proceeded down the steps one at a time on her rear end. What a tragedy. Were these women guilty of gluttony? Absolutely not. When they were children, forced feeding of young Moor girls from the highest noble caste was still a common custom. Being overweight was a sign of wealth and status. She was admired and respected and guaranteed a good marriage. Some Moorish poets eulogized a well-rounded woman and even the complexion of a hefty young girl. If she was to be married by the ideal age of 11 to 13, extra weight made her look older. She would be married to a man of her father's generation, usually a friend of her father's.

Miriem was 13 when she attended a wedding. When she got up to dance, a friend told her to sit down. When she asked why, she was told, "Because it's your wedding!" She climbed out the window, ran away and hid in the dunes. She found out later that the groom-to-be was one of her father's friends, his same age.

When a little girl reaches the age of seven or eight her parents contact a professional skin stretcher. They sign a contract. The young girl goes to live with, and is confined to the house or tent of this lady. If the girl's family is particularly wealthy, the woman may move in with them instead. She begins by massaging and stretching the little girl's skin giving it an unnatural suppleness making it easier to hold the fat that will soon be evident. She is first fed small amounts of gruel mixed with milk at frequent intervals. This is made from ground watermelon seeds or sorghum. The amount is increased until she reaches the goal of drinking more than 10 liters of milk a day. If she resists or protests there are various techniques to force her to open her mouth.

If she is especially uncooperative, the 'stretcher' lady may ask for assistance. Together they pinch the tender skin on the insides of the little girl's thighs and pour the milk into her mouth as she cries out. If that isn't effective enough, a bamboo implement devised solely for this purpose pinches and crunches her big toe. As she cries out in pain, in goes the milk. Some girls choke to death. Those who survive may enjoy the status their weight gives them for a while, but in later life they suffer from high rates of diabetes, heart disease and of course, restricted mobility.

Fortunately the custom is dying out. The emancipation of the slaves, the decimation of the herds of cattle and camels caused by the drought has reduced the amount of milk available. Urbanization, modern life styles, and equal access to education have all contributed to the weakening of the caste system and with it many of the old customs of the Saharan Moors.

Marabout

We found him sitting on the edge of his bed. He was a handsome man, but now advanced throat cancer made him weak and pale. This was my first visit. I looked around the room and was surprised that the sheets and the floor were relatively clean. We had just walked into the National Hospital.

This elderly man was highly respected in Nouakchott and in the outlying villages in his home region. In a culture where you are identified by your tribal name and then by your caste, he enjoyed a privileged position. That may be the reason that he had a private room - a room that was actually at the end of the corridor. This gave him extra privacy as no one in the corridor had any reason to walk past the door and look in.

During his life he had enjoyed adulation because he was known as a good and compassionate man. He was also a Marabout, one of a select group of people unique to North Africa. Marabouts have supernatural powers to heal their followers. They use their magic potions and prescriptions to make your fondest wish come true. If you need a job, or a wife, or good grades, he might kill a chicken and put a bit of its blood in a little leather sack, possibly with a verse from the Koran. You then would follow his instructions either to wear the little amulet or put it under your pillow.

Up north in North Africa saints tombs, small white domed buildings dot the countryside and become points of pilgrimage. The patron saints of some of the larger cities have large edifices dedicated to them. Women especially, seek blessing at these burial sites. This elderly man was known to give wise advice in addition to his powers to heal people. He was a Marabout among Marabouts.

An intravenous drip bottle was fastened to a tree branch, which in turn was taped to the end of his metal bed. He didn't act as though he was in pain as he interacted with a raspy voice with his two believing daughters and with his present wife who were seated on the floor. Quite some time before our hospital visit, one of these daughters told us that the Lord had promised that her father would join them in their faith. She was sure her Marabout father would accept the Lord Christ as his Savior!

When he fell sick with throat cancer, and none of his Marabout friends had been able to heal him, she asked if he would like her pastor to come and pray for him. She was not surprised when he gave his consent. So Bill went to this hospital room for Bible Study and prayer several afternoons a week.

I had accompanied him today for the first time. Immediately, when I stepped into the room I had the impression that we were on holy ground. The Holy Spirit was in this place.

A day or two previously Bill had returned from his hospital study. We were sitting in our living room rejoicing over his experience when his daughter rushed in. She said, "My father has sent me to tell you that he believes everything you have said. He wants to know if there is a sign that would show that he has taken this step." Then she asked us to come again and this time, bring our video camera to film the studies. I told her that I could not film a dying man. She replied that if her father agreed, would I come.

So here we were. I had walked into the hospital hiding the video camera under my clothing. Bill began the study of the lost sheep. Every so often one of the two daughters would elaborate, or launch into a song that illustrated the verse. I was standing in the corner of the room recording selections of the proceedings. The father sitting on the edge of the bed mouthed the words adding jests to illustrate the words of the hymns. The older sister turned to her stepmother who was participating in the singing by drumming on an empty water bottle. Her face was drawn and sad. The daughter turned and asked her, "And you, do you believe?" As her stepmother replied, "Yes!" her face blossomed into smiles. They hugged and it was obvious that at that moment one more name was recorded in glory. And we have the moment on video!

As we drove home our joy was unspeakable. We again discussed the 'sign' that the father had requested. It had always been Bill's policy to teach about baptism, but to let a new convert take the initiative to ask for that step. Bill was hesitating because he felt that the ideal would be to teach him a bit on the meaning of baptism. But I stressed that he was a dying man and that we should not, we could not wait.

The next day was Friday, the Muslim holy day like our Sunday. That evening we picked up a friend and headed to the hospital. The father was lying on the floor with his head lying on his older daughter's lap.

I moved to my place in the corner of the room. Bill got down on his knees on the floor with his face within inches of the father's face. Bill spoke to him softly while the other daughter filled a pitcher with water. They placed a towel under his head. Bill poured a little water on his head cupping it in his hands, saying, "I baptize you in the name of the Father," then he poured a bit more water, "in the name of the Son, and in the Name of the Holy Spirit." Then Bill lowered his head again and said, "I want you to know that your sins are forgiven without limit." From my place behind the father's head, I heard the father repeat in a hoarse voice, "Without limit." Those were his last words on this earth. Jesus did not chose to heal his body, but two days later he passed into the arms of Jesus.

Fulfilled

"What do you want to be when you grow up?" The little girl with long red pigtails always gave the same answer. "An art teacher." Through elementary school she received A's in Art. At home she drew pictures with chalk on a stand-up blackboard, erased them off and started again. Occasionally she received some encouragement. Once her sister said, "That horse is better than the picture you copied it from."

But in junior high the art teacher was not able to inspire her students. She instructed the class to cut out construction paper and to draw pictures using a compass. Bored, this 12 year old drew portraits of her classmates. Barbara must have been pleased with her portrait because she immediately carried it to the front of the room to the teacher. The teacher's reaction was surprise, and maybe approval, but there encouragement stopped. She asked who had drawn it, but she said nothing to the young girl who herself wanted to be an art teacher. So she forgot about it all. There were no art classes in high school. Timidity, or insecurity set in, as well as other activities that filled her time.

It is difficult to understand why she did not take advantage of the opportunities available at the university. Was there a fear that she would not be able to meet the expectations of her professor or even satisfy the perfection she imposed on herself?

Now she was living in the Sahara. One day she met an American lady who was also living in this out of the way place. While explaining why she and her husband were living in this city, humorously nicknamed TimbukONE, because it was 900 miles west of Timbuktu, she said that her husband was working on an engineering contract and that she was an artist and was going to start art classes. The red head's reaction was instantaneous, "I'm your first student."

Class was two hours a week, simple drawings at first, lessons in composition, shading and so on, then water color, pastels. The French Cultural Center was looking for activities to present to the international population. Well-attended art shows were some of these activities and she and some of her classmates were asked to show their paintings.

Appreciation and admiration ran high. At the age of 57, her hair no longer bright red, she sold her first painting. Within a few years she had four different prints for sale as well as several art shows to prepare in the ensuing years. Appreciation again spread through the attendees, and over the following years she sold around 50 original paintings in addition to hundreds of prints.

Age and Nobility

The original painting of the bottom left image on the following page is drawn with artist's lead pencil. The portrait is of an elderly Mauritanian man who in his youth was a camel caravan driver between Timbuktu in Mali and Oualata in Mauritania, in the heart of the Sahara Desert. Later he ran a little food shop in Oualata. One day as this portrait was in process, a Mauritanian friend came into our house and immediately started to exclaim in an excited voice, "I know that man!" She continued, "When I was a child growing up in Oualata, I bought sugar and tea from his shop." She later added more memories of links between his family and her own. Her own mother had died after the birth of her younger sister. This shopkeeper's wife had taken the baby and nursed her. She added that even though her sister is not related by blood, so not a blood sister to his children, she is considered a milk-sister and could never marry any of his sons.

Cancer Alert

And we thought that the Sahara Desert was hot. But here we were in Houston, Texas for the first time. As soon as we stepped out of the airport, we were hit with an oppressive humid heat. Our friend had arranged a car and an apartment for the three of us at no cost. The church that owned the apartment also had members who were doctors in the surrounding hospitals, and Aisha needed to see a cancer specialist.

Back in Nouakchott she had discovered a lump growing in her neck attached to her thyroid. She saw a doctor in Mauritania. He advised her to fly to Morocco. That doctor advised her to wait and see if it would go away. Many of us didn't feel that was very sound advice. A few weeks later she discovered other lumps. Knowing that adequate care was not available a friend suggested that we accompany her to the U.S. for a proper diagnosis.

For us this meant making a myriad of arrangements. Where would we stay? What doctor could we see? Who could help us finance a trip like that? We would need help for the plane tickets and for the medical expenses. Vouching for her at the American Embassy was easy. We were known there. Armed with her medical records and a promise that she would return, the visa was granted. We wrote to our own personal friends in the US, explaining her need and describing our unfolding plan. Messages came back that many would like to help with the finances. Everything fell into place very quickly.

We were taken directly to an air-conditioned apartment that was stocked with food. Two days later Aisha saw a preliminary doctor who took care of referrals and appointments. At the hospital we were taken directly to the surgeon. I translated her answers to his many questions. The doctor found her fascinating. I was delighting in translating her stories and proverbs. The examining surgeon then told us to go over to the main hospital to see the anesthesiologist. We learned that the surgery would take place the next morning! As we were driving back to the apartment in the evening, I suddenly realized that there had been absolutely no mention of payment.

The next morning the staff prepared her for surgery. As we were getting ready to pray together around her bed, a nurse walked in. "The hospital still needs her signature in two more places," she said, as she handed me a paper and I prepared to translate so Aisha would know what she was signing. When I read the paper I told the nurse that I couldn't translate phrases like that just a few minutes before surgery.

Aisha said, "Peggy, read it to me. My life is in God's hands and this paper can't change that." I translated into English for the nurse. Her face lit up and she said, "You are so right, honey. Those doctas upstairs think that they hold your life in their hands, but we know that only God does." So I translated the

151

statements on the pink paper that read something like this, "I realize that my vocal chords could be cut during this surgery." "I realize that I could die during this surgery."

I handed the nurse the signed paper and said that we were just getting ready to pray. She joined us as we held hands around that hospital bed and prayed together. Aisha was wheeled upstairs. The doctors had requested that I follow her to translate. After a few minutes an Asian nurse came around the curtain. She looked at the chart attached to the foot of the bed and saw Aisha's name. She then proceeded to speak in Arabic. She was from the Philippines and had worked in Saudi Arabia before coming to the U.S. This nurse would be with her in surgery!

Aisha didn't die. And she didn't have her vocal chords cut. The pathology reports for all of the lumps and the neck tumor came back negative. She could not return home, however, until she had time to heal. It seemed to us that the surgeon seemed to prolong the check-up visits because he liked talking to her. She continually seemed to find a story or a proverb that added spice to the conversation.

As they talked I translated. To illustrate how close humans really are despite their differing backgrounds and cultures, she told him a desert story. "A man was riding his camel in the wide open Sahara when he saw a black speck on the horizon. He was very afraid. Who could it be? An enemy? What should he do? As they got closer, he saw that the speck had become his own countryman. Squinting to be sure, he then thought he could be from his own tribe! As they got closer and closer his overwhelming fear turned to amazement. That dreaded speck seemed familiar. It was his own brother!" She considered her American doctor a brother. He thought of her as a sister despite their different cultures. As she completed this Saharan story, the editor of the hospital newspaper came in to interview her for the next issue.

We never received a bill from the hospital, or the surgeon, or the anesthetist. Our own friends' gifts covered all of her expenses including a very expensive plane ticket. The Lord had met our needs and answered our prayers beyond what we could have asked or even dreamed of.

Niki

She was a German Shepherd mix with a coat soft as satin. She didn't slobber; she didn't lick your face; she didn't scratch the screens to go out. Instead she laid her nose on our knees and waited. Sadness enveloped her when she saw a suitcase. She lay nearby, head between her paws, rolling her eyes, watching our every move.

An invisible aura made her a great guard dog. When we walked outside our yard other dogs and people passed to the other side. But she only paid attention to those who bothered her, or me. Her gentle personality changed if someone opened the gate without ringing. Visitors tried that only once. This was our house and you needed permission. During the years she was with us we never had a robbery.

Niki

As the university students and curiosity seekers came to my English language bookstore she hovered between us. I could tell when she was not happy about a would-be customer. She sensed what I sometimes did not.

She loved the dunes and the beach. She was a master wave dodger even while chasing the swooping sea birds.

We took our guests for early morning breakfasts on the dunes. With the baskets of hot coffee, croissants and brioches, we drove out of town to the largest dune, hiked to the top, ate our breakfast and watched the sun rise. But before the cool of the night air disappeared completely, turning the Sahara into an oven, we dropped down to the desert floor. The wind constantly moves the sand exposing prehistoric tools, beads and flint arrowheads. Niki assumed she was responsible for our safety. As Bill and I meandered off in different directions, she raced up and down trying to keep tabs on both of us.

Her death from liver disease was a terrible shock. Within a few months we suffered the biggest robbery of those 14 years. The culprit who took our valuables was familiar with our house. He also knew that Niki no longer lived there.

Shakespeare and Company

The summer after my first year of teaching I approached the Director of the Teacher Training College to ask if she agreed to my idea of importing English dictionaries to sell to the students at cost. I was not prepared for her reaction. She did not give her approval. I later heard that she was afraid I might be duped into losing money because the students might not be able to pay.

During the next two years I gained a greater idea of how extensive the students' needs were. A much more elaborate idea was forming in my mind. I wanted to start a full-fledged bookstore. Before finishing their fourth year, each student was required to write a 60 page thesis in English. This did not pose a problem for the fourth year teacher trainees because they had chosen their subjects during their third year in Scotland, and many of them had completed their research before returning. But the university students did not have this resource advantage.

So I wrote a formal proposal and took it to the Department of Higher Education located in the Education Ministry. The Director was a friend. He gave his verbal approval but would not put anything in writing. So I assumed I was launched. There was too much to learn. Friends offered to help. The American Embassy heard what I was attempting to do and asked if they could help me. They offered me money! I asked if it were a gift or a loan? I turned them down. Then they offered to have GSO, their service for embassy personnel, take the books through customs for me. I was very grateful. A friend in England offered to pay the bills from my new bank account there.

The first year was agony. Every time the mail including an invoice arrived, I panicked. My friend in England paid the bills as he received them, but sometimes the books didn't come. Once he paid for 50 math books instead of 50 English dictionaries. GSO was lax in telling me when the books arrived. I was very frustrated with their quality of "help." One day I went to the airport myself to investigate and found five "lost" orders sitting in the dust. Air Freight wanted to charge me to release them, adding storage fees. I explained that if I had to pay those charges they could just send them back because I would never be able to resell them. I also explained that this was a service for students where I resold at cost. There was no profit involved for me. They picked up the cartons and helped me load up the car.

I then decided that I had to centralize by paying the bills myself and picking up the books myself. I eventually began using the much faster, less complicated post office in place of airfreight. I set up credit accounts with the publishers. I could pay from Nouakchott after the books arrived. We also bought a fax machine so that information could flow more quickly. The Mauritanian government waived the importation tax on my orders. The pressure of constantly reviewing and correcting mistakes was past and the bookstore expanded. Students poured into our garage, not only to buy, but also to study from the lending library. I had collected an array of books from second hand stores in the US sometimes for as little as .20 each. These included reference, literature, criticism, history and any book that I felt would be helpful.

I presumptuously named this unique English language bookstore, "Shakespeare and Company," after the famous bookstore in Paris where the literary geniuses of the 1920's congregated. Before we retired I sold off my book stock to a new language center. "Shakespeare and Company" had been open for 10 years and closed with my ledger in the black. Bill reminds me that I did not, however, receive a salary, nor did the accounts show any payment for rent or electricity.

This bookstore served another purpose. People in the street wondered why we had so many people coming to our door. When our neighbors were curious, I showed them the bookstore. But in truth the majority of our visitors were not students. They came to the house for a time of prayer or study.

Trouble

Mamadou passed himself off as a jack-of-all-trades. World Vision had hired him to solve problems. In reality you could say that he himself caused problems. He was hired to supervise any repairs needed in World Vision's employees' homes. He was to hire a reliable plumber or electrician to do the actual work. Why, when he came to our house he decided to do the work himself, we don't know. I showed him the leaky toilet and then turned into my office just next to the toilet to prepare the next day's classes.

I jumped when I heard a swooshing sound. No explanation needed. I ran out of my office, through the water fountain shooting about shoulder height down the hall, out through the yard, opened the door to the garage book store, slid all of the books off a small two shelved bookcase, lifted the shelves to the floor, tore off the cloth which hid a large box covering protecting our water pump, lifted the wooden box which was larger than my extended arms, crawled behind the tank, reached the wall, and turned off the main water faucet.

When I got back into the house Mamadou was still on his knees hugging the toilet with his hand covering the disassembled water pipe. He was muttering 'Alhamdulillah, alhamdulillah' (Praise God, Praise God!).

I looked at the water rippling on my office floor where I had the prints of my paintings stacked, into Bill's office, and into the bedroom and finally almost to the living room from the spouting fountain.

"Mamadou, why in the world are you mumbling 'Alhamdulillah?' "

"I didn't get any in my mouth!" he replied.

I had forgotten that it was Ramadan, the Muslim month of fasting.

Post Script: It was several months later that a bank in town telephoned the World Vision office saying that an employee was there in the bank trying to cash a check for several thousand dollars. It turned out to be Mamadou. He had stolen someone's WV checkbook, and filled out the sum he wanted. He promptly lost his job and probably endured a punishment of higher order.

The "Boys"

Kacem opened our front gate. We had been away for a few weeks in the summer and left our house in Kacem's reliable hands. He was from Guinea, (Conakry) and had come to Mauritania because he had heard that jobs were available in Nouakchott. A job as a "boy" or household help (a term I didn't like to use) would enable him to bring his family out of their dire poverty. They were still back home where he had been a subsistence farmer.

It was we who benefitted most from his presence in our house. He was honest, a hard worker, and a pleasure to have around. But most of all he was discreet. I remember the first day he appeared at our door. He was looking for a job and we were looking for help. He didn't ask many questions but waited for me to speak. I asked him his name. I found out later that it was ElGassimou, but I hadn't heard him correctly and we started to call him Kacem. He did not correct me. I told him that I was looking for someone to work in the house and yard, a person who was willing to do anything. He responded, "I will do anything, if you show me how." My immediate response, "Could you start tomorrow?"

During our fourteen years in Mauritania, none of our previous employees could begin to measure up to Kacem. Our first "boy" was an older man who came three days a week but really wanted to be a chauffeur. He stayed with us about nine months. He recommended a younger fellow, also from Guinea. I didn't suspect him when I began finding items missing from the house. We didn't even suspect him when we suffered a big break-in through a window with a protective grill. We lost a camera, television, money and many other precious things. How an ordinary robber could have found that money was a mystery.

But the day I found both our car and Mohammed missing, I finally realized how duped we had been. Bill, who was away on one of his desert adventures, had left his keys hanging in the hall. They were missing. Mohammed was smart. He knew he could pay off a border guard and could take the car into Senegal even without car papers. Many hours later friends found our Honda stalled in a crowded part of the city. For some unknown reason, except the hand of God, the ignition fuse had died. The next morning he apologized profusely. We accepted his apology and did not fire him. And then one day a year later he didn't come to work. We assumed he was sick. We waited three days. Bill went to look for him only to find out that he had gone back to Senegal. This time all of our foreign currency was missing. But we still had our car.

I was trying to cook, clean away the sand every day and teach. It was just too much. So when a French friend brought her "boy" with glowing recommendations, I hired him. What I first noticed was that the kitchen was acquiring a sticky grubby look. Then I caught him out shopping buying double of everything I ordered. One of each item never appeared on our shelf. Sometimes food that I had seen him cooking didn't arrive on the table. He developed another mysterious habit. He would come to work very early and work in the yard while we were still asleep. That was highly unusual.

We rarely used our back kitchen door. One day I unfastened the double lock and pushed it open. There on the stubby branches of the trimmed trees were bottles and jars stored upside down. This man was not only stealing food from us, but he also was too lazy to take the containers to the big dumpster down the street.

The next morning I had to tell him that he didn't have to come back any more. I had to pick up the household chores again. One day as I was hanging up the clothes around the side of the house, I noticed mysterious mounds in the sand. I raked a little and right under the surface I pulled out plastic bottles, milk cartons, rags and paper. Alioune had been diligently burying our garbage right in the yard. So that was what he was doing early in the morning!

Kacem

Then I noticed mounds of sand outside our gate along the street. I began raking. I pulled out more trash. At that moment Alioune just happened to walk by. He stopped to tell me that raking was too hard for me and I should let him take over. Imagine the audacity!

Then Kacem came seeking a job. He stayed with us for 10 years until we moved to Tunis. On each of our visits back we have spent time with him, trying to express our gratitude for his years of service and to learn his latest family news. Last we heard he had seven children. How we loved that little wizened and very wise man.

Job Hunting

Abdellahi was a tall, gentle, greying gentleman from Guinea. He was a Pulaar, the majority people group in West Africa. When I started teaching I was overwhelmed with preparations, cooking, cleaning, washing laundry in the bathtub. We hired him to help me cope with the household chores. He came three mornings a week and did the cleaning, washing, and enough cooking for two days. This was not a full time job and I am sure that he was constantly looking for another job.

One day he asked, "Do you know someone who needs 'un sauveur personnel?'

I did a double take. Of course everyone needs a personal savior, but I doubted very strongly that this Muslim was asking me that. What could he mean? I thought back at other times when I had to figure a bit about what he meant in French. Then I remembered that the Pulaar language does not have a "sh" or an "f" sound. He was asking if I knew someone who was looking to hire 'un chauffeur personnel' or a personal chauffeur!

The Missing Door

"Would you consider coming back to teach at the university?" I had been sick for quite a time and was now feeling my strength again. "You can chose any course at any level you want or as many courses as you want." I told him that I was open to the idea, but on one condition. I wanted a door to my classroom. That's right, a door to close out the movement and distractions from outside. What had happened to all of those missing doors? He assured me that he would personally see to it.

When classes started in the fall, I arrived early as usual. I was shocked. There was no door. I did not hesitate. I laid down my books, asked two students who were already waiting, to come with me. We went down the row of classrooms to find one with a door. I showed the young men how to jimmy the door off the hinges. They carried it back and I helped them reverse the process.

There was only a hole where the handle should have been so it would be impossible to keep it closed completely. A couple of rocks would do the trick. That door kept out the noise from outside and of course it diminished the effect of the swirling sand storms.

I kept my door all year. No one ever stole it back.

Jesus Heals

We had been away from Nouakchott for some weeks. Kacem and Niki were waiting for us as happy as we were, to be home again. We told Kacem to go home because he had been carrying a heavy responsibility watching the house while we were away. Before he left he began telling us that his son, who was probably nine years old, had been sick for a long time. They didn't know what was wrong or how to care for him. We told him to go home and take some days off until his son improved.

And then we thought better of that advice. We sat down in the living room to pray together. Bill and I prayed for many things - that the Lord would preserve the little boy's life, that he would get the right care, that the Lord would have compassion on his parents, but most of all that God would show his glory in healing him. We then got in the car together to take Kacem home.

We walked through the wooden door from the sandy street into an open courtyard. There were lots of people milling around. Each room around the open space was occupied by a different family, probably all from Guinea. We stepped into a room on the left where Kacem and his family lived. There was one light bulb hanging from the ceiling. Bedding was folded up on the floor in the corner. Their son was lying on the only bed. He didn't open his eyes. We greeted Kacem's wife, but she only spoke Poulaar. There was no place to sit so we stood while he translated his wife's words expressing her helplessness over her son's illness.

I turned around again to look at the listless child, and then I said to Kacem, "What's happening?" He leaned over him and replied, "I don't know." Big bubbles like blisters were forming on his face. As I watched them grow larger, I said, "I know what's happening. His fever is breaking. The Lord has answered our prayers. Perhaps this healing began at the very time we had prayed back in our living room." His illness remains a mystery but his parents and siblings were very grateful. Soon he was himself again.

Parking Camels

For several years Bill spent half of each month in villages in the Sahara. One of World Vision's projects was running feeding centers for malnourished children. Later they added vaccination campaigns with the idea of immunizing every single child in each of the areas where World Vision had projects. They ran a campaign on preventive medicine and hygiene with videos on national television, small business loans, and relief to Touareg refugees from Mali.

Bill's ongoing projects were spread in different northern centers, some with no roads, no clean water supply, and no source of income. At one point he was organizing 14 feeding centers with the help of a support staffer and in cooperation with men from each town who were to run the program when he couldn't be present. Each trip required days of preparation, loading the Land Rover with supplies for a period away of approximately 15 days each month. They weighed the babies and small children. Their height/weight ratio and age determined which ones needed to enter the intensive feeding program where mothers stayed in the center feeding their children porridge every two hours.

When they returned to the capital they left behind enough gruel ingredients to last till their next visit when they would again chart the children's growth, hoping they would gain enough weight to move out of the danger zone so other children could be cycled in.

He also traveled out of the country to various meetings and conferences. I usually drove to our little airport just six kilometers out of town to pick him up. Once his return from Casablanca was reported 'late'. No prediction of how late. So instead of driving back home, I decided to play it safe and just stay, and wait, and see.

Since there was no place to sit in the little cement block airport, I returned to the parking lot to sit in the car. Even though there were remnants of white lines on the broken macadam, the cars were parked in every direction imaginable. I found a place where I could park correctly and pulled in between the mostly erased white lines. It was evening so it wasn't unbearably hot but I still left the car doors open. A man asked me if I would move my car so he could drive his out.

As I pulled back in, I noticed a handsome young man in a sparkling white flowing draa standing nearby. He came over to talk.

"I hope you're not angry because you had to move your car for him."

"Not at all," I replied.

He continued, "What you foreigners need to realize is we park our cars the way we park our camels."

I laughed and he sat down on a little curb. He obviously wanted to talk to me almost as much as I wanted to talk to him. He began to tell me more about Mauritania and about himself. He made me laugh quite a bit and maybe I did him as well, because I was enjoying myself immensely. He had been raised in the desert in traditional circumstances. He and his father tended the camels as they moved from grazing area to grazing area. His mother never left the confines of their tent except when the family migrated. She stayed within the tent area and would send a child to borrow a match or sugar from another tent.

One day he and his father were out on some isolated dunes with their animals far from their tent when a small airplane landed. They had never seen anything like that before! They watched as the pilot climbed out. To their astonishment they saw that the pilot was a woman - wearing jeans!

"Do you know what my father said?" he asked me. I waited. "I wish my wife were like that!"

We laughed again for the umpteenth time. I was sorry when the plane landed and that delightful hour was over. And yet I have often wondered since if he hadn't been pulling my leg.

What Goes Around Comes Around

We woke up on April 24, 1989 to what seemed like a calm day. Bill had a touch of bronchitis and had decided to stay home. As I returned home about noon I noticed a cloud of black smoke across town. After lunch we saw more pillars of smoke rising above the city. A short time later the American Embassy called and told us that they were concerned about disorder in the streets. They were putting us on modified alert and asked that we stay inside.

All day Monday, Monday night, and all day Tuesday mobs roamed the streets searching for any black man, woman or even a child that they thought might be of Senegalese origin. It didn't matter if they held proof of Mauritanian citizenship or not. If in protest, they tried to prove their citizenship, their papers were torn up in their faces and they were told, "Now try to prove it!" One man told us that he had a Mauritanian passport. "In every country in the world I am considered a Mauritanian, except in my own." All suspected Senegalese were to be caught and punished if not killed.

At one point I climbed up on a chair to look over our garden wall and I saw a white Moor teenager leading a group of black Arabic speakers screaming for joy as they ran down our street carrying our Senegalese neighbor's sewing machine. We learned later that our neighborhood dressmaker had been killed right there in his shop. People ran for their lives to the Great Mosque, the Catholic Church, clinics run by Catholic sisters, and even to embassy compounds. The Senegalese Embassy, duped because of promises of protection, gave what they thought was an official of the government, a list of addresses of all registered Senegalese "so that they could be protected." Their houses were raided and some occupants were slaughtered.

It wasn't until Tuesday evening that the Minister of Interior spoke on national TV issuing a warning that the pillaging had to stop. The government was imposing a curfew from 8:00 pm till 6:00 am. Calm seemed to return at least for those of us who had white skin, but the misery and fear that had started for the thousands of Senegalese or any Poulaar or Wolof speaker two days earlier would continue for days as they sat in the hot sun in the mosques or at the fairgrounds without food or water. But that wasn't all. At night the soldiers arrived to confiscate their money and jewelry, radios and watches. It became clear that they would only be permitted to leave with the clothes on their backs, so they began burying their valuables in the recently dug toilets. Then soldiers tried to sell them water.

When the NGO relief organizations offered to help feed these people, the government replied that they would cope with the situation. By Wednesday evening, when the size of the catastrophe became known, with ten thousand sequestered in the yard of the mosque and seven thousand at the fair grounds, the NGO's began to organize. A central office was set up. Volunteers were given responsibilities. We were impressed with the efficiency of these experienced aid workers. Planes began arriving with tents, extra food basics, and blankets. Doctors from Médecins Sans Frontières arrived, along with Pharmaciens Sans Frontières. Every room at the hospital was full. Bodies were lying shoulder to shoulder down the corridors. Most of them were fishermen with head wounds. At the beach there was no protection. The only ones who escaped were those who were able to get into their boats and get out to sea. A Spanish nurse told us that there so many wounded there was no place to step, let alone provide care.

Peace Corps young people who had already been trained in toilet building had set about digging latrines as fast as possible to avoid a cholera epidemic. Bill and I filled in where we could, working in the central office unless we were called on to distribute these necessities of life as they arrived.

Planes arrived from Europe and other countries in Africa, airlifting the Senegalese to Senegal, returning with loads of Mauritanians forced to leave their goods behind in Senegal. One of my most vivid memories was watching the police and army lining up the thousands at the fair grounds and loading them into buses for the trip to the airport. They were forcing the ladies to take off any garment that they thought was extra. I saw a soldier hit a young woman with his stick merely because she had stepped out of the line. Had we been living alongside barbarians? And had I been teaching barbarians? Then we began hearing many stories of Mauritanians who had saved the lives of their Wolof speaking neighbors.

At the same time that Senegalese were being flown back to Senegal, Mauritanians who had been living in Senegal were being deported back to Mauritania. It is estimated that around 200,000 Mauritanians were evacuated from Senegal to their "home" country, a country that many of them had never seen and whose language they didn't speak. They were absorbed into hastily established centers around the country. Most of the Mauritanians had been shopkeepers. Most of the Senegalese were plumbers, builders, electricians, fishermen and dressmakers.

One of Mauritania's main sources of income was from fishing. The artisan fishing industry was decimated. It is estimated that 300 were killed in those two days. I don't know the number of wounded or how many died from their wounds or from lack of care after that. Children were separated from their parents.

Husbands and wives were split apart. I don't know the number of Mauritanians killed in Senegal but we heard horrific stories. Some of my university students never returned to class. When the airlift ended, the Peace Corps volunteers returned to clean out and fill up the latrines. There was nothing left. The rumor had spread that they were full of valuables, hidden there in desperation. Men and boys had climbed the walls under cover of night and cleaned them out.

Where had all of this hatred come from? Is the answer as simple as racism? Was there more behind this horror than meets the eye? Where had this resentment been hiding all of these years?

There was growing resentment, and a desire in both countries that the other country's nationals return home. Add in the eternal conflict between herdsmen and sedentary farmers. There were specific events that ignited this violence. Only the Senegal River separates Mauritania from its southern neighbor, Senegal. At certain times of the year this river is easily fordable. Mauritanian camel herders let their animals cross the river and graze in Senegalese farmers' fields.

When the farmers determined that the animals had eaten more than their own value, they killed them. Some Mauritanian border guards then killed two of the farmers. When this news reached Dakar, the latent envy and hatred for the estimated 500,000 Mauritanians residing in Senegal - most of them shopkeepers - erupted in pillaging their shops.

The owners themselves were not attacked, but when news of these events, possibly exaggerated in the press, reached Nouakchott from Dakar, the populations reacted in retaliation. The results were far greater than just tit for tat. They erupted into uncontrolled murderous racist rage and then to reciprocated revenge.

As the mobs ruled the streets of Nouakchott I thought of the verses, "'Do not take revenge, it is mine to avenge,' says the Lord. I will repay." In other words, you leave your hurt and anger and hatred with me. Paul continues after citing this quote from the Old Testament, "Do not be overcome by evil, but overcome evil with good. If your enemy is hungry, feed him. If he is thirsty, give him something to drink."

How true it is that love breeds love and hatred breeds hatred. What goes around comes around.

Calm eventually returned, but the resulting suffering remained for years. White Arabic speaking shopkeepers, returning from Senegal, for whom certain trades were considered beneath their social status, had to learn to become electricians and plumbers. We witnessed first hand the pain and shame of men trying to make their living by fishing. But more importantly, the violence left permanent scars on the lives of the perpetrators of murder and maiming. And I missed several of our students who never returned to class.

CHAPTER FIVE -
RETURN TO TUNIS - TWICE
1997 - 2000 AND 2004 - 2006

Roman Baths in Carthage, Tunisia

Prayer Opens Hearts

In 1997 we retired from Mauritania and moved to Tunisia. It was in Tunis where we had first stepped onto African soil to begin language study. Thirty-six years of change. The prosperity, the stability, the educational level of the citizens set Tunisia apart from most other countries in Africa.

But we heard almost no mention of a Tunisian Church. We wondered why there was so little prayer for Tunisian Christians. We heard no discussion of church planting strategy. Back in 1962, we had attended two baptisms. Where were these believers? After over 100 years of Christian witnessing, there was no coherent worshiping group in Arabic in the capital city!

Some believers were meeting together up on the northern coast. But what had happened in Tunis? Was fear of persecution too great? Did disagreement divide and then bring discouragement? Had modern life become so comfortable that it interfered with any need of Christ? Was there a lack of trust in the sincerity of their fellows? Finally we met a few who had converted years earlier.

We filed requests for residence cards as retirees. Bill told the police that we had been working in the Sahara and didn't want to return to the U.S. yet, but wanted to live in an easier environment. He added that I was an artist and wanted to continue painting. After those cards were granted, a friend who worked at the French Embassy told us that the police were refusing residence cards to French retirees even though they had lived in Tunisia for many years. We were the first and only Americans granted residence cards as retirees up to that time. She asked us if we realized how wonderfully the Lord had intervened on our behalf?

A few months later a young British couple told us they had decided that they had put enough effort into church planting. They were too discouraged. The Lord had shown them that it was time to stop all effort and concentrate only on prayer. They told us excitedly of their vision. We should all concentrate on prayer for a year. They named their strategy "Awake Tunisia '99." They wanted to recruit 1,000 churches from around the world that would choose one month to pray for Tunisia. Prayer teams would visit and crisscross the country to pray that God would change lives. No one knows how many of these teams came.

A young Swedish lady told us when she and her visiting team walked down the streets of one of the holiest cities of Islam, she was crippled with fear. At their lunch break in a friend's home, they unexpectedly met another prayer team from another country. After a time of prayer together, they returned to the streets of this holy city. All fear was gone. They felt like dancing as they prayed in faith believing that God was hearing their prayers. We saw the results. It was an exciting time for us to be there watching the changes and seeing God move. There was a new openness. Religious discussions opened up naturally.

Bill had already volunteered as a tourist guide at the Catholic Cathedral on the main street. Young Tunisians streamed in during their free time, armed with curiosity and interesting questions. Looking at a larger than life wooden crucifix they would ask who is that man? Why is he there? One elderly Tunisian came in wanting to be baptized. Stories emerged of coincidences, of lives changed in God's timing. Two Christians were walking through a park praying for the city and came upon a young man sitting under a tree reading a Bible! We stayed just three years. When we left the country in Oct 2000 to settle in North Carolina, there were six small groups worshiping in Arabic in Tunis, the capital, all because of that call to pray.

Amar

We were in a grocery store when I heard a voice call out, "Mrs. Call!" I turned around to see a tall young man who several years previously had been on the teaching staff with me at the University of Nouakchott. "What are you doing here?" "Does Amar know that you are here? He added, "I'll call him when I get home." The city of Tunis had a population of 750,000. We had run into a "needle in a haystack."

The University of Nouakchott had a policy of permitting any professor of any department to sit in on the classes in any other department. I had a few Algerian and Moroccan students and some Tunisian professors, usually from the Arabic or History departments attending my classes in the English Department. The professors were older than the Mauritanian undergraduates. Some already had their doctors' degrees but still wanted to improve their English. As fellow teachers it was natural to invite them to our home for a meal.

These teachers were part of Tunisia's foreign aid strategy to help get a sister Arab nation's young university off the ground. Usually they taught for two years in Nouakchott before returning to their posts at the many different universities in Tunisia. I remembered Amar especially because when he finished his tenure in Mauritania, he wrote a letter thanking me for having "changed his life." What was he referring to? Was it his improvement in English that was helping him as a professor? I was not at all sure what I had said or done that merited that kind of a compliment and there was no further clue in the letter.

Amar invited us to his home where we met his wife and two sons. He had not been married when I'd seen him last. His wife was a mathematics teacher and he had resumed teaching as an Arabic professor at his university. As we sat down to eat, he said, "When I ate at your house, in Nouakchott you prayed before the meal. Would you pray here too?" We were surprised. After the meal he wanted us to see his research material for his doctoral dissertation on pre-Islamic poetry. He seemed anxious to explain that Muslims use the "unmatched beauty" of the Arabic language of the Koran as one of the proofs that it came directly from God. They say that only God could have created such depth of harmony and rhythm. God had dictated that beautiful Koranic language and Mohammed had written down his exact words.

Much to our astonishment Amar then said he had discovered that claim baseless. In his intensive study of pre-Islamic poetry he found the Arabic already spoken in the Arabian Peninsula more beautiful then the language of the Koran. He showed us his filing system, discussed some of his outline, and then he turned around and took a book off his shelf. "This is the Bible that you gave me many years ago." I had no recollection of having given him a Bible.

It became increasingly clear that he was telling us that he was abandoning Islam. We wish today that we had asked him more questions to jog our memories about those conversations of the past and to respond to any questions he still had. At that time there was no church of Tunisian believers in Tunis for him to meet. We have only seen him twice since. We can only pray that God is continuing to speak to him bringing understanding of the love of Christ into his life and to his family.

We only stayed in Tunis a brief three years. When we returned to the U.S. in October 2000, we settled in North Carolina.

To Tunis Again

What a great idea. Our ex-landlord, in a letter from Tunis to us here in North Carolina was suggesting that if we were missing our friends there, why didn't we just come back! Someone else said that if we weren't doing much in NORTH Carolina why didn't we come back to NORTH Africa. We had been living in Durham for four years. So in October 2004, we rented out our furnished Durham house and flew back to try to get our feet on the ground again. Our landlord also said that our old apartment was already rented to a student.

Some close friends took us in while we searched for housing. One of the first visits we made was to our old proprietor, to see if he knew of any apartments for rent in the area. His answer: "Upstairs! I saved it for you."

Another friend was packing up to retire to France and gave us several pieces of furniture. Then we heard that our little red Opel car was up for sale. So we lived in the same apartment and drove the same car as we had four years previously. But by far the most exciting part of this return was seeing the growth of the national church under the direction of Tunisian leadership.

We were again asked to host Thanksgiving for the same group of young people. The difference was that they were married and had children. Bill and I knew that might be our last big, open invitation for Thanksgiving in Tunisia. Some day these guests would become our hosts and hostesses. Today a few of those kiddos are now near their teens with their younger siblings not far behind, a second-generation Tunisian Church.

A Kitchen Gaff

Whole turkeys were expensive in Tunis so Bill and I came up with a solution. It would give us just as much meat, and if I could pull it off would look almost as good as a whole roasted bird as we carried it to the table for that dramatic moment before carving. My father had always squeezed every moment of drama he could, swinging his arms as he ceremoniously sharpened his carving knife at the table and then sliced the meat as thinly as he could without the slices breaking.

The French say that the presentation is as important as the taste, and I love the dramatic moment when everyone is seated around the table, vegetables, salads, dressing and rolls in their places, when it's the bird's time to make its grand entry.

I gave Bill instructions to buy three large deboned turkey breasts and two large drumsticks and attached thighs from our butcher down the street. I laid the smallest breast down, sewed the two other breasts to each side, sewing them together at the front and top, then placed fistfuls of spiced dressing inside. Next came the two thighs with the attached drumsticks. I chuckled as I sewed them on, buttered, seasoned my version of a turkey and put it in the oven.

The moment of reckoning came. Our enthusiastic guests arrived, chatting and laughing, happy to see each other. I called them to the table. We said the blessing, thanking the Lord for this abundance. I returned to the kitchen for the turkey that I had worked over so carefully. It was beautifully brown. Just perfect. I laid it on the table to be carved. I don't recall that anyone cheered. This was an international crowd, experiencing my version of Thanksgiving dinner, some for the first time. Eyes were focused on this most important part of the meal. At first there were only a few chuckles. Then laughter broke out.

The butcher had sold Bill two left legs.

One was pointing down toward the missing tail and one awkwardly pointing upward. What would a Frenchman have thought of that presentation?

The Best Part

The most wonderful experience of this part of our adventure was seeing how the church had strengthened during those four years. Numbers had grown. Individuals had matured. The recent growth began and grew because of that vision for concentrated prayer, AWAKE TUNISIA '99. Many were still planting the seed but God was producing the fruit. "This is what the kingdom of God is like. A man sows seed on the ground. Night and day, whether he sleeps or gets up, the seed spouts and grows, though he does not know how. All by itself the soil produces grain…." Mark 4:23. Good soil of the heart prepared by prayer receives the mysterious power of the seed, the seed of the Word of God resulting in new faith, growth and then maturity.

In 2014 a selected group of 200 Tunisians from many walks of life and representing each political spectrum, had reflected and debated, and made concessions over a two-year period before they voted in the most remarkable Constitution in the Arab World. It assures equal rights for women before the law, freedom of belief and conscience. You can be a Tunisian and a Muslim, or an Atheist, or a Buddhist or a Christian - legally. The word 'apostate' is outlawed! But persecution from family pressure continues against young converts who may be ostracized or thrown out of their homes. Many around the world still pray for the country of Tunisia every day.

CHAPTER SIX - IT HAPPENED HERE AND THERE

Reverse Culture Shock

When we arrived back in the US after spending more than half our lives overseas we did not anticipate a severe readjustment curve. We had been born here in the U.S., had attended American schools. Bill had served in the American military and had pastored American churches. We spoke American and wore American-bought eyeglasses, and we walked like Americans. We had returned to the U.S. periodically down through the years, and we thought that we belonged to the "American Club," in our logical thinking patterns, if not so much in our opinions or in our view of the world.

So, we were caught off guard when it came to living here and adjusting to the myriad of changes that we had to face. First of all there were the way-of-living adjustments. We bought a house in Durham, North Carolina. Our understanding real-estate agent caught wind of how lost we were feeling. She gave extra advice and made some decisions for us. It was the first time that we had a cordless phone, automatic washer, clothes dryer, microwave, toaster oven, dishwasher, an automatic remote-controlled garage door, smoke detectors, garbage disposal, gas fireplace, wall-to-wall carpets. We didn't know how to get the electricity and gas turned on or how to answer the questions asked us when we tried to get a telephone number. I would rather have done it in French in an African land of few options where life was simple: Take it or leave it, then wait for it.

In fact just getting a phone line in one country where we lived turned out to be fun. I had been to their office several times with no results. This particular day the employee said, "Oui, Madame. We have your phone ready to go. See that box on the counter over there. That is for you."

So I waited and watched. An Egyptian came in. He passed some money to one of the technicians and my phone slid off the counter into a truck destined to his home. I didn't say a word. Instead I decided to try an experiment - not pay, just stay. I hoisted myself up onto the counter and sat there. After a while someone realized that they were not going to get rid of me, nor was I going to slip money to anyone. The only solution was to get a couple of technicians to follow me home with another one of those little boxes. It worked like a charm. The final installation was quite a site with rabbit ears at intervals linking small strips of cable hanging over our neighbor's yard, lying on the roof of our garage, across our yard and down the side of the house. But those wires did the trick for years carrying our faxes and voices where we chose.

I can't explain why the same challenge was such a daunting task for us here in the US, but it almost overwhelmed me. I called the gas company, gave our moving in date, set up an account, then the telephone company. They asked me so many questions I couldn't answer, so I had to turn the phone over to Billy. Then I called the electric company. All went well until they asked my name. I repeated as I had with the others, "My husband's name is..." He interrupted and said, "What's the matter with your name?" I was so nervous that I said, "I don't know!" So all of the utility accounts are in Bill's name except Duke Power.

But we were 'different' in other ways. In reality, we were oblivious to the extreme differences between our new friends and us. We had a worldview that was different or even contrary to those around us, and I guess we expressed what we thought. We were sorry that America was not worried enough about its image, but put its own national interests ahead of caring what other people felt, or thought, or needed. Were our leaders unable to see issues from others' viewpoints? Why were they so naive about the consequences of their words and actions? Where had that reputation established after WWII for being GOOD, acting with compassion and concern, gone? The casual and oft made remark heard here in the US, "America is the greatest country on earth," may be true, but it still upsets me, because it is naively and proudly quoted so off-handedly. Do we have the right to parrot that we are better than the rest of the world when we don't know the rest of the world? Why do so few people in the U.S. have any knowledge of a subject like world geography?

I was asked to speak to a Sunday school class in Pennsylvania. I asked the class of about 12 middle school boys to name as many countries in Africa as they could. I was afraid that they might have assumed that Africa was one country instead of over fifty. There was dead silence. Finally I heard, "Egypt?" in a soft fearful voice. "Yes! Another?" I said. Silence. Then their teacher filled in the silence with, "Pakistan?" What could I say?

About two years later a friend from Durham went to live in Central Asia for a few years. When she returned, she said, "Now I understand you. When you first came to Durham I thought that you were from another planet. You were so different. You had completely different opinions from the rest of us."

This lostness inside us, this disconnection that we were experiencing that only time could heal, was compounded because we actually were different and acted strangely in the opinion of others. In some ways we felt more at home on the other side of the ocean. We were aliens in our own country.

You Are Never Alone

It was November 2000. Bill and I had been in the U.S. less than a month and were on our way to North Carolina to settle on our new house. We stopped for lunch and changed drivers just before arriving at the entry to the West Virginia Turnpike. Why did this state look different? Was it coal dust grubbiness? Was that graffiti typical? "HOG WASH" had been slashed across one of the bridge support pillars. The little restaurant looked aged and worn. The door handle was so dirty I didn't want to touch it. I had not hesitated to mention my observations with scorn.

We passed through the tollgate. That red dashboard warning light was on again. It had gone off while we ate lunch, but now we could no longer ignore it. I pulled over right next to a small building. As Bill jumped out a man wearing an iridescent orange vest came up beside him. They stuck their heads in under the hood at the same time. He said, "I'm glad you stopped because I saw you were losing water as you came through the toll booth." He and Bill came to the same conclusion that the problem was too serious to be remedied there in that cold biting November wind, so he invited us into his little office for a cup of hot coffee.

As we entered the building we noticed a sign opposite the front door, "YOU ARE NEVER ALONE ON THE WEST VIRGINIA TURNPIKE." What comfort! He went to the phone, had a short conversation and then gave us clear instructions. "I want you to pull out into the entering traffic, then cross the median making a U-turn. Go right back out the exit booths. Be careful of those oncoming cars. Go a couple of miles, exit at the next opportunity and turn on such and such a street. You will find a garage called...." We couldn't repeat what he said but it sounded like Lodo. "They are expecting you." We did just as he had said returning back to the nearest town and found a garage called LO-DO.

Two men immediately came out and said, "Pull her into that door over there. As I walked in behind the car I read little signs of encouragement posted on the walls. I wish I could remember them today but they were reassuring. Bill stayed with the car and I walked to the front of the building where a couple of people were working behind a desk. The toilet had a sign, "Out of order" smacked across it. I started to read a magazine but looked up to see the owner singing as he came out of that toilet, "Jesus loves the little children, All the children of the world…." After he let me use it, we started to talk. "What does LO-DO mean? Is that you and your wife's names?" I asked.

He responded, "It means just what it says: Low Dough." He asked about where we were headed and the usual chitchat followed. He was a pastor of a Four-Square Gospel Church down the road. His congregation had grown. They had just bought an abandoned movie theater.

Surprisingly soon the car was finished. He handed me the bill. I didn't understand car mechanics; what I was interested in was the price. They had replaced the thermostat and the seal for the huge sum of $27.00 and some cents. "That's not enough," I said. So he replied, "Okay" and changed it to $29.31, tax included! We left with our hearts full of gratitude.

As the hours of driving rolled by I had time to reflect on my critical attitude of the state of West Virginia. We had laughed as we pulled off for lunch some miles before reaching the turnpike entry. Those words, "HOG WASH!" were still vivid in my mind. I felt rebuked and guilty. I had to learn again that appearances are deceiving. My critical attitude had been reciprocated with generous hospitality, genuine concern for our welfare, and excellent repair help. And the price! Those men had not only said they were Christians but had proved it by exhibiting the spirit and love of Christ. We thanked God for leading us to such wonderful people, especially when we felt so lost.

A friend told us later that a typical West Virginian would give you the shirt off his back. It was a lesson I needed. I still have that receipt!

Why We Came to Durham

Choices, options, decisions. Wouldn't life be boring if there were no options? Much simpler, but boring. Suppose we were all pushed around by someone else, to be here or there or to do this or that. Making the best choices forces us to think, to weigh the 'good' and the 'bad' against each other. That's freedom.

But suppose the choices are between several 'goods.' Then we face a greater challenge to choose what is best or even what we feel is right. People still ask us why we settled here in Durham. We sometimes look at each other not wanting to answer. Or do we look at each other because we're not completely sure why?

When we made plans to leave North Africa in 2000, our son said, "Why don't you stay there one more year and make it 40 even." What he did not add was, "But when you do come home, we want you to settle close to us." We didn't find out they felt that way till years later.

We had spent the summer of 2000 looking around. The one goal we were sure of was our desire for continuing contact with young people, hopefully from North Africa, probably on university campuses. We did our research. Where did we already have ties? What options were there? Too many including U Mass, U of Texas at Austin, U of Cincinnati, Virginia Tech, and Florida. We visited each one including some real estate agents. When we returned to Tunisia to close down our house, we took our indecision back with us. One of our friends there was a recent graduate of North Carolina State University. He suggested we investigate the Triangle area. So in October we did. We contacted one person who worked with a group at NC State University and he suggested others, till we had met people from Duke and UNC. There are three universities within a short distance of each other. We also met a real estate agent who made an appointment for the following Tuesday. Houses were less than half the cost of Massachusetts. Utilities and food were much cheaper. The weather was more moderate than Texas and Florida and Amherst, MA. Here was a happy middle ground.

Billy, Chloé and Anita at UNC, May 2013

We found a house we loved with landscaping challenges, moved in December and started working with one of the student ministries at Duke University immediately after our move. What we did not discover until a few years later was that the largest concentration of Mauritanians in the U.S. is in

Florence, Kentucky, 10 miles from our son's house! I have recently spoken on the phone with one of my former students.

But the crowning confirmation of our choice is that our only granddaughter, Chloe came as an out-of-state student to the University of North Carolina. We saw her occasionally during the year, but she lived with us during her summer school sessions and we have finally come to know that cute little girl as an adult.

Mercenaries

After living in our new house for a few months we were supposed to let the builder know what things needed repairing. I certainly didn't realize that we had the right to insist that all the repairs be done correctly.

But Joey, his repairman came. He started with the small lock on the inside door to the garage. I sat down near him to watch. I thought that it probably wouldn't be necessary to supervise him as I would have done in West Africa, but I wanted to watch to learn as much as I could. Wherever we had lived I was usually in charge of plumbers, electricians and the like.

Joey eventually began chatting.

"I hear you guys were mercenaries." There was a pause before I said, "What?" He repeated, "I hear you were mercenaries." And again I said, "What?"

Then I replied, "Well I don't think I'd say it exactly like that." When he repeated it again, I replied, "Well not in the usual sense of the term."

The next day he came back a bit flustered, waving his hands in the air, he confessed, "I didn't mean 'mercenaries.' I meant 'missionaries!'"

Precious Souvenirs

"I told them that your house is like a museum," our Tunisian friend said. I was sitting with a group of my best Tunisian women friends during a return trip to North Africa. She was reminding them that on her last trip to the U.S. she and her husband had visited us here in Durham.

So she thought that we lived in a museum? It is true that the large brass plate in front of the fireplace is from Morocco, and the old camel box sitting on the left of the hearth is from Mauritania, and the beautiful old clay storage pot on the other side of the hearth is from Algeria, and the small intricate shelves on the wall are from Egypt. The little perfume bottles on the window ledge were bought in Tunisia. Despite the fact that the seller had sworn that they were authentic Tunisian, I happen to know that they were made in Egypt. The little brass figurines of Africans playing drums and flutes, which Bill prizes, are from some sub-Saharan country, maybe Mali, or Ghana, or Senegal.

We have a wall featuring photos of our ancestors reminding us of our roots. Above them are two shelves highlighting Bill's mother's pewter collection. I don't think that there is any piece that can be attributed to Paul Revere, but the communion set came from a defunct church in Algiers, when at independence it was closed and turned into either a city hall or a mosque. The Christian contents found their way to flea markets. We have leather wall hangings which date from another era of nomadic life in the Sahara Desert and clay pots dug up in the desert remind us of a more verdant time and of a civilization that was fading before our eyes.

But the most precious of all of our souvenirs are not quite so obvious. Before we retired to Durham I mentioned to Bill that I would really like to have a display coffee table. Then I could lay out some very precious items that couldn't be displayed any other way. We found one in a damaged furniture store when we arrived in Durham. We purchased it along with several pieces of furniture and the salesman threw in, as a gift, its matching smaller display table. It's glass top was missing, but that was easy to remedy.

The smaller one contains, just under the glass, a leather bound, hand written and hand sewn Koran. There are pages missing. But the memory of how we acquired it is a long and fascinating story. Beside it, sits my collection of ankle bracelets from Mauritania. The coffee table in the center of the living room contains a varied display of arrow heads, prehistoric hatchet heads, camel harness buckles, necklaces from the desert nomads, olive oil lamps, some of which are authentic - and coins, some Carthaginian, some Roman and some Byzantine and some imitation, circa 20th century.

The globe, which Bill used as a child to learn world geography, sits on a shelf and his mother's sleigh bells hang beside the fireplace. This worn leather strap of brass bells accompanied her, hung around her horse's neck as she drove her sleigh from the farm on the mountain to the valley on her way to high school. And I have my mother's cedar chest and doll cradle.

That's probably more than a half of it.

Flashing Lights

The police car's siren and flashing lights behind us were getting closer. He was following US! What should we do? Bill pulled over, got out of the car and headed back toward the lights. He thought he was doing the policeman a favor until he saw the officer's hand jump back to his holster and heard him yell,

"You get back in that car!" How were we to know that Rule Number One when stopped by the police in the U.S. was: Stay seated with your hands on the steering wheel?

We were on our way from western Massachusetts to Boston's Logan International Airport, 100 miles away and risked missing our flight. The night before had been full of uncertainties. We had planned to profit from the free tickets Delta Airlines awarded parents of their employees. We had given our son, Billy our expected itinerary. He procured the tickets down in Texas and sent them FedEx to us in Massachusetts. The only problem was that they were lost. When by late evening FedEx still hadn't found them, I stopped packing and we went to bed. We were staying in the house where Bill had grown up. Both of his parents had died so the house was empty. Early the next morning FedEx telephoned that the tickets were found and that they would bring them to this house out in the country.

My reaction was swift. "No, we can't wait here. Bring them to HoJo's parking lot in Greenfield," which would be on our way to Boston. We threw our clothes into our bags, closed up the house and jumped into the car.

Within seconds of our arriving at the parking lot, the FedEx truck pulled in. I jumped out of the car, signed a paper, took the envelope and Bill sped out onto the road to Boston. That's when we saw those flashing lights. As Bill got back in the car, the policeman stuck his head in the window and said, "Where do you think you're going at 70 miles an hour?"

We explained a bit of the FedEx story and told him that we were headed to Logan Airport in Boston. His reply, "No, you're not. You are headed toward Vermont and Canada." He didn't give us much time to think about that before he said, "Show me your car papers. "We rifled unsuccessfully through the glove compartment of this rented car when he came to our aid and said, "They're usually behind the visor." He looked them over and asked Bill for his driver's license.

Then he astounded us again by saying, "What's this? You have a Massachusetts driver's license with a Pennsylvania address!" We had decided that using the Massachusetts address of Bill's folks' empty house might not be wise, so he had applied for renewal using what we thought was a more valid address in my home state.

He fairly shouted, "Where do you live anyway?"

We sheepishly replied, "West Africa." Silence.

"I catch you speeding. You tell me you're headed to Boston, but you're not. You have a Massachusetts driver's license with a Pennsylvania address, but you don't live in either place. I guess you have enough problems already. I'm not going to give you any more. Just don't let me see you cross the median." And he let us go.

We did not cross the median but went all the way to the next exit and turned around. And we did make the flight.

A Christmas Memory

There are countries around the world that don't follow our western calendar. The Muslim calendar begins the week with Monday, not Sunday. I tried using one once but very soon decided to switch back. But if you really want to be confused, try using a calendar based on a lunar month where the months with their Arabic names move forward a few days each year. For example, the holy month of Ramadan, when Muslims fast during the daylight hours, might occur in the summer one year, but then advances 10 days each following year. So it eventually moves to the spring, then winter, to fall, and eventually to summer again. January 1, 2013, reads the 19th day of the month of Safar Rabi 1434. The year is based not on the date set as Christ's birth but on the Hijira, Mohammed's flight from Mecca to Medina.

This really is logical reasoning for a Muslim who feels that his life is being controlled by Christian ideas instead of Muslim principles, but it seems that not many Muslims are tempted to live out of step with our calendar. One effort to assert Muslim principles, which we experienced firsthand, was the change of the weekend. If the Christian holy day is Sunday, and the Jewish holy day is Saturday, Muslims celebrate on Friday. The 2:00 pm Friday Prayers are the main mosque event of the week. So we scheduled our usual weekend activities on Thursday afternoon and Friday. So in our minds we went to church on Friday. Saturday became Monday and Thursday became Saturday, etc.

This had serious consequences for American oil companies who were joint owners of Algeria's gas and oil industry. American offices were closed on Saturday and Sunday. Algerian offices were closed on Thursday and Friday. And with the time zone differences between Algeria and Texas, there were only six hours a week when telephone calls could be made from office to office!

The Algerian government figured if they were to carry through on Islamization that they would also have to outlaw Christian holidays. Christmas, which only a few Algerians were celebrating in imitation of the French colonial celebration with a tree, and dancing all night, became illegal.

The absence of Christmas was even starker in the Sahara than in Algeria. We made our own Christmas in both places in church and with guests in our home.

So perhaps you can feel what I felt one mid-December when I arrived flying from the heart and heat of the Sahara into JFK airport in New York City. After clearing police controls and customs I came out into the entry hall of the huge international terminal. As the sliding doors opened, I saw a two-story lighted Christmas tree and a huge beautifully decorated colored glass chandelier.

But most of all the music, amplified through the hall, moved me more than I can express, *Hark! the herald angels sing. "Glory to the newborn King!"*

Margaret

I must have told my mother that I wanted a doll for Christmas. My brothers scorned that idea by telling me I was too old to play with dolls and I figured that was that. I remember getting up Christmas morning and going straight to the living room. There she was. The first thing I saw was a beautiful doll sitting on a little wooden rocking chair. The little chair was for my youngest brother. The doll I named Margaret, not because I liked the name, but because that meant that she was truly mine.

When we came home from North Africa in 1965, the old homestead had already been sold with its attic treasures, and Margaret was nowhere to be found. I had not adequately communicated by mail to my folks that if they were able to keep anything of mine and take it to be stored in their new house, that I would like the trunk of old letters and Margaret. My great love was gone forever. You have to admit that she probably wasn't in the greatest condition. I remember that the toes on one foot were chipped, but she had socks and shoes to cover that from view. I try to imagine today what Margaret would look like if she were lying in my mother's doll cradle that was saved for me. Maybe she was smaller than my imagination makes her and she would have been lost tucked down in there anyway.

Airport Shenanigans

There were only two seats open from Hartford to JFK. We had to return our car rental and leave extra time if we needed to change our schedule at the last minute. There is always a bit of anxiety flying 'standby.' We arrived at the airport early, picked up a sandwich and headed to our gate. It was our plan to enroll the help of a gate attendant to see if she would suggest that we get listed on another route. There were two Delta agents at the computer desk. I told them that we were standby passengers, headed to Raleigh/Durham, NC through JFK. She reviewed the seat situation, thought a while and finally suggested that we not change our plans.

So we were comforted and sat down to wait for two hours. From time to time we wandered around. I noticed that the same two ladies were helping out the agents at other gates as planes came and went. Suddenly one of them came running in her heels back to our gate. She punched in a combination on the secure lock and ran down the jet way. I decided to watch to see what drama was unfolding because a plane had just arrived. I could see her face in the window of the jet way. It never occurred to me that she could see mine. She finished advancing the jet way to the plane door and then returned back up to the waiting room. I decided to stay there and tell her that I hadn't realized she had to be a jack-of-all-trades, but before I could say anything she said, "You freaked me out!"

What could I have done? She continued, "I thought you were my mother. The last plane to arrive at Gate 4 was from Minneapolis and that's where she lives. You look just like her, same color hair, same cut…"

Before long the other employees were laughing and calling me "Mom."

We were relieved to receive our boarding cards. Her advice to wait was right on. At boarding time the wheel chair passengers went on first, then the special elite passengers. As we waited I saw my 'new daughter' take the microphone, her voice reaching the surrounding gates,

"Now I want to make an announcement. I would like the passenger who looks like my mother to board next!"

Bill assumed that that meant he could, too. As I walked past her she said, "I couldn't resist. I just had to do that!"

When we got on the plane the flight attendant said to me, "Hi, Mom!" She was an African American. Thinking she might not have heard, I told her about the announcement over the PA system. A while later she came down the aisle. As she handed each of us a little package of cookies she said, "You are two of the cutest little cookies I've ever seen." The flight was too short to serve drinks and snacks to the other passengers so we didn't eat them then. As we disembarked I told her that when we did eat them we would think of her.

We made the second flight from JFK as well and arrived home 11 hours after we had set out for the airport.

Contraband

The woods around us were quiet and only moderately dense. It looked like a perfect campsite. From the area where we had set up our makeshift blanket tent and pup tent, we would be able to see any movement through the trees for quite a distance. Dusk was still about an hour away so we puttered around snacking and making sure that all was ready before darkness set in. The four of us, plus a small white poodle, were alone in a strange country and in a strange place. We pushed our fears aside. It seemed as though we were the only people for miles around except for the border guards who were on duty about 50 feet behind us. They were quietly chatting in Spanish. The presence of these guards was the reason that we had been guided to this area to spend the night.

Two days before, we had set out early from Algiers with our friend Mary Ellen Shoup and her beloved (by her) poodle, Pierrot. Our destination was Europe for a few weeks' vacation. Our intention was to drive across western Algeria, into Morocco, turn straight north and reach the coastal Spanish enclave of Melilla by nightfall. Bill and Billy were in the back seat. Mary Ellen was driving and Pierrot would periodically let me know that he didn't appreciate my taking not only his seat, but also some of his space on the floor under the dashboard.

We had carefully calculated the travel time with two drivers, leaving ample time for delays at the two border crossings. Our ferry from Melilla to Malaga in mainland Spain would leave port at midnight. We had booked our berths for the night, planning to be in Malaga by 8 am the next morning. But about halfway between Algiers and Oran we had a disastrous flat tire. Each of the many small towns along the way gave us the same negative response about the possibility of replacing the spare. The hours were speeding by as we drove, worrying about another flat, across western Algeria through customs into Morocco, before turning north toward the Spanish enclave on the coast.

We arrived after midnight. We'd missed our ferry. The next three days were big Spanish holidays and all berths were booked for the next two nights! We were stuck in this Spanish enclave in northern Morocco. Melilla had been part of Spain since 1497. This chunk out of northeast Morocco was only twelve square kilometers surrounded by barbed wire. The total population numbered about 80,000 Spanish citizens.

Since we had already planned on camping across mainland Spain on our way to France, it was logical to inquire about where we could camp here in Melilla. We were directed to the public beach. Mary Ellen had a two-man pup tent but since it was already well into the night, we decided that we could simplify the set-up. Bill and I did not own a tent but had intended to camp under a blanket fastened to the baggage rail on the car with clothes pins and draped down to our suitcase handles. Since the car was an essential part of the setup we decided to spend the night, not actually on the sand away from the road, but right on the sidewalk along the road at the edge of the beach. Billy slept in the car.

We didn't think of any danger and of course we had Mary Ellen's little white poodle to protect us. I have to admit that it never occurred to us that we would need protection. Bill and I blew up our air mattresses, placed them on the sidewalk and crawled into our sleeping bags. Mary Ellen unfolded what she called her banana bed, faced it in the opposite direction head to head with us and crawled in. At least our heads were all under the blanket tent.

I was awakened by Pierrot's growling. I crawled out, stood up and saw a drunken man trying to get into bed with Mary Ellen. That would have caused enough of a problem but he had a large German Shepherd with him. I kept my distance and yelled for him to scram in English. That didn't work. Then I yelled in French, and then in Arabic. Nothing moved him. My last resort was 'pst, pst!' which I suspect means 'come here' in any language. By then Bill was up. Mary Ellen crawled out holding Pierrot. None of us could speak Spanish. We had camped very near an all-night bar, and one of their unstable-on-his-feet customers had come over to check us out. What would his huge dog do if we touched his master? Our visitor was not interested in moving off.

Finally a car stopped and asked us what the problem was. One of the passengers spoke to us in French and then in Spanish, he convinced the drunk to leave us alone. He meandered off, and we crawled back into bed. The night was almost gone.

Where in the world could we spend the next night? Not here in any case. We did some shopping for food and asked where we could camp out. We must have received good instructions because we drove up a winding hill and came across many tents spread out in the woods. It was a beautiful site. We found an empty space but would set up our blanket tent closer to nighttime. Then we went to visit our neighbors. They were really well equipped with chairs and tables, even TV's, so we joined one family to watch the bullfights. To our great surprise as the afternoon wore on, one by one, each family began to pack up and wend their way back down the hill. Eventually it was clear that everyone was leaving. They explained that it was far too dangerous to stay in those woods at night!

What were we to do? One of the men told us to gather our things and follow his car. He led us to the area where the border guards were on duty. He assured us that we would be safe there.

We had a snack and began to set up camp for the night. Billy would spread out on the back seat of the car. This time Mary Ellen set up her pup tent and she and I would leave the blanket arrangement to Bill. He would use the banana bed to keep off the ground.

Before the sun set, mysterious movements began a little distance away. Through the trees two vans appeared from nowhere and pulled into the woods. The men jumped out, opened the rear doors and rolled huge bales, wrapped in burlap, into a ditch. Just as they finished, a large number of mules seemingly from nowhere, also came tearing into the woods. As the men tied the bales onto the mules, two other men walked to the border guards, chatted for a moment, obviously negotiating some arrangement and then returned to the trucks.

We stood there puzzled and in awe at the drama unfolding so close to us. All of a sudden we realized that just on the other side of that flimsy barrier was the country of Morocco. As the vans returned from where they had come, the remaining men mounted the loaded mules and started running straight at us. They then veered left toward the border guards. As they approached at top speed the guards lifted the barrier and they sped through and disappeared into the woods on the other side.

It all happened so fast. We sat down in shock to try to find an explanation and to speculate about what those bales contained: Radios? TV's? stolen goods? And what products would then make their way back into Spain on those mules? And what was it that those Spanish guards had received for cooperating so efficiently?

The night with its mysteries, at least for me, the light sleeper, was not over. I awoke to the sound of heavy sniffing around the tent. There was a pack of wild dogs outside. As worried as I was about Bill's welfare, I could not bring myself to open the tent flap. In the morning another piece of this story unfolded. It had nothing to do with those dogs. I could not stop scratching the numerous welts on my hips and legs. We had set up the pup tent on an anthill. As the French say, 'Le comble!' (The last straw).

How we spent the next morning and afternoon I can't remember, but I do know that we were the first in line to board the ferry that evening.

Les Faux Pas

We recently listened to a message where the pastor had difficulty finding the right words. He would hesitate and then fill in the pause with a word that sounded like the word he was searching for. So we heard sentences about 'analogues to life' or 'the prices were exultant.' Rather amusing yet very distracting!

I wish that I could say that our own language learning 'faux pas' were not catastrophic. Our gracious listeners often let them slip by, but some of our French friends did point out mistakes, and I am still grateful for those corrections. I have selected some of the most amusing mistakes that we English speakers made while learning French and then blamed them all on one fictitious person:

It was the first time the American found himself in the pulpit having to preach in French. Since few of his audience knew him, he thought it would be a good idea to introduce himself with a little background information which, of course, made no significant difference to his French audience. But then again it did!

So he started out, "Je suis ici un ane." The congregation was a bit restless. (If you look up 'un âne' in a Larousse Dictionary, you will find that it is 'un animal avec une grosse tête et de longues oreilles,' (an animal with a large head and long ears). He meant to say, "Je suis ici depuis un an." (I've been here for one year.)

But our hero was not deterred, and continued explaining more about his parents' roots in the U.S., "Mon père était sudiste and ma mere était nudiste." Because he sensed more restlessness, he repeated, "J'ai dit, mon père était sudiste et ma mere était nudiste!"

What he wanted to say was: My father was from the South and my mother was from the North. What his French speaking audience understood is clear, I believe.

As the laughter calmed down he switched the focus to his audience. Trying to explain that we should not think of ourselves more highly than we ought to, that we are all sinners he said, "Mais vous pensez que vous êtes les gens bons! Mais vous n'êtes pas les gens bons. Vous êtes nés dans la malle." And then he finished his talk in typical American fashion with a challenging invitation. "Si vous n'êtes pas sauvez, sauvez-vous!" (See note)

We never heard how that congregation responded. No doubt, dumbfounded, puzzled, and unexpectedly amused.

NOTES:

By 'gens bons' he meant good people, but 'jambons' (ham) is pronounced the same. La malle is very different from 'le mal.' 'La malle' (trunk) is not 'le mal' (evil).

'Sauver' means 'to save'. But the expression 'Sauvez-vous' means get out as fast as you can! (If you are not saved, then get out as fast as you can!)

Spice and Sand

I was speaking to a group of children at a conference in France, showing them where Mauritania was on a map and telling them what life was like. I talked about the caste system and the different languages, the tribes and ethnic groups. I dressed them up in Mauritanian garb. I also explained that when the wind blows, the sand does too. It is everywhere: in your hair, your food, you name it. Among the objects I had brought with me was a bottle of sand. When I'd left Nouakchott the design of eleven distinct colors of sand in that little bottle was an illustration of the beauties of the Sahara. Unfortunately, the trip in our suitcase caused its contents to settle. The colors of sand at the top of the bottle once separate and swirling in design, had settled and mixed into one another. The beauty was mostly gone. The children, however, seemed interested.

But for me that sand was of no further use. I intended to throw it away. As the children left the room and I was gathering up the objects, a crazy idea hit me. Maybe I could get more mileage out of that sand after all. I went straight to the dining hall, picked up two salt shakers, emptied the salt from one into the other and laid the filled one back on the table. Then I poured some sand from my little bottle into the empty saltshaker, all the while planning my strategy. As the dining hall began to fill I found Bill and we sat down for a 'quiet' lunch.

I ate a bit and then started walking from table to table, reciting my little speech. I said that Bill and I had lived in the three countries of North Africa where most of these people were presently living, and I had learned something about North African recipes and their spices. We were the only attendees living in Mauritania. I continued that there the food was very different. Would anyone at the table like to try a little Mauritanian spice?

At least one person volunteered from each table. They took the shaker, shaking it on one of the food items on their plate. Most of them caught on immediately. They were good sports. But one lady told me that she didn't taste anything and asked for a second shake. As she dosed her lettuce, a wave of exhaustion passed over me from trying to control my laughter. One big forkful and she said, "Pe-e-gggyyy!"

Sitting at the last table were people I didn't know. But three of the children had been in the morning class. As soon as their father took the shaker, their hands flew up covering their mouths. I signaled them to be quiet. They had recognized the sand and they knew their father! I guess he liked my spiel and decided to try some out.

Oh, my! He was not happy! I still, to this day, do not know if his anger sprang from the fact that I had wasted a bit of his food, or if he didn't like being the butt of my shenanigans, or if he thought that the sand might be dirty, or if it was because he had been taken in, in front of his children. I was very, very sorry and returned to my own seat immediately.

I had had my fun. That was enough. I threw the sand away and filled the shaker with salt. My joke had succeeded far better than I ever dreamed. Every person laughed after falling for my spiel, except one.

And me? I was exhausted.

Mauritanian Visas

We had been invited to lunch at the Residence of the Mauritanian Ambassador to the United States in Washington DC. We entered the large dining room. Only two faces, both Mauritanian, were familiar, the assistant to the Ambassador to the U.S., Abass, and Mohamed Ali, the assistant Consular Officer. The other Mauritanian was our host.

It was definitely not a lunch. The large round side table was laden with several chicken and fish dishes and salads and couscous. We were to serve ourselves, but there were so many people bringing me food that I never really was able to see all the options. The seats at one end of a long table were completely filled with the guests who had arrived before us. They were obviously all American. Three were introduced to us as various employees of the State Department, Finance and Commerce. They were not very interested in us, however, but the meal passed pleasantly enough with the Ambassador telling a few jokes and the usual chitchat. It became obvious that "Finance" and "State" had spent time in Africa but "Commerce" was a bit left out. I was very happy to be sitting next to Abass. It was an easy enjoyable conversation.

Why were Bill and Peggy there among this group of 14 or 15 people from the U.S. government? Well we were unique only in that we had actually lived in Mauritania. We also had received a personal invitation. And you could blame it on FedEx.

We had special flight privileges because of our son's job with Delta, so we could easily visit friends in both Mauritania and Tunisia each year. Visiting Tunisia was simple, but Mauritania required visas. In the spring of 2002 we assembled the required documents including our request forms, passports, photos, money and FedExed them to the Mauritanian Embassy in DC. FedEx billed us twice for their trouble. In 2003 the passports didn't arrive back even though we had paid for their return. After many phone calls they arrived in Raleigh 20 hours before our departure and we had to drive to Raleigh to pick them up.

Rather than repeat the tension of FedEx's mistakes again, in 2004 we decided that it would be safer to drive the visa requests from Durham to the Embassy, a trip of almost 6 hours each way. We found a parking space on the crowded street in front of the Embassy and expected to walk into a poorly maintained building reflecting life in the Sahara. The reception area was freshly painted with clean white walls. We walked up to a receptionist and said that we hoped to procure visas. A man came up behind us and asked us to follow him upstairs.

He had us sit down in front of a large desk, introduced himself and the other official. Why did we want to visit Mauritania? They couldn't believe that we had already lived there for 14 years. What had we done during all of that time? When they heard that Bill had done relief and development work, and that I had taught at the University, they asked if I knew so-and-so and so-and-so. I was pleased to be able to say, "Yes, one of them was my student."

They told us that they had grown up together in the same town up north. They reminisced about their childhood days together and even about their homemade contraptions to catch locusts. They added that the Ambassador, too, was from the same town. Ah, that was the Africa we knew, where you get a job if you know the right people. We were having a very happy, animated discussion. I felt at ease, at home.

From time to time the man behind the desk would look at our applications. Finally he handed the envelope back to us. I opened it up. Inside were two returned ID photos - we had furnished two each - and $180.00, the whole fee for two visas. We left, not with the three-month tourist visas that we had requested, but with one year-multiple entry visas, marked "GUESTS," and a reminder that we had the right to apply for Mauritanian citizenship!

On the way home we wondered how we could return the kindness of those two men. We decided to take some of my art prints to decorate those empty embassy walls. As soon as we got home I started working on getting them framed, two desert scenes and a portrait of a Mauritanian.

A few weeks later we returned north again, gifts in hand. While we were still in the reception area a tall young man approached us and asked me if I wasn't Mrs. Call. He said, "You don't know me, but you taught my sister." Fortunately I remembered her well as a good student who was now a high school English teacher. Then we proceeded upstairs, to present our gifts. As we were standing in the hallway we heard a voice call out, "Bill and Peggy!" Coming toward us was a Peace Corps volunteer who had often been at our house in Nouakchott. She was a photographer who had written a book on Mauritanian children. We chatted and she said that she too was there to give the Embassy some of her photos to decorate those bare walls! We lined up with her photos and my paintings and took pictures.

Bill and I then sat down to pick up where we had left off with these two friends who had been so kind to us. When we got up to leave Mohamed Ali said, "You can't go yet. I'm taking you out to lunch." He drove us to a Moroccan restaurant. We were spoiled with a huge meal served on one platter. Then in saying our goodbyes we realized that if Mohamed Ali's tenure at the Embassy ended soon, we would never see him again.

That was not to be though, because that Friday back in Durham the Ambassador's assistant, Abass telephoned saying that the Ambassador wanted to thank us for our gifts and was inviting us to lunch on Monday. Could we face another 12 hours in the car so soon? Of course we accepted, and headed back on Monday at six am to arrive in D.C. at noon. When we pulled up in front of the embassy, Mohamed Ali was in the driveway with the Ambassador preparing to leave for the Residence. We parked and got out of the car. He came running down the driveway and enveloped me in a big hug. Then he did the same to Bill. This was unheard of. White Moor men of their culture and tribe do not even touch the hand of a woman outside of their family.

So here we were having a meal with the Mauritanian Ambassador to the United States in his home in D.C. The visit finished with Mohammad Ali pinning a Mauritanian and American flag flying side by side on our lapels.

We never thought of thanking FedEx for messing up those two previous years.

Peggy and the Pope

I was surprised that he was so short. He came slowly down the aisle in his brilliant red robes and his little white skullcap. He turned to the left side, pouring out his blessings with gentleness and care as the nuns, lining the elbow high barrier set up along the center aisle, reached out to touch him. Just as he arrived toward the center of St Peter's, he changed strategy and crossed over to our side. A spontaneous whoop of female voices lifted to the vaulted ceiling, filling the sanctuary, similar to a room full of teenagers reacting to a rock star. He approached, leaned forward taking each nun's hand in his.

How in the world had we found ourselves in the midst of this exciting event? There was nothing in our transit through Rome that could possibly have foreseen this experience. It was Billy who had insisted we not continue straight home but spend at least four days sightseeing. Bill had been to Rome when he was a soldier stationed in France in the 1950's and had actually been at the celebration when the Pope declared Mary the Queen of Heaven. I had visited in the 1970's. Billy's words still ring in my ears. "You've never seen Rome together, why wouldn't you do it now?"

The first morning we set out to see the Sistine Chapel. The beauty of the Vatican Museum was beyond words. The effect of the soft lighting illuminating the long corridors lined with paintings, not only on the walls but also on the ceiling, overwhelmed me. I hate to admit it but the climax, the Sistine Chapel itself with one of the most famous of all paintings, God touching life into his creation Adam was a disappointment simply because I had expected it to stand apart. I felt it was overwhelmed by the numerous detailed paintings surrounding it. But I hardly know better than Michelangelo.

After a quick lunch we went around the corner to St Peter's Cathedral. We immediately joined a short line in the center court. We tried to chat with the sisters in their black garb in front of us, but they were from Poland. The line did not move. Then we heard French behind us. Two Belgian couples sounded impatient. "Why was the line not moving?" We chatted on and off for another hour. As time went on, thousands joined behind us. The air danced with excitement.

We learned that the doors would not open until four. It was not yet 3:00 and we had already been there on that spot for an hour. The Pope was scheduled to appear for a special ceremony dedicated to the sisters from around Europe. We were unaware that it was Pentecost. When the doors opened the line disappeared. Everyone from every side began to run. We were being carried along by a mob. We didn't know where the best seats were but I saw the Polish nuns running to the center aisle, so we followed them.

The sanctuary was immense. Everything seemed oversized. There was so much to see. As the procession entered, Bill's camera batteries ran out. My little camera was set in some sort of delay mode so I only got smudges. The Polish sisters smiled and gestured as we tried to communicate and then one of them handed me a small plastic crucifix. The booklet programs were beautiful. We could follow through the long ceremony even if we understood very little. The music soared. Unseen choirs sang.

When the ceremony was over we piled up the chairs and joined the line along the railing on the center aisle. There was one sister between the barrier and me. As the Pope came slowly down the aisle and held one of the Polish sister's hands in his, without reflection I reached over her shoulder and laid my hand on his hand! I was shocked at my audacity. How had I dared do such a thing? I turned around to Bill behind me and in the hearing of those around us, I said, "I touched the Pope's hand!" Bill's response was, "The Pope blessed the people, but Peggy blessed the Pope!"

I still felt giddy that evening as we arrived back at our hotel. I had to tell Billy. I picked up the phone that he had specified was to be used in the case of an emergency and called him. His anxious voice responded, "Mom what's wrong?"

"I touched the Pope!"

"You did not!"

I assured him that that was exactly what I had done and he interrupted with, "Wait, I want to put you on speaker phone."

Pope Benedict XVI

The only disappointment of the day was that we had no photos from inside St. Peter's. The next morning we visited the Spanish Steps, then the Trevi Fountain. Again, I was awed at the size of the beautiful sculptures and the spraying water. Those surging horses were exquisite. I scanned the scene from street level and then my eyes dropped to the pools of water. There, talking together, were the two Belgian men that we had talked to for so long in front of St. Peter's. I started down the steps just as they started up. One of them yelled, "Madame! Where did you go yesterday when everyone was running?" I explained that we had lined up at the center aisle. I had actually touched the Pope's hand. They were incredulous. Then they said that they had run up to the front and were seated in the seventh row and had been able to take tremendous pictures. A few weeks later after we got home, an email arrived with five photos! And they are good!

Running Out of Tears... Well, Not Quite

Public speaking? I was too shy. In 3rd or 4th grade my teacher asked us to prepare speeches to be presented in front of the class. I went to school one morning and found out that I was to present my speech that afternoon. I was scared to death. Rather than cry in front of the class, when I went home for lunch, I feigned being sick. I had a make-believe stomachache. My mother put me to bed for the afternoon.

I had succeeded in not having to suffer unbearable humiliation before my classmates, but I was suffering a worse pain of another kind, a guilty conscience.

I had lied to my mother. In the years to come, the pain of regret and guilt resurged every time I remembered that afternoon. I knew my mother had never lied to me, so why had I lied to her? I don't think that I ever confessed.

Despite the years of teaching, the fear of public speaking outside the classroom persisted. Those tears that were right there under the surface, waiting to burst forth, interfered with my desire to do a good job. It went a little like this. I would stand up, start to speak, and my chin would begin to shake. The tears would begin to form. My nose joined the flow. I never reached the sobbing stage but this weakness could become quite off putting if I was speaking about something I felt strongly or cared very much about. My tears blocked my sight and I couldn't read my notes. I had to have a handkerchief handy for that nose. Someone told me once that people really paid attention when I spoke in public. I made it such an emotional experience.

Even today if I read a simple story or watch a movie that is in any way touching, sad or joyful, for example about a sick child, or a sentimental event, I am touched to the core and the tears flow. My mother was like that, too. But today when I have to speak before an audience I just ask myself, "Do I have something to say? Do I feel that I am prepared?" Then I pump myself up, go for it and stay the tears and love it. At least I don't have to feign illness again.

In most public speaking situations, but not all, I have run out of tears. Well, not quite, not entirely, and not always.

Billy and Anita, Alister and Chloe

We only had one child. After one miscarriage and a failed attempt at adoption we accepted that this was the way it would be. Billy was about six years old when I told him that we were contemplating adoption. His reaction included some advice; "I just hope he isn't a French kid because then we'd have to speak French at home all the time."

When he was about 12 years old I read an article written by a lady who had just returned from her son's wedding. She recounted how she had started to pray for her son's choice of a bride when he was 12 years old. She was recounting how wonderfully the Lord had answered. Billy too was twelve years old.

The summer he turned 16, after passing his Brevet Exam in Lycée Descartes. in Algiers, he transferred to the U.S. spending two years at Ben Lippen High School in North Carolina and then four years at the University of Massachusetts, before starting pilot training. The Air Force posted him to San Antonio, Texas. Bill wrote him a note suggesting that he attend the church where Bill had met the Lord and was baptized 30 some years earlier. He asked him to write back and describe what the church was like. It was in the Young Adults' Sunday school class in that church that Billy saw Anita for the first time.

We were thrilled when we received a telegram from Billy. It said simply, "Anita said, 'Yes!'" I wrote back a one word answer spread out in large letters across an Air Form. "DELIGHTED." We had been able to spend several days with her one summer while they visited us in France. She is beautiful in every way, and has a marvelous testimony.

They were married in 1985. Most of Billy's buddies were also pilots in training. Just before the close of the wedding ceremony, these friends, in full dress uniform, raised their swords to form an archway for the newlyweds to pass under as they left the church. The animated reception served as our introduction into the customs of a Mexican-American wedding. The beautiful decorations and music by the Mariachis and a second orchestra added to the joy and enthusiasm of Anita's warm and loving family.

We have two beautiful grandchildren. I wonder what Alister would think if he knew I called him beautiful. He is a graduate of the Air Force Academy and is presently flying one of the same model planes that Billy flew during his Air Force career before being hired by Delta Airlines. Chloe graduated from the University of North Carolina and has now moved back to Kentucky.

Alister Ritchie

Chloe Kristen

I Was Amazed

In Tunis we lived in an upstairs apartment. The owner downstairs had a fairly ugly mongrel that sat on our doormat every morning waiting for us to open the door. We never enticed him with food and he never tried to put his foot over the threshold. He just waited until both of us, especially Bill, had given him a pat with some kind words. If I greeted him when Bill was off somewhere else in the house, Lucky went around the balcony to the windows to find Bill who patted his head, scratched his ears, and spoke a few kind words through the open window. Lucky would then pad back downstairs for the rest of the day.

Once we had guests in the bedroom right next to the front door. I opened the door to let the sun shine down the hallway and there sat Lucky. As I spoke a few kind words, our guest called out, "Does that dog understand English?

I replied, "No, but he understands love."

It seems to me that, with perhaps some exceptions, most people understand love. That is the language we all should give top priority to learning. One of our friends said that she could not understand how anyone living overseas could understand the culture if he didn't know the language. That is quite self-evident. But is that the most important language to learn? Is our ultimate goal to understand the culture? Or is it to learn how to effectively love the people, hoping they will be drawn to Christ? "Though I speak with the tongues of men and angels it is all to no avail - if there is no love."   I Corinthians 13:1

How can I be sure that I love someone? Is it merely an emotional attachment? Is that what Christ meant when he said, "Love one another as I have loved you." Or is that what he meant when he instructed his disciples about the greatest commandment? "Love the Lord your God with all your heart, soul and mind." Or the second, to love your neighbor as you love yourself!

I once asked a retired Anglican vicar who had lived in the Middle East for many years, "How do you know that you love someone?" His answer, "By what you are willing to do for them." Jesus loved us so much that he gave his life for us. Greater love than that does not exist.

An Algerian convert to Christ told Bill the story of his conversion. He often visited, 'Old Mister Liley.' They would speak of Christ. Kabayli angrily tore down every argument Mr. Liley presented. He tore up and stomped on the tracts he was given to read, but every time he went back, Mr. Liley would open the door with these words, "Kabayli, it's great to see you!" He added, "I was amazed. I could not resist that love! That is what softened my heart."

About the Author

At the age of ten Peggy accepted Christ into her life in a small country church in the heart of Bucks County, Pennsylvania. That event brought purpose and stability and eventually a desire to show and share the love of Christ overseas.

Peggy Call and her husband lived in four countries of North Africa: Tunisia, Morocco, Algeria and Mauritania from 1961 till 2000.

While her husband served as pastor, translator, and teacher during those years, she entertained an almost steady stream of guests. Their son attended French schools until the age of 16.

While teaching at the University of Nouakchott, Mauritania, she founded and managed an English language bookstore called, "Shakespeare and Company" as a non-profit service to university students of English and English teachers. She also was able to fulfill a dream from childhood. She learned to reproduce on paper the beauties of the landscapes, as well as the weathered faces of the Sahara Desert.

CPSIA information can be obtained at www.ICGtesting.com
Printed in the USA
BVOW08s1333200215

388648BV00004B/9/P